UPTON 1
CHESTER

A community for 150 years

Phil Pearn

Léonie Press

Supported by The Chester Civic Trust
as part of its Millennium Festival

ISBN
1 901253 25 2
Published December 2001

© Phil Pearn

All rights reserved. No part of this publication may be reproduced, stored
in a retrieval system, or transmitted in any form or by
any means, electronic, mechanical, photocopying, recording or
otherwise, without the prior permission of the copyright owner.

Edited and designed by Anne Loader from
the UPPA website created and researched by Phil Pearn

Published by
Léonie Press, 13 Vale Road, Hartford,
Northwich, Cheshire CW8 1PL
Great Britain
Website: www.anneloaderpublications.co.uk
www.leoniepress.com

Printed by Anne Loader Publications

Foreword

In these days of rapid change and uncertainty, and with the significance of a new Millennium, there is a mood of retrospection and a blossoming of interest in local history. Where better to start than in our immediate neighbourhood?

From its beginning, some 150 years ago, the entity that is Upton Park has grown organically. It is not a 'housing estate' but it is an estate of residences which reflect changing architectural fashions and the changing ways of life and tastes of the community which has developed. It has grown like a small village. In recognition of this integrity it was designated a Conservation Area in 2000.

Only two things have remained constant, from the first landowners and the covenants they imposed, to today's Upton Park Proprietors Association's elected committees – and these are the determination that the Park should be well-maintained and its residents considerate of their neighbours.

There is a wealth of historical record and anecdotal information, but they are lodged in hundreds of source documents, public and private, and in the memories of past and present residents – many of us elderly. It has taken a prodigious effort to bring all this together. It has needed a person with the skills and, above all, the perseverance and patience to produce a record of our community and its environment in book form. We are indeed fortunate in having Phil Pearn, our present UPPA Chairman, willing and able to carry out this project.

Jean Garrod
Erstwhile UPPA Chairman and Secretary and City Councillor
Currently Parish Councillor

Preface

Two years down the line, and my publisher giving me sections of the book to read, leads me to reflect on how this project started and the nature of the published book.

The seed for this history book project was our decision to pay off the remaining mortgage on our house. Thanks to careful storage back through history, we received from the building society a two-inch (5cm) thick set of documents containing manuscripts of indentures and deeds of title stretching back to the 1850s. My inherited nature for hoarding and nostalgia was excited and as early retirement had given me that precious commodity – time – I was eager to find out more, even if it meant considerable time spent indoors.

Having got to grips with these documents and with reference to relevant material in the Cheshire Record Office, it became clear that some of the stories about the house passed down through previous owners were more myth than fact. Similarly stories I'd heard about the early days of the Park didn't stack up with historical records. Discussing this with others in the Park and exhibiting my enthusiasm to know more soon meant a shelf full of old Upton Park Proprietors Association records and residents recounting stories faster than they could be captured.

Given that I'm not naturally tidy and organised, how was all this information to be analysed and pieced together? The computer age with its hyperlink files was the answer and basing the material on a website meant that others could monitor my progress, correct things I got wrong and be triggered into recalling more history. While I have one-finger typed in most of the text, my wife Lynne has transcribed lengthy documents including the legal ones. She has also been a necessary sounding board as ideas have swirled around in my head.

So the website grew and even those households reluctant to get involved in the early days were soon happy for their house to be featured. The website guest book was receiving entries and reuniting old friends who had grown up in the Park and were now spread around the world. The telephone network of past residents grew as each new contact provided links to others of their days in the Park.

My discussions with past residents, hearing their enthusiasm about their days in the Park, have been my greatest incentive to continue with a Park-wide history. My star contributor must be Mrs Margaret Millett, whose mother was born here in 1881.

Many of those interested in the project are not internet users and were wanting printed sheets but the files were constantly being updated. Even those following the progress on the website were pressing me for a book. My image of the website was for it to be on-going, knowing that I'd never have a complete story or never be sure that all the recorded facts were completely true. However, to have a book before the end of 2001 seemed like a good target deadline and another Millennium celebration. Although I had written many reports during my working career these were always technical and had a half-life of rarely more than a few months. The idea of writing a book that might be even more appreciated in the future provided the energy and inspiration to go for it.

With our good friend, Anne Loader, the possibility presented itself for her to take my website files, evolved over the last eighteen months, and produce a short run of a professional looking book. Part funding was soon resolved thanks to a handful of Park residents who well represented the full spread of all current residents. The final funding came through The Chester Civic Trust as part of its Millennium Festival following chairman Stephen Langtree's enthusiasm for local history projects such as this. Team-working to a deadline with a very sympathetic Anne has maintained my enthusiasm and has encouraged me to tidy up many of the loose ends while retaining pleasure in the whole project. I am indebted to her for her editing and attention to the detail of minor inconsistencies.

So now at the deadline for publication, we have the content of a book and a website waiting for all the *errata* and the new burst of facts from people asking *'why didn't you include this?'* The emphasis has been on validating and recording those facts and memories most susceptible to being lost. My apologies in advance for *what's missing* and *what's incorrect* – I have sought to include and validate as much as seems appropriate within the timescale.

I hope you enjoy the content as much as I have enjoyed researching and compiling it. I hope also that the reference aspects of it are useful, but I must emphasise that I have no legal training and have seen only a small fraction of all the relevant legal documents, hence any interpretations are just from a willing layman. Anyone pursuing legal enquiries should only regard this as general background briefing prior, to seeking professional legal guidance.

My thanks go to the helpful staff of the public records offices as listed under acknowledgements and to the residents past and present who have dug out old family snapshots and documents and have recalled times past so that they can be enjoyed by future generations within this framework of a history of Upton Park Chester.

Phil Pearn
September 2001

Formal acknowledgements

Cheshire and Chester Archives and Local Studies for permission to reproduce sections of early Ordnance Survey, tithe maps and indenture plans as well as access to census records of the 1800s. Reproductions of extracts from Ordnance Survey maps older than 50 years are with permission of Ordnance Survey.

Chester Community History & Heritage for permission to reproduce an early photograph and for access to electoral rolls of the early 1900s.

Upton Park Proprietors Association for access to its archived information and permission to reproduce certain summarised records.

The cover and the eight centre-spread photographs are courtesy of Mrs Barbara Cottrell for the historic photos and Alison Pantony for the recent colour photos. I have failed to trace the aerial photographer but acknowledge the use of their work.

Sketches
The 'Yarn' sketches and the bonfire sketch are the work of Patricia Kelsall.
The Mill and Elm House sketches are the work of Arthur Garrod.

All material belonging to private individuals has been reproduced with their kind permission. The list is too long to publish here.

Book Advisory Panel & Production Cost Underwriters
Stephen Langtree – Chairman of Chester Civic Trust
Charles Buck, Susan Creeth, Pat Feakins, Prof Robert Roaf, Pauline Rourke and Lynne Pearn – all of Upton Park Chester

Proof reading
Jean Garrod and Pat Feakins – both of Upton Park

Finally my thanks to past Chairman of UPPA and local Councillor Jean Garrod for writing the **Foreword**.

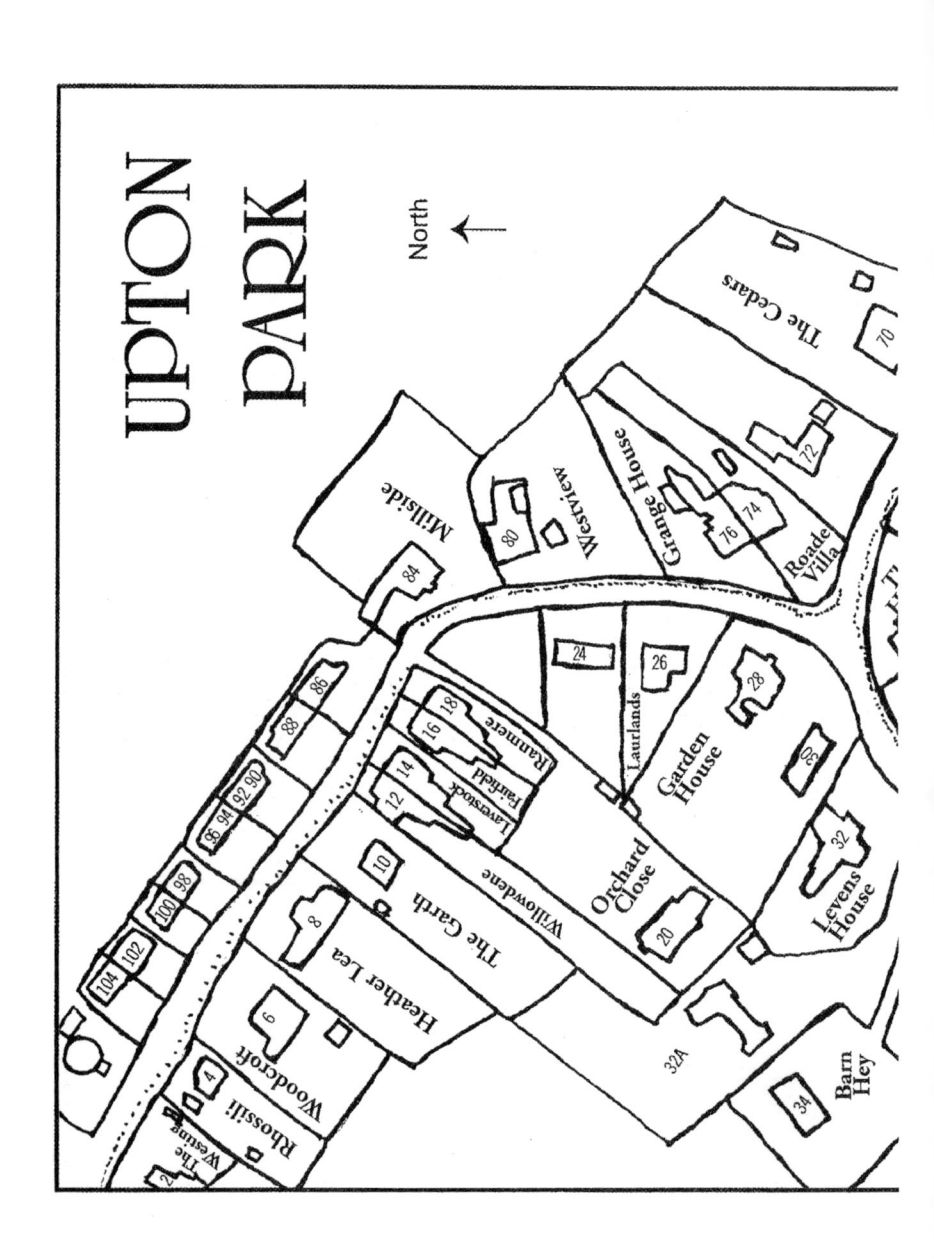

UPTON PARK

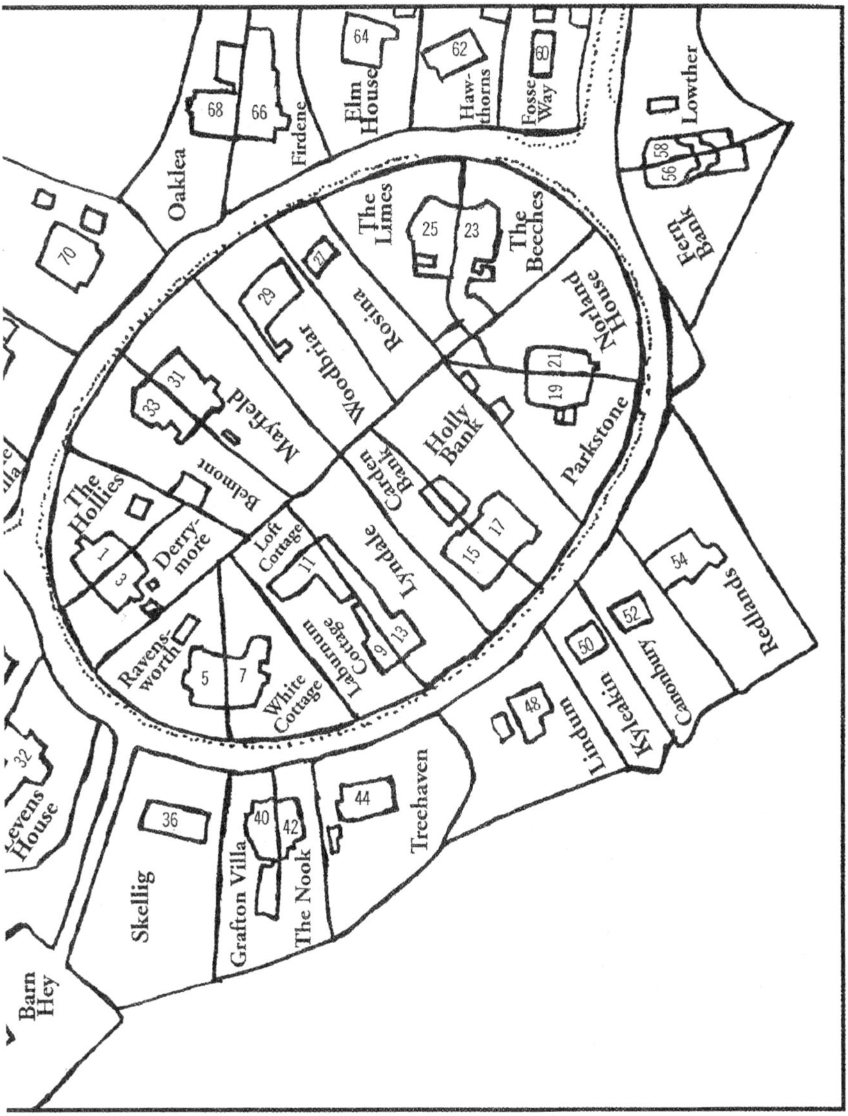
Oaklea
68
66
Firdene
64
Elm House
62
Hawthorns
60
Fosse Way
Lowther
58
56
Fern Bank
70
The Limes
25
23
The Beeches
27
Rosina
29
Woodbriar
Norland House
21
19
Parkstone
31
33
Mayfield
Holly Bank
Garden Bank
Belmont
The Hollies
1
3
Derrymore
Loft Cottage
11
Lyndale
17
15
13
9
Laburnum Cottage
Ravensworth
5
7
White Cottage
54
Redlands
52
Canonbury
Kyleakin
50
Lindum
48
Treehaven
44
The Nook
40
42
Grafton Villa
36
Skellig
32
Levens House
Barn Hey

Contents

Foreword i
Preface ii
Formal acknowledgements v
Upton Park map .... vi-vii
Introduction ix
Chapter 1 - Establishing the Park 1
Chapter 2 - The Covenant 22
Chapter 3 - From plots to households 26
Chapter 4 - Maintaining the Park 134
Chapter 5 - The Proprietors Association (UPPA) 145
Chapter 6 - The Social Scene 152
Chapter 7 - Park People 160
Chapter 8 - Reminiscences 177
Chapter 9 - Military connections and wartime experiences ... 192
Chapter 10 - Yarns 196

Reference Section:
Abstracts from the Minute Book 203
A typical indenture for initial plot ownership 225
The Release of Covenant 230
Census Records 235
Electoral Registers 243
The Chester Civic Trust 256

Introduction

Many local history books have been written about towns, villages and suburbs. Often tracing their roots back for many hundreds of years, they have community centres such as churches, schools, pubs and local businesses.

This history has a far narrower focus, recording a residential estate that until the post-WW2 period had under 50 households and no community centres or businesses. Its Chester neighbourhood is only covered sufficiently to provide context – the book is not a local history of Upton. Nevertheless it has abundant interesting history, both in the archive records of its Association and in the memories and records of residents past and present.

The residential estate was conceived as a truly 'green field site' development but grew quite slowly with a covenant obliging its gradually increasing community to ensure the well-being of the Park and its residents.

Today, the residents of Upton Park enjoy a community spirit rarely found in modern suburbia. The need to raise annual funds and maintain the roadway does have a galvanising effect on this community spirit and leads to a sense of common ownership of the whole Park. With this and the various annual social events there is a strong feeling of belonging and of knowing one's neighbours. There is a good mix of ages and a young family new to the Park is likely to have immediate neighbours still enjoying a happy life here after many decades.

How has the Park brought this about?

While most expansion of housing during the 1850s was still ribbon development panning out along the roads leaving the town, this proposed development of 30 properties in a rural setting on the outskirts of the city was generally ahead of its time. Planned during a 'boom' period but then with slow initial growth in the ensuing slump, the first properties were more modest than the original plan and are believed to have been built very much as one-off developments. Gradually the Upton area grew and the appeal of Upton Park caught on so that by the end of Victoria's reign – some 50 years later – most plots were developed and those still not taken for property development had become extended

INTRODUCTION

gardens and paddocks for residents. All this resulted in a good mix of properties and yet retained the tranquil setting. A feature of the grand initial plan did survive – the tree-lined avenue Park entrance.

Today Upton Park has swelled to some 65 households and is surrounded by suburbia of predominantly post-WW2 vintage. However on entering Upton Park via the Avenue one gets a sense of leaving suburbia, passing down a country lane and then alighting on a tranquil enclave of housing nestled behind characteristic holly hedges and established trees. Add to this the interesting architecture of many of its houses and it is not surprising that it has been declared a Conservation Area.

A leather-bound minute book started in 1899 records the meetings of the Upton Park Proprietors Association (UPPA). While today's affairs are recorded with word processing, the minute book, which was used until the mid-1970s, is still in the archives and has provided much information for this history. Similarly the accounts ledger started in 1921 records house and proprietor names with their assigned rates.

This history attempts to strike a balance of providing reliable reference data while being an enjoyable read. Old manuscripts paid little attention to the spelling of names and places and hence various versions have been encountered and often transcribed here verbatim. Reminiscences have been quoted and even yarns have their own chapter, while the author makes no claims for their authenticity other than that some Park residents have related them in a convincing way. It is hoped that any amusement they may cause is not at anyone else's expense.

Chapter 1
Establishing the Park

Upton and the land before the Park

England's first well-recorded 'census', the famed Domesday Book, describes Upton as having two Manors and a population of between 20-29. These would have been the male heads, hence the true population is usually considered to be five times this figure to include the families. Only one other village in the surrounds of Chester had a population above 20.

From the 1839 Upton-on-the-hill parish tithe map held in the Cheshire Records Office, we see that the site of the original covenanted Upton Park was pastureland. The fields are numbered for tithe purposes as 33, 34 and 35 and named as:

33 - Field adjoining with lane (2 acres, 3 roach, 23 perch)
34 - Little Sour Field (3 acres, 0 roach, 9 perch)
35 - Sour Field (7 acres, 2 roach, 20 perch)

The name suggests poor damp agricultural land and Sour Field is adjacent to a pond. It would follow that this land would be cheaper for building development than good quality farming land. It is interesting to note that many of the early Park deeds refer to Lower Field rather than Sour Field. The word 'sour' was often spelt 'sower' in northern districts of England and in old script the letters 'S' and 'L' are not dissimilar. So either the name got confused by the manuscript writers or possibly it was a useful marketing ploy when selling building plots for grand houses to avoid the name 'Sour Field'.

The lane into field 33 was in existence and the Park Avenue was later taken along the boundary between fields 36 and 37.

Fields 33, 34 and 35 were all owned by Samuel Brittain, a Chester solicitor, and occupied by Joseph Lloyd who appears to have lived in the house on the corner with Mill Lane (shown as 31 on the tithe map) and also used the orchard plot (shown as 32). In common with much of the district the tithe rent was payable to the Earl of Kilmorey and for fields 33, 34 and 35 amounted to a total of £2 13s 4d.

Upton Mill, with its yard and associated buildings including the mill house and garden (shown as 30 on the Tithe map), was also owned by Brittain and occupied by William Carter the miller. Carter used field 36 and other fields within the parish.

Upton Villa (later known as Upton House and then Stanton House) is the house standing in field 29. The house and field (named as White field) are recorded as owned and occupied by Frances Dickson and her husband James.

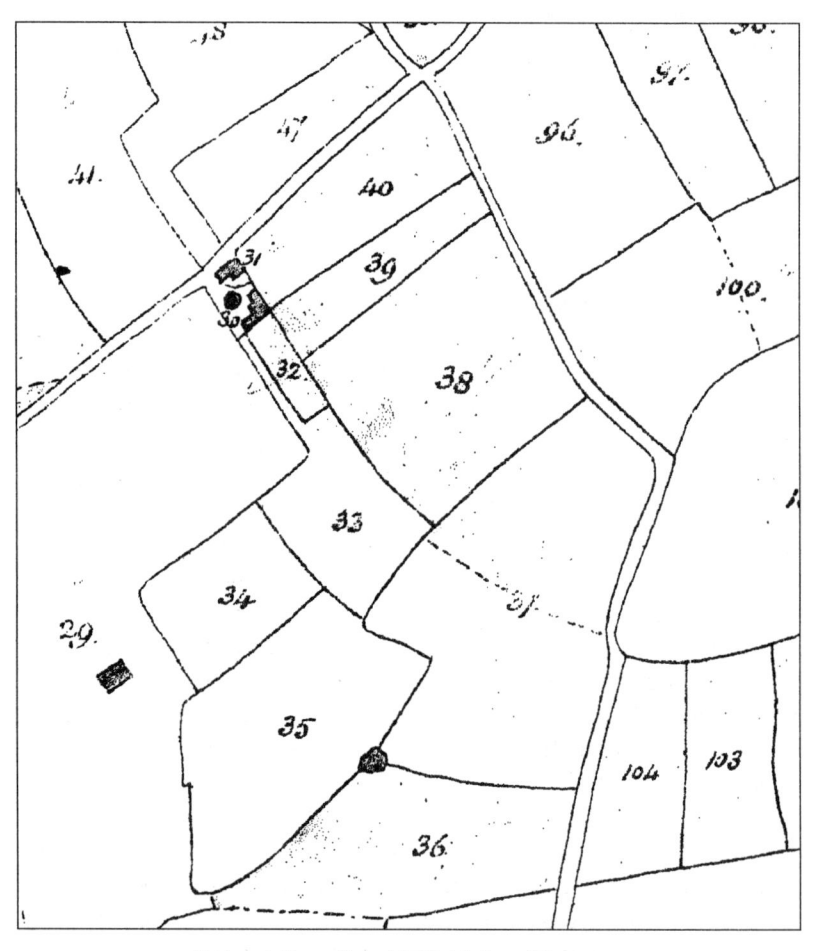

Extract from the 1839 Upton tithe map

The full 1839 parish tithe map shows two clusters of housing in Upton – one around the junction of Church Lane and Upton Lane and the other at the junction of Upton Lane and Mill Lane.

Around the middle of the 1800s, Upton began to grow. In 1840 the Chester to Birkenhead Railway started on a line along Upton's western boundary although Upton was not to get a train station until the next century. Upton had been in the parish of a Chester church, St. Mary's-on-the-hill, but a 'chapel-of-ease' was built in Upton, consecrated in 1854, and became an independent parish around mid-1880s. With a public house (the beginnings of the Wheatsheaf Inn) from around the mid-1850s, a chapel built in 1860, and a school finally built in 1885, the population was clearly growing.

The need: conception of the vision and land acquisition

The 1850s were a prosperous growth period with new technologies, increased communication and public demand for better sanitary living conditions. In Roger Swift's book on *Victorian Chester* John Herson notes a 46% growth in Chester's businesses between 1840 and 1878 but he also notes the appalling insanitary conditions and the 1845 Chester Improvement Act. Chester had a cholera epidemic in 1848 and again in 1866 followed by typhoid in 1887. The population of Chester and its surrounds was growing fast from around 30,000 in 1851 to around 40,000 in 1871. In the 1850s Chester's housing stock increased by nearly 20% – the sharpest rise of the century – and building continued at a relatively high level in the 1860s. Chester's bright future as a port was over but the railways were establishing it as a retail centre. Northgate railway station opened in 1875 and the Manchester Sheffield & Lincolnshire Railway Company opened a Liverpool Road station in 1890.

The new wealth of the artisan class meant that people could demand, and afford, better living conditions with households renting if not buying their homes. Queen's Park on the south side of the River Dee, across from the city, was conceived and the foundation stone of the first house was laid in July 1851. Although not

UPTON PARK, CHESTER

The grand plan drawn by John Hitchen

ESTABLISHING THE PARK

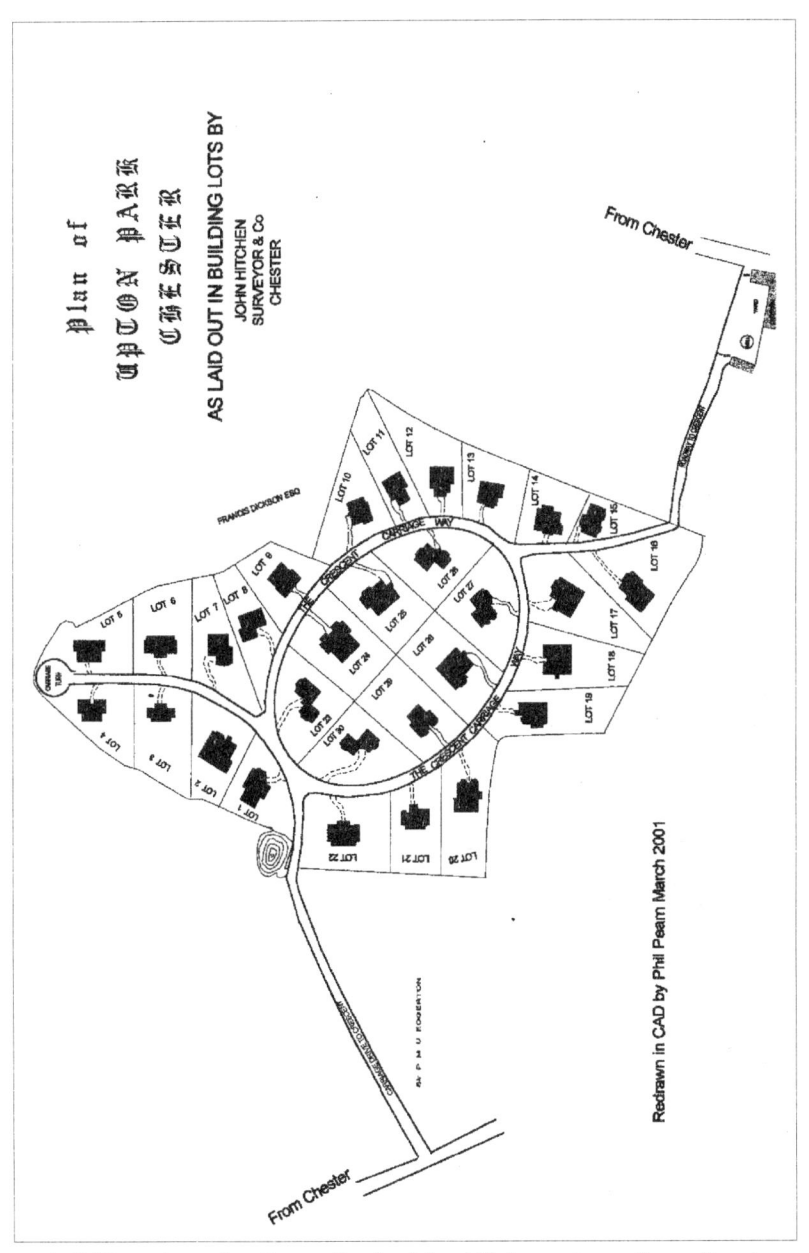

A CAD redraw (by the author) of the Hitchen plan, attempting to copy the original faithfully where it can be discerned

seen as 'rapid progress', some 20 to 30 houses had been erected by the time of an 1852 report.

A group of three fairly young Chester entrepreneurs, William Pitt, William Shone and Thomas Wood, saw the opportunity for a similar but smaller venture just north of the Chester city boundary. A suitable site was available, offering views of the Chester skyline and the Welsh mountains, meadowland towards Upton Heath and the immediate surroundings of a working sail-decked Mill and extensive nursery gardens. Most of all, it was light and airy, could be laid out as a country park and yet had easy access to Chester and the rail network.

Surveyor John Hitchen, who was responsible for Queen's Park, was engaged to draw up a grand plan (see pages 4 and 5), with 30 plots each having a single individually designed property. While on a smaller scale than Queen's Park, the similarity is clear with a central circle and crescent carriageways. Again, like Queen's Park, all plot proprietors would be covenanted to preserve the high standards of the plan.

Most of the land was available from the estate of Samuel Brittain and comprised the three previously-mentioned field plots totalling 13.5acres. Pitt, Shone and Wood bought them on 4 June 1856 as tenants in common.

Conveyances name the sellers as Richard Barker and Ann Brittain, William Walker Brittain, William Brittain and Thomas Brittain.

The Avenue would provide access from Wealstone Lane and this was acquired by Pitt, Shone and Wood on 5 June 1856 from Sir Philip de Malpas Grey Egerton. Access at the other end needed the lane down through the Mill yard and onto Mill Lane. This was acquired by Pitt, Shone and Wood on 4 May 1857 from William Carter.

Finally on 7 May 1857, Pitt, Shone and Wood, seemingly in league with James Dickson of the nurseries, acquired land from Charles Dutton and James Smith. The location of this land is not clear.

ESTABLISHING THE PARK

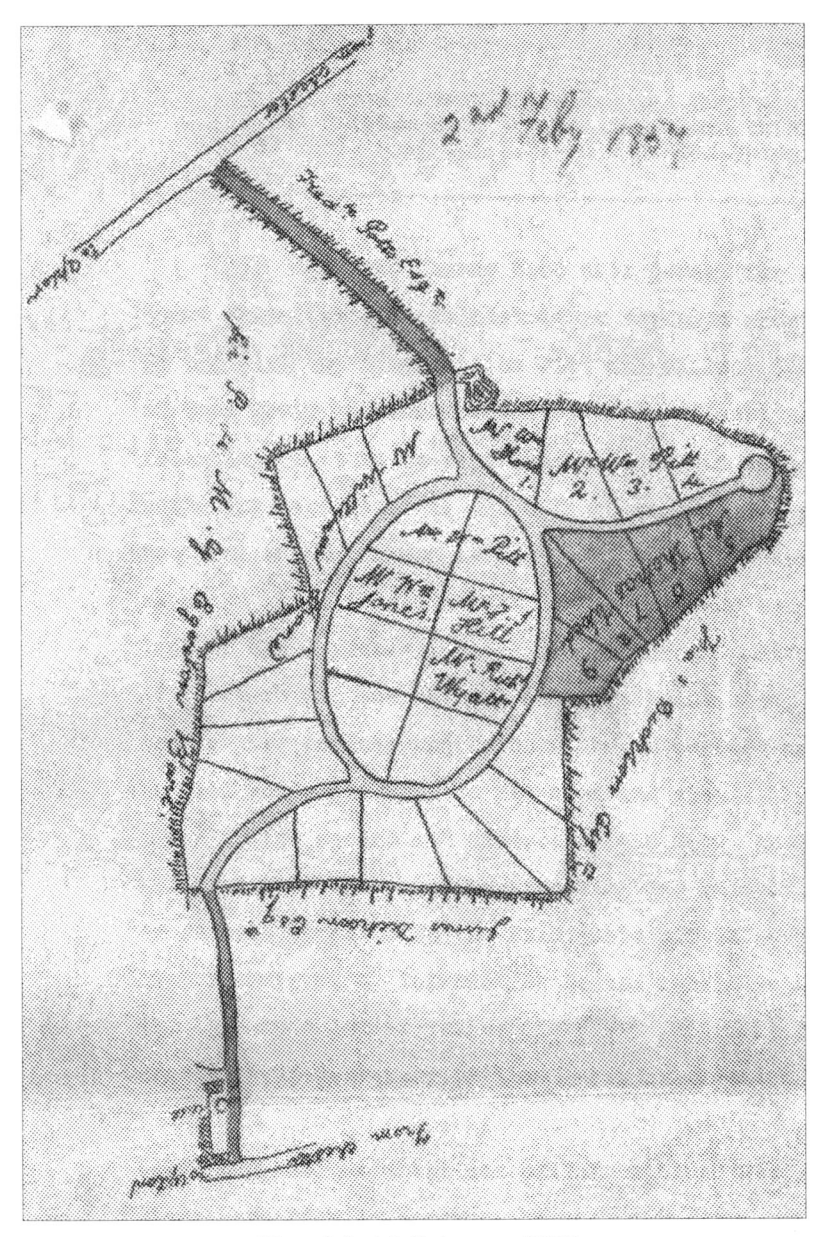

Plan dated 2 February 1857

Pitt and Wood move in, and the first plots are sold in the late 1850s

By 1857 the three founders had reorganised their tenants-in-common arrangement into individually owned specific plots. Some plots had also by this time been sold on to third parties.

This plan dated 2 February 1857 (see page 7) shows allocations in the southern half of the Park.

By 17 August 1857 a plan (see page 9) covering the full covenanted area was included with indentures. This records changes since the February plan, interestingly showing division of plots indicating the intention to build double properties.

The named plan is difficult to read hence the following table gives the named plots (plot ownership is shown related to the current postal numbers).

- plot 1 (now Nos. 56, 58) to Griffiths, Foulks
- plots 2 thro' 7 (now not in the Park) to Dickson the adjoining land owner
- plots 8, 9, 10 (now 54, 52, 50, 48, 46) also to Dickson
- plot 11 (now 42, 40) to Haswell, Denson
- plot 12 (now 36) to Denson
- plots 13, 14 (now 32, 28, 30 and drives to 32A and 34) to Woodward
- plots 15, 16, 17 (now 26, 24, 84, 80, 76, 74) to Pitt
- plots 18, 19, 20, 21, 22 (now 72, 70, 68, 66, 64, 62, 60) to Shone
- plot 23 (now 21, 19) to Holland, Pitt
- plot 24 (now 17, 15) to Wood
- plot 25 (now 13, 11, 9) to Wood, Roberts
- plot 26 (now 7, 5) to Evans, Wilkins
- plots 27; 28 (now 3, 1, 33, 31) to Wilkins
- plot 29 (now 29, 27) to Jones
- plot 30 (now 25, 23) to Pitt

Despite the apparent advanced state of these 1857 plans, by the Spring 1861 census, the Park had only four households.

Two were founding fathers Pitt and Wood. Pitt lived at No. 84 (possibly a double originally) and Wood lived at No. 13 (a double). Whether the other two households were the other halves or whether they were another one or two properties is not certain.

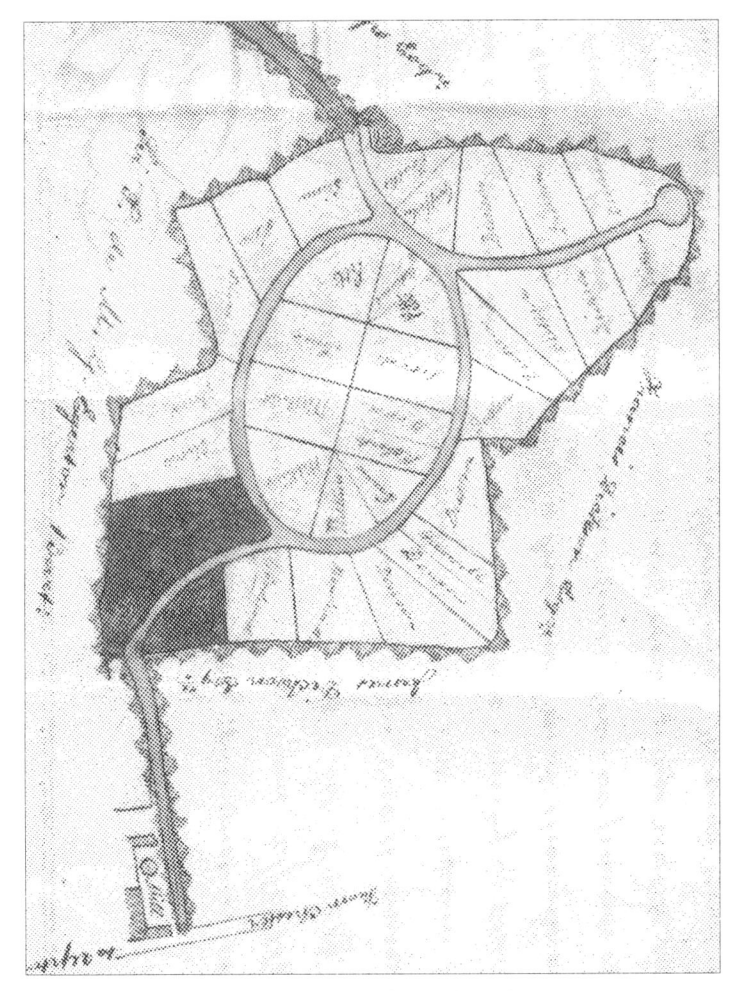

Plan dated 17 August 1857

However, they are not signatories on the 1870 Covenant Release document and hence it is a reasonable assumption that they were tenants to Pitt and Wood in the other halves of their double properties.

Details of these four households can be seen in the 1861 census.

Pitt had built his house in the top northerly corner of the Park at the end of the Mill yard and orchard. Presumably this helped with access. Wood's house may have been built after Pitt's when the roadway was usable. Quite possibly the Avenue access was later than the Mill access.

During the 1860s it is likely that other properties were built, the most likely being:
- Nos. 5/7
- Nos. 40/42
- Nos. 1/3
- Nos. 56/58

All these first properties were doubles (although the original state of No. 84 has not been fully established). The practice appears to have deviated well from the original Hitchen plan.

Why wasn't the grand plan working out?

It may have been that the property market was slumping a little after the high activity of the 1850s. The Queen's Park history also tells of this slowdown. Maybe it took time to persuade home-seekers to come to Upton Park when Queen's Park was more established and, with the new bridge, much closer to the city and the railway network. It may simply have been the building boom causing over-supply or the Upton Park prices being too high.

Release of covenant and revision agreed

The covenant included in early indentures can be seen in the Reference section and the Release of Covenant is fully explained in its own chapter.

A document duly signed by many plot owners and dated 12 January 1870 released the original covenant which restricted building to only one property – double or single – per plot. It then established a new covenant whereby each of the 30 building plots were now allowed either one double or two single properties.

Only one certified copy of this Covenant Release document is known to exist – it is dated 18 December 1874.

The assumption is that the Release document is between all the plot owners at that time, however, this is not specifically stated. Most of the current owners' deeds, that have been seen, refer to the 1870 covenant. To date it is only the deeds for plot 19 – The Cedars – which was sold for building in 1933 that makes no reference to the 1870 revised covenant but rather refers to the early 1857 covenant. This is surprising since William Shone was the holder of the 1870 revision and he had interests in plot 19 right up to 1919.

Six days after signing the 1870 revision, Pitt, who on 1 October 1869 had just sold his property on part of plot 16, sold much of the unused plot 16 to William Beswick who then built a single property (No. 80). The conveyance "Pitt to Beswick" shows the existing property as a single but the first OS survey in 1872 shows it still as a double. If it was still a double then this appears to be in total defiance of the new covenant.

Pitt may have either already converted the existing property Millside (No. 84) into a single or covenanted the new owner – David Horsefield – so to do. No record is known of any such conversion until after the survey of 1898.

Millside is known to have been a single property since 1920 and believed to have been so since the late 1800s. So the evidence is conflicting as to whether it actually was a double that was made a single as part of the 1870 Release of Covenant agreement.

Why was the covenant released and a revision agreed?

- surely the legality and cost (nearly £2 in stamp duty) of the release would have been better used to split plot 16 into two plots if the only need was two singles on plot 16?
- why the need to build again on plot 16 while so many other plots were vacant?
- did the other plot owners really see this as a benefit to them when none of them actually made use of it?

Whatever the reasoning for the rethink of covenant the interesting fact is that other than for the building of Westview (No. 80) the revision of the covenant was not exploited again for nearly a century.

Maybe Pitt had great foresight of the building demands a century later – if he did some later proprietors are grateful to him while others wish the original rules had stayed!

Pitt built and moved into one of the Hawthorne Villas (No. 19) or Chatham Villas (Nos. 23/25) – in either case facing at the head of the now established tree-lined Avenue. He left the Park a few years later seemingly having sold or mortgaged all his interests in it and, some evidence suggests, not a wealthy man.

A final point: it is not known today whether all the then current plot and subplot owners signed the Release of Covenant document – although the document implies this. There is no signature from Dickson, for example.

Assumption down the years has been that for all those covenanted plots remaining in the Park, this revised covenant applies – except apparently the deeds of The Cedars which gives no mention to the 1870 change.

Early 1870s and still with only eight resident households

The 1872 OS survey shows 16 dwellings, suggesting that development was finally underway. However, the 1871 census records only eight households (see Reference section) and the Upton area having several unoccupied properties. Some of these buildings though appear to be owned by absent landlords – possibly speculative rental building not yet drawing tenants.

The early indentures embedded the covenant and are difficult-to-read legal documents comprising one continuous sentence manuscript on a sheet between A1 and A2 size. (See a transcript of a typical indenture in the Reference section).

In essence (paraphrased by the editor) each indenture of a property states the following:

Three Chester speculators, William Shone, Thomas Wood and William Pitt acquired the 13.5 acres of poor farmland for Upton Park from the Brittain family on 4 June 1856. One of the three or A N Other then acquired a number of plots, a single plot or a part-plot for £xxx xs 0d (and then sometimes sells on a subset to a third party), who then sold on for a specific property to be built generally for the first owner. All the rights established by Pitt, Shone and Wood are 'in perpetuity' i.e. established for their heirs and for anyone that they assigned by such action as by selling any of the land. Pitt, Shone and Wood had acquired right of way through the Mill yard. Each owner takes on the obligation to fund their proportion of establishing all road, sewer, fences, etc, and then maintain these. For each property sold on, the owner took on this maintenance obligation in proportion to their ground area. Every owner took on the revised covenant obligation regarding dwelling density. This states that only one double or two single dwellings were to be built per original plot and that these should be to a standard (in current parlance) of not less than Council Tax band F or G. Every owner was restricted by covenant to not set up unsightly animal sheds or carry out any business to give nuisance or offence to others.

Property development now fully underway

Well before the end of the Victorian era, the covenanted area, as we know it today, was established, mainly with double villas – the grander style of villa coming after the first few properties. The only villa with black and white top-half timber cladding seems to be the last but it was still built and lived in before the 1891 census. The few vacant plots on the outer circle were generally used as orchards or gardens.

Before WW2 a few single dwellings were built within the covenanted area and along the lane, opposite the mill yard and orchard.

After WW2 the explosion in housing development led to the demolition of Upton House (formerly the base of Dickson's nursery). Plots 2 through 7, which never really became part of the Park, left the covenanted area and were absorbed into a new and separate modern estate.

Meanwhile the 50 post-war years saw completion of the Park with 12 single dwellings within the covenanted area and a further 13 dwellings in the northwest of the now expanded Upton Park. Of the 12 in the covenanted area, eight have exercised the relaxed covenant allowing two single properties within an original plot.

Throughout, no dwelling has been demolished.

Journey through the Ordnance Survey for the development story

The 1st edition Ordnance Survey map (see page 16) published in 1880 shows the result of survey work on Upton Park in 1872.

Already several houses existed, some named: five doubles on

the inner circle, two doubles on the outer circle, and two singles on the lane towards the Mill. It is interesting to note that several vacant plots are shown with orchard or gardens possibly in use by the occupied plots.

The 2nd edition Ordnance Survey map published in 1899 (see page 17) shows the result of survey work on Upton Park in 1898.

The circle was now complete as regards intentions at the time. Census records suggests this may have been fairly soon after the 1872 survey with the exception of plot 24 which stayed as Thomas Wood's garden grounds until Nos. 15 and 17 were built in the 1880s. By this 1898 survey, several outer circle properties had also been built.

It must be remembered that these maps only show the existence of dwellings without indication of their occupancy. The available census records cover 1891 but 1901 is as yet unavailable.

As properties were developed several were in the hands of other residents presumably seeing them as investments and taking on tenants.

By the 3rd edition OS survey map published in 1912 (see page 18), no further dwellings are shown within the covenanted area but two doubles have been built c.1904/5 opposite the Mill orchard along the lane to the Mill (Nos. 12, 14, 16, 18).

By the 1932 OS survey (see page 19), two single dwellings were added to the outer circle and five singles completed the length of lane opposite the mill yard and orchard. Park accounts record these latter five as built in the mid-1920s. Only one further single dwelling was added to the outer circle in 1935 and was featured on the next edition (post 1936) OS map (see page 20).

Immediately after WW2 a further single (No. 44) was added to the outer circle, restricted in size at the time due to post-war regulations. In the 1980s it was enlarged to its current state.

While no dwelling demolition has occurred, early OS maps show a glasshouse on the site of the New House (No. 72). Some UPPA maps referred to this as 'the ruin'.

Over the last 50 years, there has been a number of new dwellings infilling in accord with the covenant restrictions, built in a variety of styles of the day but none replicating the original period design. Hence all the period properties are original although some of these have been modified or extended.

An interesting reflection on shifting fashion trends is that for the few decades post WW2, the older buildings were seen as less desirable and some owners of older properties were buying the orchard/garden plots and building new dwellings offering the comforts of advancing technology. Rateable values based on potential rental income were much lower for the older properties which all added to the environment in which buyers of some older properties would have preferred the newer ones but could not afford them. Towards the end of the 20th century trends had swung with period houses becoming more desirable again and often bought by those wishing to reinstate the period look.

During the WW2 war effort iron railings and gates were removed in great numbers and it is unlikely that Upton Park escaped. Evidence suggests that many of the 19th century dwellings had iron gates but only some of these remain. Some have clearly been added in recent years to restore the original appearance.

While trees remain a major feature of the Park, residents' grounds are generally landscaped now to today's style of lawn and flower beds. Although some keen vegetable gardeners are still around there is now little in the way of orchards and allotments when compared to past times.

Property extensions and upgrades are on-going, often occurring at change of ownership. As regards new dwellings, the Park is now probably full. Although the covenant could not restrict a few plots from adding new dwellings, the covenanted area is now within a Conservation Area which adds a new perspective to any planning application.

UPTON PARK, CHESTER

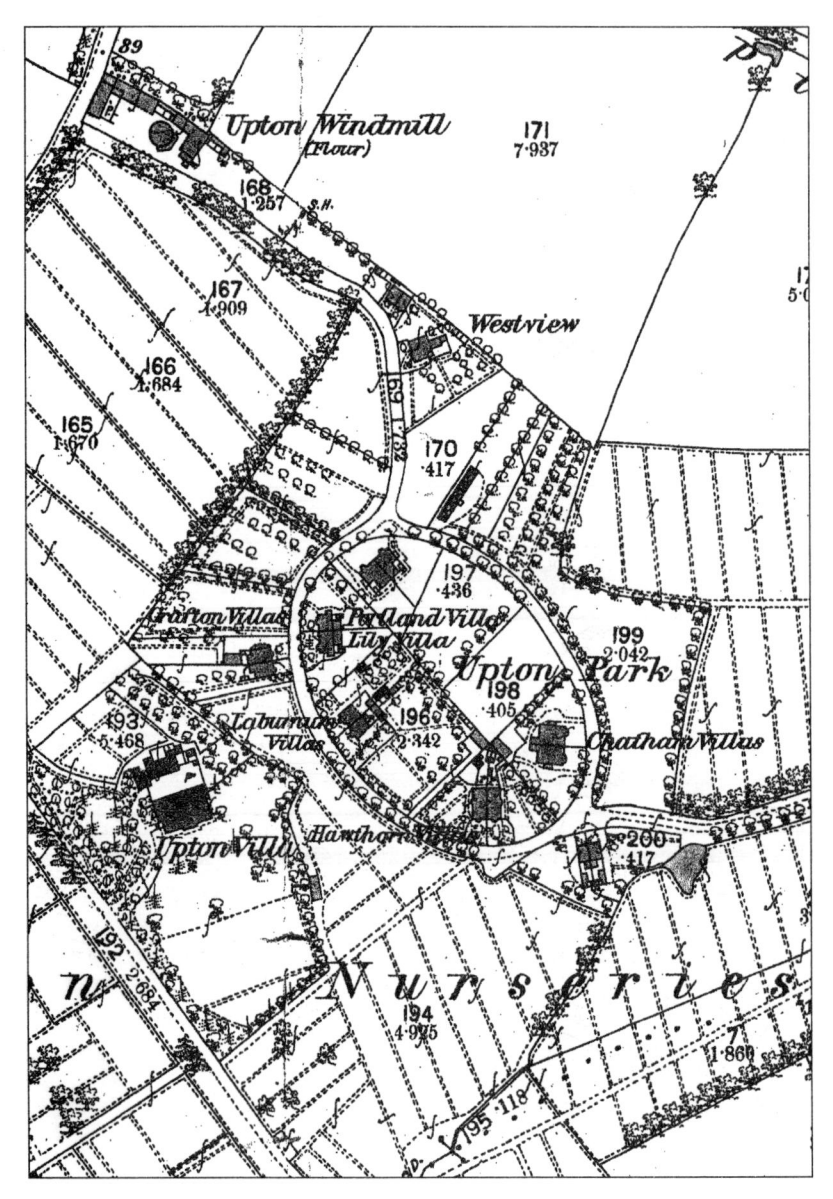

Extract from the 1872 Ordnance Survey

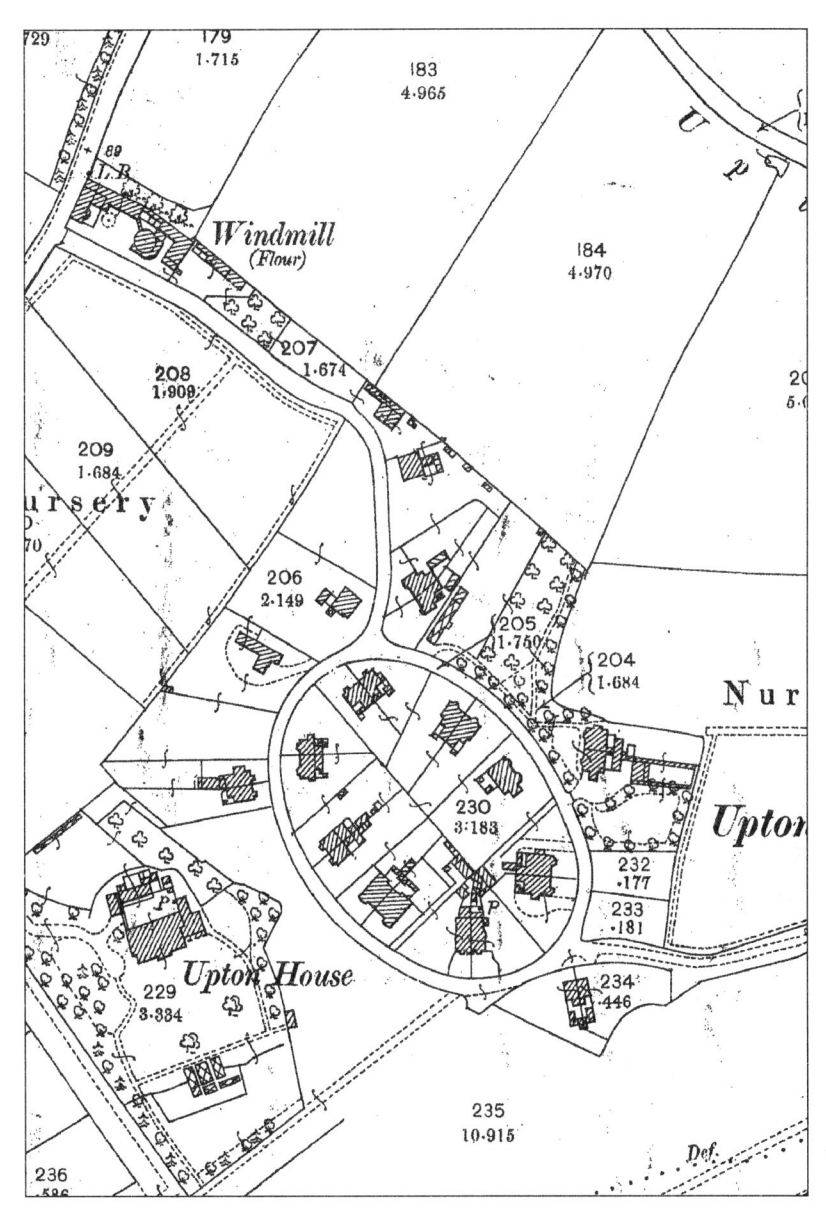

ESTABLISHING THE PARK

Extract from the 1898 Ordnance Survey

UPTON PARK, CHESTER

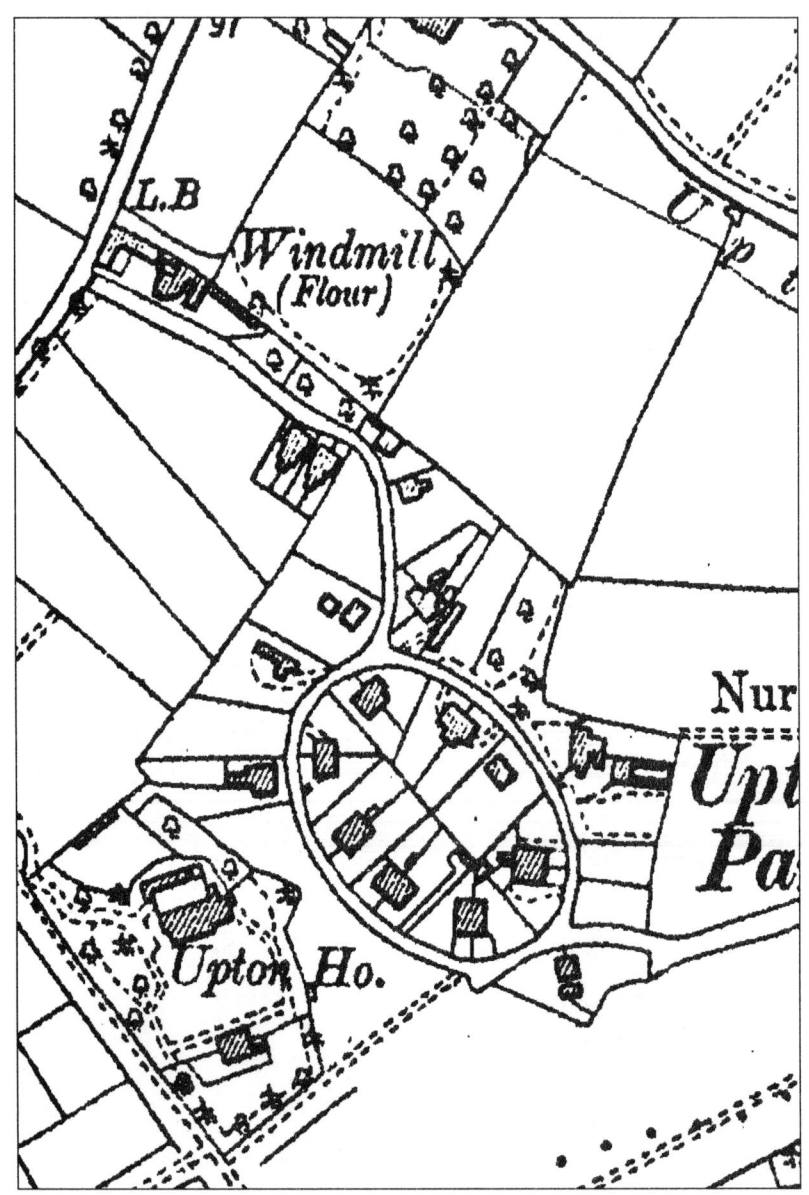

Extract from a 6" 3rd edition Ordnance Survey map published 1912 believed to be from a 1908 survey

ESTABLISHING THE PARK

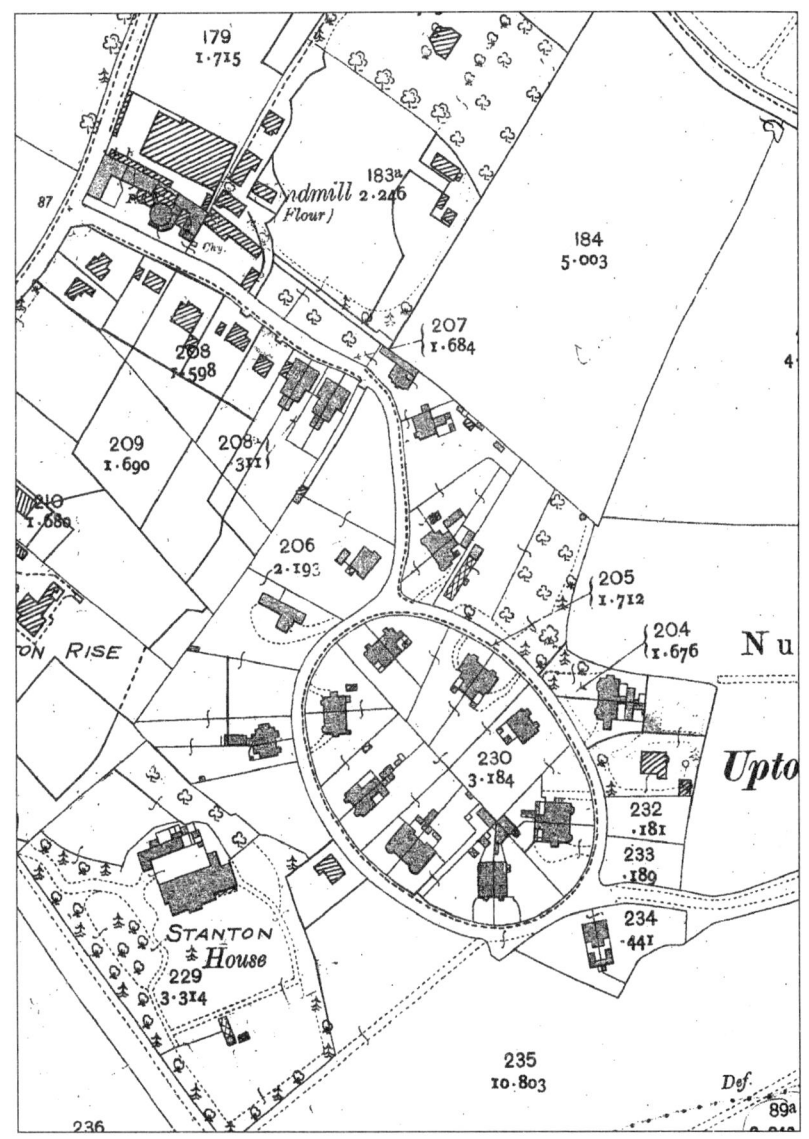

Extract from the 1932 revised Ordnance Survey

UPTON PARK, CHESTER

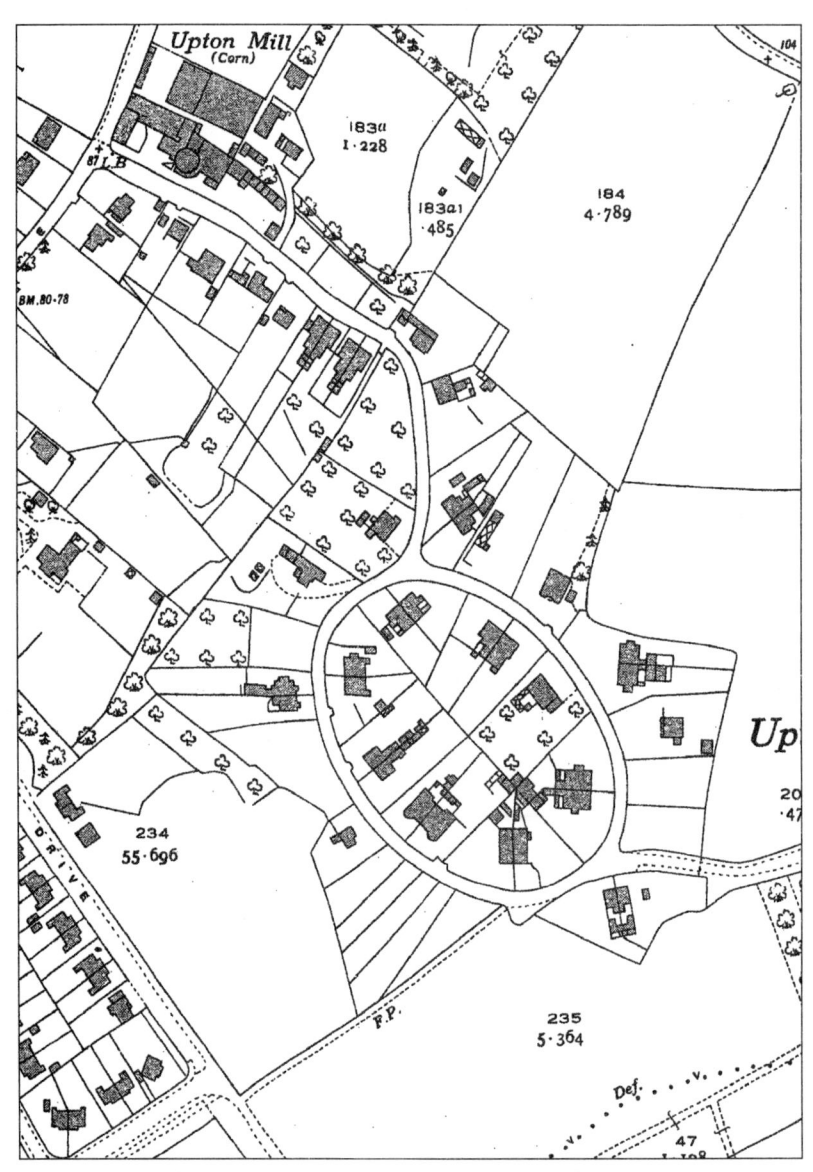

*Extract from the Post-1936 Ordnance Survey map
but date of survey not identified*

ESTABLISHING THE PARK

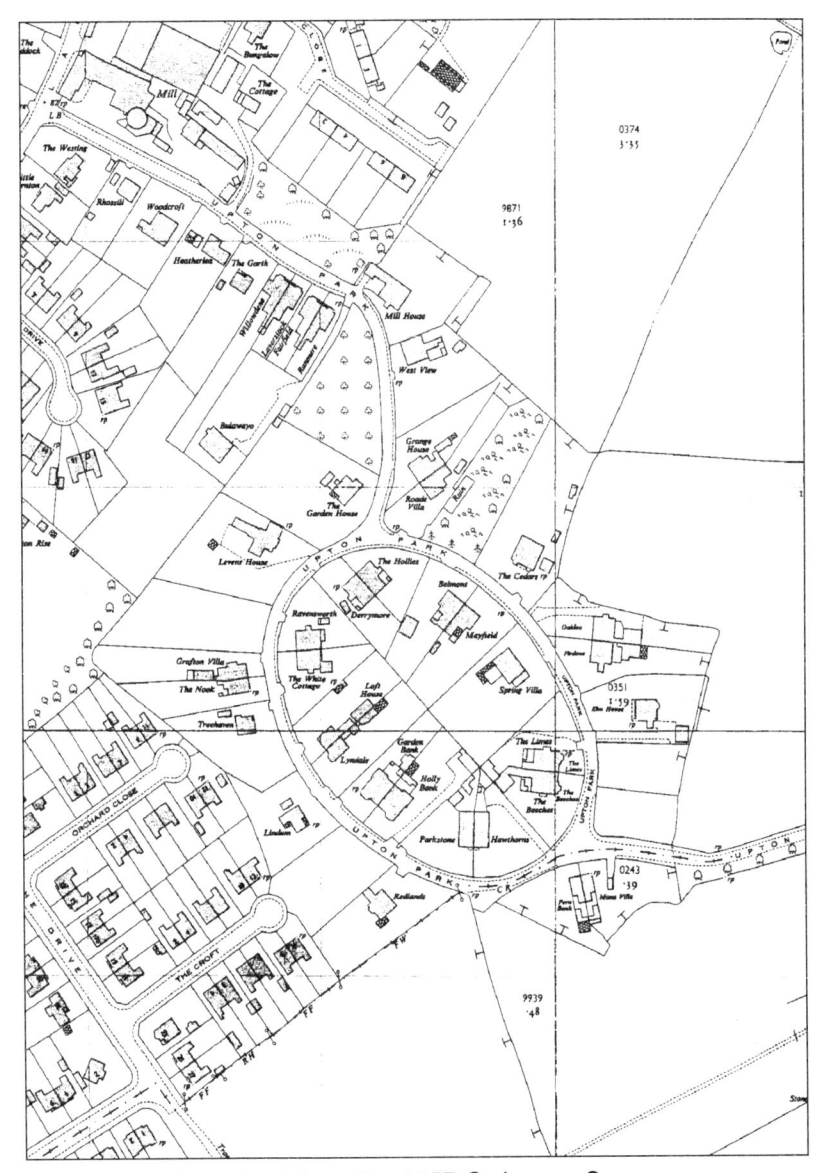

An extract from the 1957 Ordnance Survey
Reproduced by kind permission of Ordnance Survey
Crown Copyright © NC/01/25951

Chapter 2
The Covenant

Understanding the Covenant

Disclaimer: *The following has no authoritative legal standing and has been compiled by an engineer with no legal training. However, the research for this history has surely been far more extensive than that carried out by any conveyancing clerk and by HM Land Registry at any conveyance of a property. It is written here to aid a wider understanding based on a good spread of supportive evidence and systematic analysis rather than folklore, emotion and isolated questionable pieces of evidence.*

To many residents of Upton Park, 'The Covenant' has a majesty as its 'Bible' governing the heritage of life in the Park. Emotions can be raised and it is often discussed like folklore without fully informed knowledge.

In essence it is a perpetual binding agreement between fellow proprietors for the wellbeing of the Upton Park community. Custom and practice has allowed variations where this is seen by all as beneficial and within the spirit of the original agreement.

The covenant is similar to that of Queen's Park but is more liberal. It does not, for example, restrict the use of land so that it cannot be used for purposes connected with the Roman Catholic religion such as a Roman Catholic church, chapel, monastery or nunnery. Neither has it, for many years, controlled the positioning of buildings or been so specific in their allocation of use.

The first covenant seems to originate from when the 30 building plots passed from tenants-in-common ownership by Pitt, Shone and Wood to individual ownership of specific plots.

Either the founding fathers wanted to retain control of the standards on which the Park would develop or they were obliged to do so by the previous land owners. Roger Swift's book on *Victorian Chester* states that the Cathedral Dean and Chapter owned much of the land to the north of the city which as they sold it off from 1845 had covenants to ensure high quality building.

However, areas such as Kilmorey Park have seen their covenants lapse.

One covenanted area near Upton Park is Flookers Brook. Its covenant is enshrined in an Act of Parliament dated 1876. The Flookers Brook Improvement Trust has a board of trustees including Flookers Brook proprietors but also appointees of the original land owners.

On 12 January 1870, Pitt, Shone and Wood signed a document claimed to be with the full set of owners of the 30 plots making up Upton Park. This released the original covenant restriction on housing density and established a new slightly relaxed restriction.

Down through the years, the covenant with its 12 January 1870 revision has been referenced or reiterated or interpreted and restated in all the household conveyances within the covenanted area.

This has resulted in HM Land Registry having a variety of references to the covenant as each property has been recorded within its system:

- "the original conveyance contains restrictive covenants but neither the original deed nor a certified copy or examined abstract was produced on first registration."

- A version of the covenant then stated is often lacking in certain aspects (possibly those considered outdated) and some embellishments have crept in such as restricting "any trade whatsoever" rather than the founding father's intention of not causing nuisance or offence.

- However, the following is also found: "will at all times hereafter observe and perform the covenants contained in the original Indenture of Conveyance between the initial developers and the first owner of their property."

Conviction since the passing of the founding fathers' era, down through the years, has been that only the support of all covenanted proprietors could lead to any changes in it. How the Park rate is shared out is the only real alteration since 1870, this having been changed significantly twice.

Original covenant documents still exist within the indentures of the first individual land owners (e.g. Pitt for plots 15, 16, 17).

Only one certified copy of the 12 January 1870 release document is known to exist and is in private ownership.

Unofficial transcripts of an original pre-1870 indenture and of the 1870 Release of Covenant can be found in the Reference section.

In plain English, what does the revised covenant say and imply today?

Essentially it covers three topics:

- **Density and quality of properties:** Only one double or two single properties on each of the original 30 plots, built to a standard with a value not less that that which would align with today's Council Tax band F (or maybe G). The positioning of the building within the plot is not defined other than to restrict unsightly outhouses and animal sheds away from frontages. Pitt, Wood and Shone possibly expected the estate to be completed within their time of interest because they specified that they should approve the building plans. They made no provision for this authority after their deaths.
- **Establishing and maintaining the common areas:** Common roadways, pathways, boundaries and services had to be established and maintained in what was an area outside the provision of the local council. On several occasions throughout its history, UPPA has investigated the adoption of the Park by the council but the question has been dropped since 1947 when the Council estimated a prohibitively high cost to bring it up to the desired standard. To this day it remains independent for certain services such as roadway and roadside maintenance. Provision and service of all utilities is funded by the utility provider.

Proprietors are obligated to share the funding of this maintenance. The 1870 covenant stated sharing as in proportion to the square yardage of each proprietor's ownership (including vacant lots as gardens). In later years this was applied even to electrical suppliers for their substation and to the War Office for a gateway off to their land. At a general meeting of UPPA on 16 December 1927 it was resolved to adopt rateable values as the basis of the sharing. At the 1966 UPPA AGM it was first proposed to adopt equal shares. Although rejected on that occasion it was later agreed. Both these changes have been by general agreement between proprietors.

- **Use of the properties:** No businesses are allowed which cause nuisance or offence. This is not as specific as for Queen's Park and today's legislation of public nuisance acts has surely superseded this covenant clause.

As previously stated, no unsightly animal outhouses are permitted. Unlike Queen's Park, no specific animals are named as prohibited but again this is now controlled by modern legislation.

The density of use of the property (e.g. multiple family occupancy or servants' quarters in outhouses) is not covered. Again, not as strict as Queen's Park, the covenant does not prohibit the renting or selling to 'unrespectable' families although some residents have occasionally wished such a clause had been copied!

The only real challenge to the covenant has been with regard to property density. This point is strongly guarded by proprietors and has survived many challenges. The recent Conservation Area status should hopefully further help the case to retain it.

As recorded in the 22 March 1958 Estates Gazette, Mr. J R Laird, member of the Lands Tribunal, ruled that the indenture dated 12 January 1870 be modified to permit the Dickson Drive development on what were plots 2, 3, 4, 5, 6 and 7. In reality these plots had never been part of Upton Park and no road to them had been built – they were just a footpath through to Dickson's nursery.

The covenant was successfully used in a 1996 hearing to stop over-development of plot 15 when two permitted properties had been erected in such a way that a third could have been possible. Hence the 'plot' opposite Nos. 80/84.

A few residents have argued that today we accept a far higher density of building as still offering a desirable environment and that the 1870 thinking is now outdated. They have always been persuaded otherwise.

Chapter 3
From plots to households

Introduction to the history of the individual houses in Upton Park

Although the postal address house numbers belong to fairly recent history they are used as the definitive locator of a dwelling since house-names have often been changed over the years. However to journey through the houses in numerical order would not be helpful and so the order in the book has been set very much from the historical relationship between the dwellings.

As has been discussed in Chapter 1, the covenanted area originated with 30 plots although only 24 were developed to provide 42 dwellings. A further 23 dwellings that form Upton Park are outside the covenanted area and cannot be associated with any early plot plan.

Section A – See pages 30-43
Plots 16, 17, 18
House numbers **84, 80, 76, 74** and **72** – plots originally owned by Pitt and then having some inter-connected ownership for many decades.

Section B – See pages 44-49
Plots 19, 20, 21
House numbers **66, 68, 64** and **70** – originally Shone's estate with one double villa, for many decades, until the grounds were sold for building development between the wars.

Section C – See pages 50-57
Plots 22, 30
House numbers **23, 25, 62** and **60** – originally owned by Pitt with the one double villa and ground opposite, until developed post-WW2.

FROM PLOTS TO HOUSEHOLDS

Section D – See pages 58-60
Plot 1
House numbers **56** and **58** – a double property built in the early days of the Park.

Section E – See pages 61-63
Plot 23
House numbers **19** and **21** – a double property built in the early days of the Park

Section F – See pages 64-76
Plots 24, 25
House numbers **13, 9, 11, 17** and **15** – originally owned by Wood and one of the earliest double properties which then some 25 years later had another double property built in the grounds.

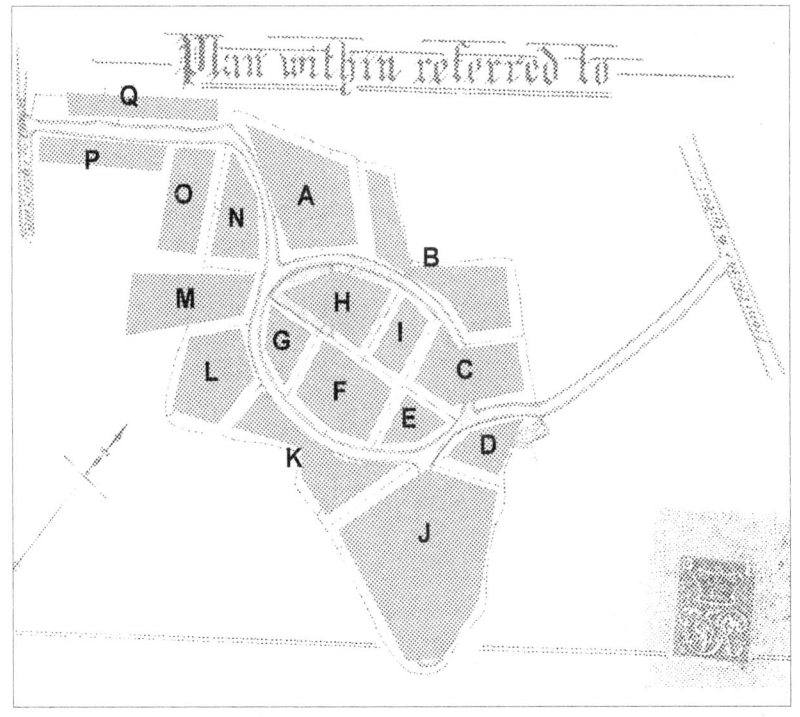

Plan showing plot sections

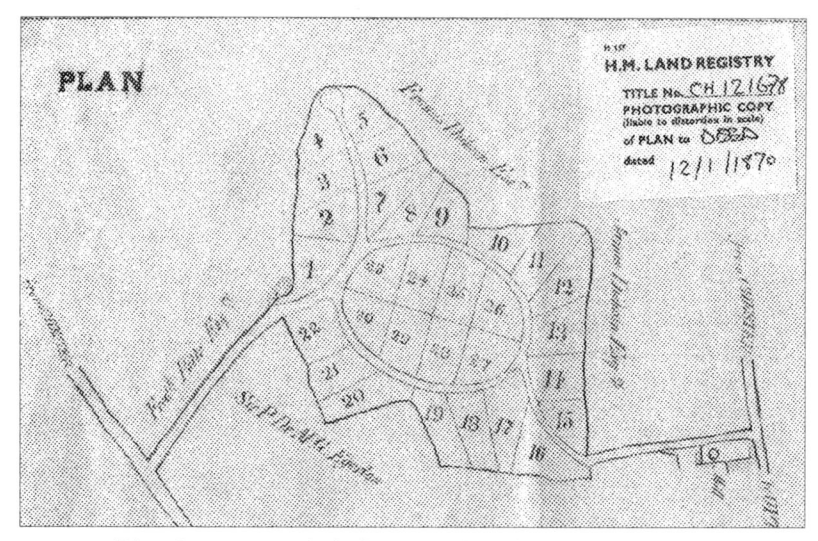

Plan from an early indenture, dated 12 January 1870

Section G – See pages 77-81
Plot 26
House numbers **5** and **7** – a double property built in the early days of the Park.

Section H – See pages 82-88
Plot 27, 28
House numbers **1, 3, 31** and **32** – a double property built in the early days of the Park and a second double property a decade or so later.

Section I – See pages 89-92
Plot 29
House numbers **29** and **27** – the only Victorian single property on the inner circle with a second property built in its grounds post-WW2.

Section J – See page 93

Plots 2 – 7
No Park houses built – plots taken out of the Park in the 1950s.

Section K – See pages 94-99
Plots 8, 9, 10

House numbers **48, 44, 54, 50** and **52** – plots used for many years by Dicksons Nursery and then developed 1930-1965.

Section L – See pages 100-104
Plots 11, 12
House numbers **40, 42** and **36** – a double property built in the early days of the Park and a single property built in its paddock in the mid-1970s.

Section M – See pages 105-108
Plot 13 and non-covenanted land behind.
House numbers **32, 34** and **32A** – a single property built in the 1890s which then used some of its grounds to provide access to two modern bungalows built in 1960 and 1979.

Section N – See pages 109-112
Plots 14, 15
House numbers **28, 30, 24** and **26** – a single property built in the 1890s which acquired an orchard plot, later used to develop two single properties in the 1960s, and then in 1985 built a bungalow in its garden grounds.

Section O – See pages 113-119
First development area on the south side of the lane to the Mill.
House numbers **12, 14, 16, 18** and **20** – two double properties built early in the 1900s and a bungalow built behind them in 1955.

Section P – See pages 120-124
Second development area on the south side of the lane to the mill.
House numbers **2, 4, 6,** and **10** – five single properties built in the 1920s.

Section Q – See pages 125-131
The Mill and its former grounds
House numbers **86-104** – Upton Mill House, formerly in Upton Park, and the residential buildings developed in the 1960s.

Section A: Plots 16, 17, 18

House numbers
84 built c1859
80 built 1870
74 & 76 built c1890
72 built 1959

On 17 August 1857, William Pitt bought out the two-thirds shares of Shone and Wood for plots 15, 16 and 17 totalling 6722 sq yds for the sum of £336 2s. It appears that this was funded by railway clerk Evan Reece Evans, who may have been Pitt's father-in-law. He then died before 1861.

Early records suggest that William Pitt then built Millside (No. 84) in the northern corner of plot 16 and lived there with his family and mother-in-law. They are recorded in the 1861 census but simply with an Upton Park location and no house name. On 1 October 1869, Pitt then sold the property on a 775 sq yd sub-plot retaining the remaining larger sub-plot of plot 16. The original covenant allowed only one property, double or single, on each plot and so his remaining part of plot 16 had no development potential.

On 12 January 1870, Pitt had the agreement of Shone and Wood, and certain other plot owners, to release the restriction on building and allow one double or two singles per plot. Six days later this enabled Pitt to sell the remaining 1613 sq yds of plot 16 to William Beswick to build Westview (No. 80).

It appears that Pitt also sold plot 17 in 1870, to Bell and Evans, who may have been his father-in-law. If he was then it returned to Pitt again on Evans' death shortly afterwards. Whether Bell built the double property (Nos. 74 and 76) is not known but it appears that the first owner of the double property was William Smith of Westview following its building c1890. On 25 January 1873, Pitt sold plot 15 (some 2219 sq yds) to widow Margaret Anne Higginson. Plot 15 lay undeveloped for many decades.

Plot 18 is included in this cluster of houses because although initially it was part of the Shone estate (along with plots 19, 20 and

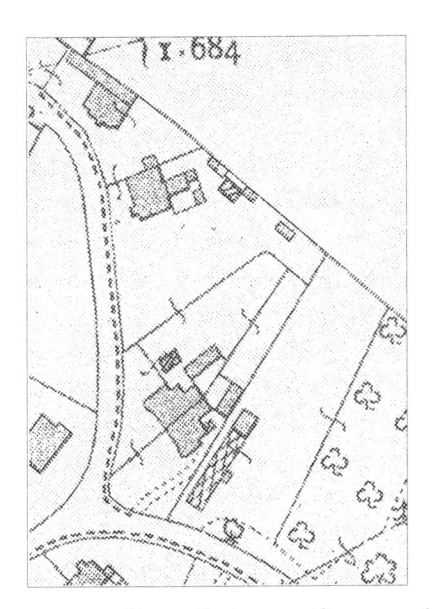

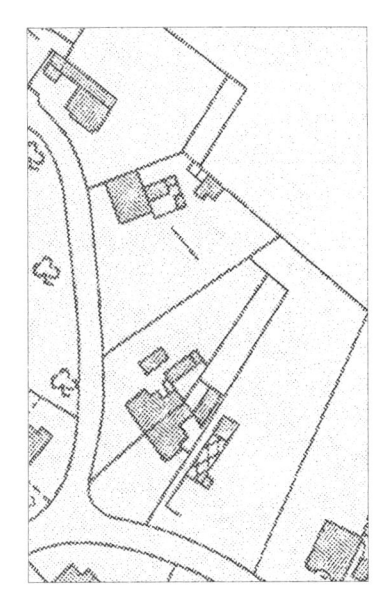

From Ordnance Surveys during the 1930s showing boundary changes

21), its history has been more associated with plots 16 and 17. The 1872 OS survey shows a greenhouse on plot 18 and a 1912 mortgage deed refers to a vinery and as well as an orchard. When the owner of Westview built the double property (Nos. 74 & 76) their boundary was such that Westview retained back access to plot 18 probably renting it as allotment from the Shone estate. After the former Shone estate was acquired by the Furleys they sold plot 18 to R W Gardner of Grange House (No. 76) who also acquired the interconnecting piece of land from Cecelia Pearson of Westview. Plot 18 with the back strip then stayed under the ownership of Grange House for about 10 years until it was sold by the new owner, Mrs Iva Williams, to Elsie Lotitia Roberts on 19 September 1936. The plot stayed undeveloped until after the death of Miss Roberts in 1955. Inherited by her cousins, bookbinder Frank Sconce and retired policeman Samuel Jones, they sold the land in March 1958 for building by Dr John Cameron Doran. The 1950s OS is the first survey showing the greenhouse as a ruin.

No. 84 Upton Park
Now known as Millside
formerly Mill Cottage but Millside since pre-1920

The 1872 and 1898 OS surveys show the property as a pair of cottages. All the other pre-1870 properties were pairs and it is likely that William Pitt and family lived in one half with tenants (see 1861 census) in the other half. Although the layout of internal walls with the central staircase does not support a notion of two equal sized halves, nevertheless there are enough indicators that the property was a double later converted to a single to satisfy the new 1870 covenant regarding the building of Westview (No. 80) on the same plot. The front porch appears to have been added early in the 20th century and at some point a ribbon line of bricks has been painted yellow probably following the fashion of many 1870s Park houses which feature a course of yellow bricks.

The first owner after William Pitt was railway goods guard David Horsefield. The 1871 census records him at 32 years residing with his wife Mary (also 32), nephew David Horsfield Dodd and lodger Miles Hodgson Towers, the Upton curate, who was later to move into Westview.

In 1876 the property was acquired by James and Elizabeth Prince who moved in shortly after their marriage. Subsequently the home of their daughter Mrs Gowings, the property stayed in the Prince/Gowings family for a half century. Although recorded in the 1881 and 1891 census records and the early Park accounts ledger, much of the history of this era comes through daughter Margaret's recollections of the house and garden (see Chapter 8).

The 1898 OS survey supports the belief that James Prince had the back of the house extended out and the stable/coach-house block built.

Graham Hinde of No. 3 relates that whilst he was at Oswestry School, his art master, George Roland Harding Webster, informed him that he had previously lived in Millside. Webster died c1951 while in his mid-80s and it is likely that he lived at Millside some time in the period after the Gowings left. Graham further recalls that Webster was a talented artist/craftsman who had studied at The Slade and worked in a Pre-Raphaelite style.

Captain (later Major) John Sidney Smith and his wife Kathleen Lily acquired the property in 1927 and then in 1934 it was bought by army dentist Major Henry Erasmus Flavelle (b 1894). He lived at Millside with his first wife and three daughters – Margaret, Moyna and Diana. Mrs Flavelle died in 1938 and the Mary Margaret Barton recorded in the 1939 electoral roll was the nanny engaged to look after the young family. During WW2 Henry was stationed in Edinburgh and Colchester and the house was let out.

Stories suggest that during WW2, three Free French pilots were billeted at Millside and Windmill girls up from London were entertained with no shortage in the flow of drinks and the resulting display of 'empties'.

Henry Flavelle married his second wife, Cecily Rowland, at the outbreak of war in September 1939 and the family returned to Millside after the war, now

Major H E Flavelle

33

with a further daughter Alison.

The garden was significantly increased post WW1 to take in non-covenanted land originally outside the Park area. During the Flavelle era this featured a tennis court and Mrs Flavelle is remembered as serving silver service tea after a match. In 1975 the Flavelles sold Millside to the Beard family

Brian Beard first occupied Millside on his own while renovation work was carried out. His wife Olive and their children Caroline and Nicholas joined him later. The roof was rebuilt, with one large tree causing major problems. A damp-proof course was established and the electrics improved whilst the remains of the early gas facilities were removed. The roof of the coach-house had totally collapsed and Brian built a double garage with a flat roof in its place.

When the Beards took over, the lounge had a small room at the back, a butler's pantry, accessed down two steps. Brian integrated it with the lounge, raising its floor level. This involved removing the partition wall – an exercise which revealed some interesting historical finds. Brian's renovation work also revealed that the extended back portion of the house had been constructed from old ships' timbers bolted onto the (then) exterior wall of the house. The timbers still had the large bolt-holes of their earlier life.

The Beards played a major part in the social life of the Park and hosted the adults' 'street party' for the Royal Wedding celebrations in 1981.

After the Beards, the next owners were Simon and Sylve Kirk who built the conservatory on the north side between the garage and the kitchen. They moved to the USA and the house was vacant for several months before being acquired by Simon Nixon in 1998.

FROM PLOTS TO HOUSEHOLDS

No. 80 Upton Park
Built 1870/1 and originally named Westview
(the name is no longer used)
The Westview name was appropriate a century ago but years of housing development render 'Westview Gone' more appropriate, and now No. 80 is making more of its southerly aspects.

Above, Westview from the front, and, right, from the garden taken in 1999

On the 1872 OS survey, Westview is the only single property and the only one not named as a Villa. The ground level of the Park rises towards its northern end and plot 16 may have had a very open view west at that time but exactly why the covenant was rewritten to allow its building is not clear. Plot 17 would appear to have had similar aspects and was still unsold and owned by Pitt.

As built it was a square Victorian house and an adjoining cottage with its own yard wall. The folklore of a dairyman's cottage preceding the house is disproved via the deeds and the OS survey. The 1871 census records the Beswick family with eight children but without servants, although the adjoining cottage design suggests facilities for servants. Also, William Beswick was a Chester schoolmaster, implying his need to commute daily into Chester and yet there was no significant stable and coach-house. A number of small outhouses shown on the OS survey may have been modest facilities for a horse. The well is unusual in that it is nearly six feet in diameter compared to the usual three to four feet. The large external water tank above the coal store may have been used as a header tank with water hand-pumped up from the well. The wash-house within the enclosed courtyard is not featured in the 1872 OS survey but appears in the 1898 survey.

On 24 June 1873 the property was conveyed to William Smith, then passed to his daughter Cecilia Pearson and subsequently to his granddaughter, staying in the family until 1940. The Smiths did not have servants but their lodger the Rev. Miles Towers did

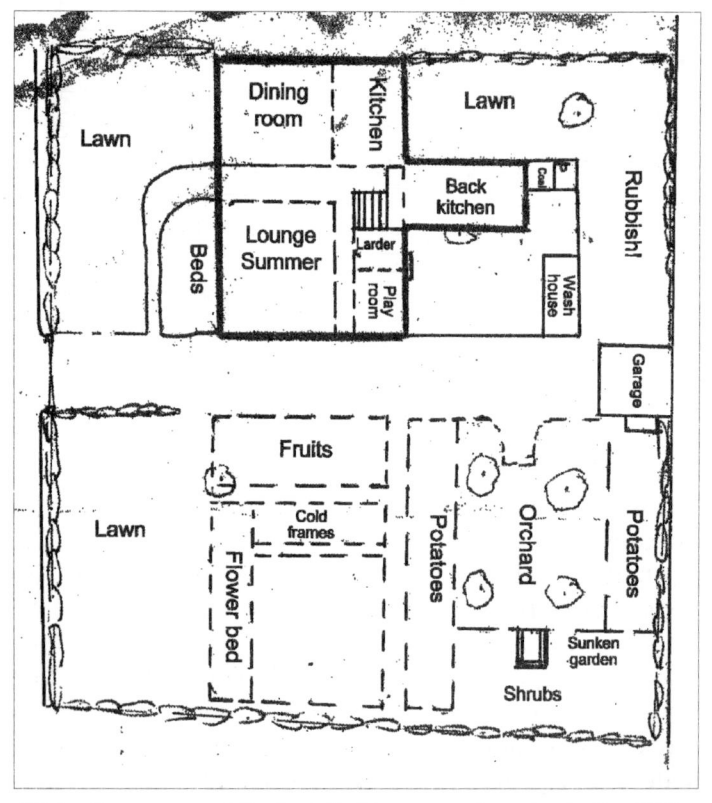

Michael's memory of the layout of house and garden in the 1950s.

have. The family lived in the Park for 80 years and are covered within the account of the Smith/Pearson family in the section on 'People of the Park'.

Westview was sold by Constance Pearson for £875 on 15 October 1940 to Robert Charles Harris, Chartered Electrical Engineer, of Fairholme, Chester Road, Poynton, and his wife Magdalene Ethel Harris. Their daughter Olwen was on military war service during 1945. Magdalene died on 30 March 1947.

Westview was conveyed on 6 January 1949 to Alexander (Sandy) Brown, who moved in from Hoole with his wife and three children. Sandy had been a Major, a civil engineer and in 1949 was with the Water Board. During 1951-52 he worked in East Anglia following the region's bad floods. Michael and Barbara (who were five and eight years old when the family moved in) revisited on 13 June 1999 to recount the history of their time at Westview and their memories of their life in the Park.

Michael and Barbara recalled that:

• The outside loo was functional but only used in an 'emergency'.

• The cottage upper floor was derelict when they arrived. Sandy refloored it to make a bedroom for Michael, cutting a door through from the main house stairway. Michael used the pear tree to leave his room!

• They considered the wash-house was large enough to serve the whole house.

• The cottage larder still existed – not then as a loo – and was used for shoe cleaning.

• The walk-in larder had large slate slab shelf (larder now integrated into a room)

• There was a fireplace in the upstairs north front room but it was not used.

• The bottom of the wooden garage was rotten so it was cut out and given a brick base (the garage was totally demolished in the early 1980s).

• The boundary to the field was a 7ft high tight holly hedge. The bridge into the field was much as it is today.

Westview was conveyed on 30 September 1960 to Malcolm Kermode and the family moved in from Vicars Cross. They would have preferred one of the post-WW2 Park houses but in 1960 these

The back cottage and outhouses as they were in 1978. The green water tank can just be seen on the outhouse roof on the right.

were much more expensive. Malcolm became Town Clerk of Chester leaving the Park when he retired. The family were his wife Kay and their three children Gillian, Simon and Honor Kermode who spent much of their childhood in Westview. The Kermodes carried out many changes and adapted the house name to Westmead. They cleared the garden beds and many trees to establish an open lawn area marked off as a tennis court. They

Better view of the water tank just prior to its removal. Below it - the coal hole and the exposed whitewashed walls of the outside toilet.

created a porch with an inner door and relocated the door into the dining room. A downstairs reception room was created by combining a side hallway, a pantry and a small room, and adding a french window into the garden. The kitchen chimney blew down during a gale in the mid-1970s and was removed.

When Malcolm Kermode retired he and Kay moved to Neston, selling the house to the current owners on 1 March 1978. Phil and Lynne Pearn moved from Leicester as Phil joined ICI. At the time their son James was three years old and Toby was just 10 months. Lynne was UPPA Secretary for a short period in the early 1980s and Phil became Chairman in 2001.

Since 1978 they have carried out considerable refurbishment and extension, in keeping with the period property. A double garage was built using bricks salvaged in the early 1980s from the demolition of the nearby army mansion - The Firs. The back cottage and outhouse area has been opened out to overlook the garden and a conservatory built. Of the greatest historical interest is that while excavating the outhouse area, early drains and wall foundations enabled a realisation of how things were in the Victorian and Edwardian era. A filled-in six foot diameter well was discovered and reinstated to 12ft depth complete with a working handpump.

Showing the old outhouse wall line and drains, and the well.

No. 76 Upton Park
Now known as Grange House
formerly Fammau View

The 1898 OS survey shows the property with the detached two-storey outhouse believed to have been a stable/coach-house block built in tandem with servants' quarters above. In the 1930s a further detached outhouse is shown – possibly a garage – which had been demolished by the 1950s and the current lean-to garage was subsequently built.

The Smiths were the first owners and with their own house (No. 80) named "Westview" they then named No. 76 as "Fammau View" – in those days the Welsh hills would have been clearly visible. Margaret Smith was born in Llangefni, Anglesey and may have named this side, her husband having named the other half (No. 74) after his birthplace.

The 1891 census names the residents (assumed to be tenants) as John and Jane Griffiths and their four children. John at 46 years was a retired corn dealer. The Griffiths name occurs frequently among past residents of the Park.

In 1895 William Smith of Westview died and in 1898 No. 76 passed onto a Miss E Frith who died in 1906. William Shone was her sole executor and the property then appears to have been rented out, first to a Mrs.Wright and then a sea captain Heard. The 1911 electoral roll names John Burgess, suggesting he was the owner-occupier.

The property was willed at some point to William Shone (probably William Shone 3rd) and Horace Pritchard of 70 Watergate Street. They sold to bank cashier Ralph Wilson Gardner on 22 April 1922 for £900. The earliest Park accounts, for 8April 1921, show the house name already changed to Grange House and record Mr R W Gardner already responsible and having paid for the 1920-21 year. The 1921 electoral roll also names the Gardners – Ralph Wilson and Elizabeth Emma – suggesting that they may have rented the property prior to their ownership. Other Gardners – Ernest and Nora – are listed under Upton Villa.

The property was conveyed on 4 May 1934 to Mrs. I H Williams for £1300. She then, on 19 Sept 1936, sold plot 18 that had been acquired 10 years before by Ralph Gardner.

Mr T E Williams is named in the accounts ledger as settling the Park rate until 1939 when Rev W J McEldowney is named and active in Park minutes. At this time, Donald and Rosalind Mountney were residing here with the Rev McEldowney.

The property was then sold on 19 September 1942 for the lower sum of £1000 having lost much of its garden. The new owner was Ivor Thomas Williams with his wife Elizabeth. Different sources have him as a production engineer and as running the aquarium at the Zoo.

The Gilmours bought on 7 March 1949 for £2,500. They had three sons including John, who recalls many happy times in the Park. Mr Gilmour had a full career with Shell retiring in 1961 and died in 1966. Mrs Betty Gilmour stayed on until her death in 1978.

Keith and Sandra James acquired the property on 11 August 1978, with their family – Melanie and Angela. They have carried out significant refurbishment in keeping with the property.

No. 74 Upton Park
Known as Roade Villa

Roade is a village in Northamptonshire, the birthplace of William Smith of Westview who is believed to have been the first owner and landlord of the property.

The 1891 census records the tenant occupants as John Davies, bank clerk, with his wife Esther and two young sons. They also had two domestic servants.

After the death of William Smith in 1895, Roade Villa was inherited by William and Cecilia Pearson who continued to rent it out. The tenants of Roade Villa in 1921, and still in 1929, are recorded as George and Elsie Matthias. By 1939 the electoral roll shows George and Florence Crane as tenants. Henry Ebrey Crane was Cecilia Pearson's executor.

Following the death of Cecilia Pearson in 1936 it appears that her son Marshall inherited the property and by 1945 he had moved in himself with his wife Leonora.

They stayed until 1953 when they sold to Lt Col Arthur French, who moved in with his wife Margaret and their daughter, Gillian. After Gillian's marriage she moved with her husband Paul Stevenson to No. 19.

No. 72 Upton Park
Originally named 'The New House',
(the name is no longer used)

In November 1957 GP Dr John Cameron Doran acquired planning permission to build a detached house and garage on plot 18. The plans record approval of both UPPA and the current owners of the former Shone estate (Nos. 66/68). In March 1958 he bought the land and began to build using architects R S Biggins & Associates of Chester. The house is believed to have been featured in a house style magazine of the time.

By 1960 Dr Doran and family had moved overseas and the house was acquired by Edward Harold Mason, a county librarian. In 1963 it was recorded in Park accounts as having the highest Council Rateable Value of £210 just beating Bulawayo's £202.

In 1984 the Mason family sold the house to the current owners, Martin and Alison Pantony who moved in with their daughter Helen, in April 1984. Martin and Alison have both served on the UPPA committee and Martin was Chairman in the 1989-90 year. Alison is a distant relative of the Dickson family who previously owned plots in Upton Park and the surrounding nursery.

Section B: Plots 19, 20, 21

House numbers
66 & 68 built c1877
64 built c1930
70 built 1935

When Pitt Shone and Wood divided the Park into their individual ownerships, William Shone acquired plots 18-22 as shown in the 1857 layout plan. All these were plots on the eastern side of the outer circle. This was the first William Shone who never lived in the Park himself. By the 1872 OS survey there was still no property development on these plots except for the glasshouses on plot 18. The boundary was tree-lined and plot 19 established with an orchard.

By 1881 the large double property (now Nos. 66 and 68) had been built, with Shone's son William, now 33 years old, in residence with his wife Grace, their baby son William and a few years later baby daughter Grace. The OS surveys all indicate the house as a double but only the southern side (No. 66) had a stable/coach-house block and the early records only show the one household. This William Shone (the 2nd) was an estate agent and he acquired the double property (Nos. 23 and 25) on plot 30 in 1893. It appears that when he sold plot 30 with its property he also sold the vacant plot 22 with it. The Shone estate based on plots 18, 19, 20, 21 remained the largest estate within the Park for many years. William (the 2nd) died in 1911 and although his son William (the 3rd) took on interests in other Park property, the Shone family had left the Park by 1921. Company records have not revealed how they used the property.

By 1921 the Shone estate had passed to Brookhirst Switchgear, a large industrial company based in Chester.

On 12 November 1926 Brookhirst sold the estate to A W S Furley with a mortgage from William Shone (the 3rd). He soon sold off plot 18 to Gardner of Grange House (No. 76) and c1930 developed plot 21 with a single property (No. 64) demolishing the stable/coach-house block. He later sold off plot 19 for building development in 1933.

No. 66 Upton Park
Known as Firdene

By the time of the 1921 Park accounts ledger, Firdene was separately noted as 2680 sq yds, had a tennis court and coach-house, and incorporated plot 21 as its grounds. The 1921 elecoral roll does not record any occupation.

After plot 21 was developed the Furleys moved into it and rented out No. 66. The electoral rolls show the Taylor family in 1939 and the Tregoning family in 1945 living there.

When the Furleys moved to Scotland post WW2, their son stayed in Oakley (No. 68) but they sold Firdene.

The first new owner appears to have been A O'Nians, possibly as an absent landlord. In 1951 Firdene was acquired by Miller and Joyce Broadfoot who stayed into mid-1980s. Miller is believed to have been with the CEGB and to have been aged 89 when he left. They had a son and a daughter.

No. 68 Upton Park
Known as Oaklea

The earliest Park accounts ledger of 8 April 1921 records Oaklea at 5844 sq yds incorporating plot 19. This property was the highest Park rate payer (£4 17s 4d – more than twice any other single named plot/property) in the days when the rate was based on plot area. The ground area reduced to 3906 sq yds after plot 19 was sold.

Under Furley's ownership, Oaklea appears to have had tenants: 1921, George and Elsie Matthias; 1929, Esther and Thomas Mathias; 1939, George and Francis Coleman; 1945, the Cook and Sinclair families. After WW2 A W S Furley moved to Scotland and the Park Accounts ledger records son R Furley until 1954.

1954 accounts record Mr Beeley although Mrs Broadhead is believed to have lived in Oaklea during the mid-1950s. Ron and Joyce Ross then bought the property in 1957 moving from Upton Drive. Ron soon installed the letterbox by the gate and as recalled by his wife, he was rewarded by the very first letter being a £300 winnings on the football pools. They stayed for 12 years selling in 1968 to the Docherty family who moved to the area from Scotland. David, who contributed to the Park tradition for vintage cars, soon joined the UPPA committee. They stayed until the late-1990s.

No. 64 Upton Park
Known as Elm House (formerly Wyeby)

A sketch by Arthur Garrod dated 28-2-1988

The property was built in the grounds of Firdene (No. 66) on what was essentially plot 21. The exact build date is not known but it first appears on the 1932 OS revision.

It is not until 1935 that the house-name "Wyeby" first appears in the Park accounts ledger with the rate paid by Mr A W Snead Furley. The 1939 Electoral Roll names Arthur and Daisy Furley as living in Wyeby. In 1945 it was briefly owned by L Marcuss and by 1946-7 by J G Carver who changed the name to "Elm House".

In the late 1950s the Park rate responsibility passed to the steel-makers John Summers Ltd. Dr. Jeffs and family then acquired the property until 1975 when it was acquired by the current owners Arthur and Councillor Jean Garrod. Jean served as UPPA chairman for several years during the 1980s.

The Garrods were told that the house had been built by a retired 'Foundry master' as his home with his wife reputed to have done the bricklaying, and coal mining waste used in the construction. This story may account for the 'missing' years' pre-1932 until 1935 when it was acquired by Furley.

The house is distinctive:
- The back has regency-style bays made from steel.
- The frontage is constructed in a colonial style with pillars.

No. 70 Upton Park
Known as The Cedars

This is a 1930s dormer bungalow built on plot 19. Arthur Walter Snead Furley sold the 2000sq yd plot 19 on 23 July 1933 to builder William Foden of Mt Pleasant, Saltney for £170.

Although William Shone had had a interest in the Oaklea/Firdene estate up to 1919, the conveyance of the land to build The Cedars refers only to the initial covenant of 1857, making no reference to the 1870 Release and new covenant of which he held the original.

It would appear that Foden built the house possibly extending the back to cover in the back porch at a later date. Ground floor rooms except for the modernised kitchen still have their exposed beam ceilings.

The property is first mentioned in the ledger in 1934-5 as owned by Mr W Foden with a council rateable value of £32. It is shown on the post-1936 Ordnance survey.

The 1939 electoral roll names William Foden as resident with his wife Florine May and another William Aubrey Foden. By 1945 the house was vacant.

On 19 July 1944 Ronald Foden – following the death of William – conveyed the property to Shell Refining & Marketing Co Ltd. The Park Accounts ledger names Shell Research and occasionally under the name of L Eisinger.

Various Shell staff were tenants. Bill Nash and then Barbara and John Kane on two occasions between 1957 and 1961. Barbara recalls the horse from the field next door being attracted into the garden by the compost and then getting stuck in their greenhouse.

Iain and Peggy Pender bought the house in 1962 when Shell pulled out of owning property. Iain worked for Shell and from 1968 the family were only there during annual leave from overseas. They kept the house until 1984. The Pender children, Judith and Jonathan, have fond memories of their childhood formative years in the Park (see Chapter 8, 'Reminiscences').

Reg and Joan Thomas with their two sons then acquired the property and carried out some refurbishment including adding a third dormer room.

The Cedars has been the home since 1994 of Will and Pam Webb and their family, Jack and Harriett.

The rear of the house in 1968

Section C: Plots 22 & 30

House numbers
23 & 25 built c1870
62 built 1962
60 built 1967

The 1857 plot layout shows William Pitt owning plot 30 and William Shone owning plot 22. The 1872 OS survey (extract below) shows the double property (Nos. 23 and 25) as Chatham Villas on the 2441 sq yd plot 30 but plot 22 not separately marked, just part of the as yet undeveloped Shone estate. By the 1898 OS survey with the Shone estate developed on plots 18, 19, 20 & 21, the 2313 sq yd plot 30 is already shown divided into two sub-plots. A conveyance for the double property in 1893 states the ownership of *'that piece of land (now divided into two) situate immediately opposite the said hereditaments and separated therefrom by a road'*. The garden plot was divided and allocated such a way that each semi property had a ground area of 2337 sq yds.

It is believed that William Pitt had the double villa built either for his own use or for letting. After October 1869 when Pitt sold

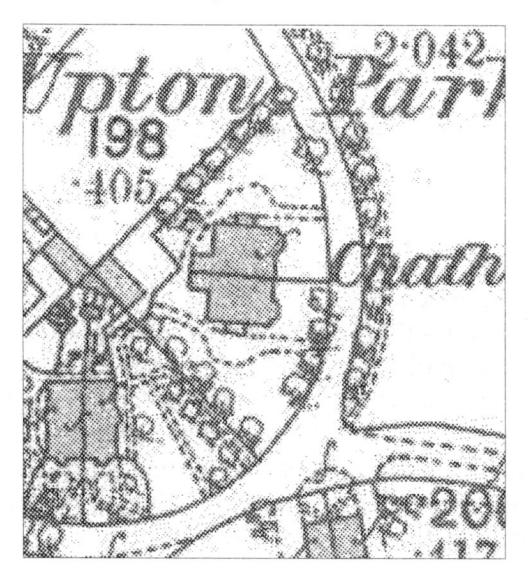

Millside (No. 84) it is not clear whether he lived in Chatham Villas or in No. 19. With both these double properties Pitt was establishing the Park in line with his original vision of grand-style housing.

The 1872 OS survey shows a drive down the north-eastern boundary of the plot 30 with, presumably, a stable block in the corner of the plot. By the 1898 OS survey this is shown as part of The Limes (No. 25).

By indenture dated 9 August 1873 William Pitt mortgaged the full property (Nos. 23 and 25) for £1700 to Charles William Duncan, a City of London Gentleman living in Mansion House Chambers. The assumption is that Pitt then became an absent landlord – he is not mentioned in the 1881 census as living in the Park. The names shown in the censuses of 1881 and 1891 are believed to be tenants. In 1886 Arthur Pritchard took a share with Charles Duncan as mortgagee. Arthur died 8 September 1892

By indenture dated 29 November 1893 the property was conveyed for £1125 to William Shone (the 2nd) believed to still be living at Oaklea/Firdene (Nos. 66 and 68). Charles Duncan remained as mortgagee until 1896 when John Griffiths of Hoole, a corn merchant, and Norris Alfred Ernest Way became the mortgagees. John Griffiths is recorded in the 1891 census as living in Grange House (No. 76).

William Shone (the 2nd) died in 1911, his properties passing to William Shone (the 3rd).

While owned by the Shones, the two halves were rented out on yearly tenancies. Robert William Hughes is recorded in the 1901 and the 1911 electoral rolls. Reginald and Augustus Hughes are recorded as lodgers. During at least the latter part of this period the other half was let to Mr J Burgess.

Harold Sabine acquired The Beeches (No. 23) first and then acquired The Limes (No. 25) on 19 February 1919.

The 'over the road' garden of No. 25 was sold first to allow the building of the new 'Hawthorns' (No. 62) in 1962. The 'over the road' garden of No. 23 had apple trees and chickens during the 1950s and Mrs Sabine, the owner at the time, would not part with it. It was not until after her death in 1963 that Harold Sabine agreed to sell and No. 60, Fosse Way, was built.

No. 23 Upton Park
Known as The Beeches since early 1900s
*With No. 25 named as Chatham Villas when built c1870.
Records suggest other names in intervening years: Sunnyside in 1881,
Woodbine in 1891, The Baden and then becoming The Beeches once the
trees became established, at least by 1920.*

Originally the property was a 'square' main house with a back annexe on a smaller scale (e.g. lower ceilings) presumably as kitchen and servants' quarters. Further extension, as first shown on the 1936 OS, provided a single-storey further back room and a double garage.

The 'swing both ways' serving door in the corridor between the scullery and the main house has been retained. The servants' quarters upstairs are now integrated with the rest of the house and reached by taking two steps down from the height of the main upstairs corridor.

Small buildings shown in the courtyard in the early OS surveys, presumably an outside toilet and wash-house, have been demolished and the yard has recently been enclosed in a conservatory.

Owners from 1919
- The ledger from 1921 to 1963 shows Harold W T C Sabine as

the owner of the property. A civil engineer, he was Chairman of the Park for over 20 years and established the committee as we know it today. He was clearly one of the lead players in the history of the Park. Mrs Sabine died in 1963 but Harold continued to live there until his death. Their grandson Tony, son of Roger, recalls visits to the house during his childhood.

- Ian and Anna-Marie Morris became the owner-occupiers in 1967. Ian became Park Treasurer in 1970.
- W R Carter and family were the owners from 1976.
- Peter and Heather Holmes and family owned the house from the early 1980s until 1987. Peter had one of the beech trees felled which caused much concern and disgust among some fellow residents who considered that it had been done simply to gain more light and enable a lawn to grow. A lament written by Ken Starkie was circulated with the AGM notice, which led to heated debate at the AGM. Peter Holmes responded with his own poem in the style of Rudyard Kipling's 'If" (see 'Yarns', Chapter 10).
- The Beeches has been the home since 1987 of Chris and Katie Quartermaine and family. The Christmas Eve 1997 gales took out another beech – almost a clean snap at about one metre high. Only one old beech now remains.

No. 25 Upton Park

Known as The Limes with No. 23 named Chatham Villas when built c1870.
No. 25 retained the Chatham Villa name probably until the lime tree-lined track to the stables/coachhouse became integrated within its grounds c1920.

Owners from 1919

The property was conveyed on 15 December 1919 from H W T C Sabine to Annie May Carbutt from Sherwood, Nottingham, wife of Benjamin Carbutt. The mortgagees were silk and velvet manufacturer William Fox and James Fox. Her daughter Betty Carbutt is remembered living at The Limes although by 1945 both she and her mother were tenants at No. 18.

On 25 March 1924 it was conveyed from Mrs Annie M Carbutt to C Blandford who was possibly already renting the property. By 1940 the records show only Mrs Annie J Blandford, who sold it on 10 July 1946 to A Proctor.

It was then conveyed on 1 April 1949 from A Proctor to Cyril B Davies and his wife Jessie. On 31 October 1958 it was sold on to J H and H Taylor.

FROM PLOTS TO HOUSEHOLDS

On 3 July 1962 The Limes was conveyed on to J F Johnson.

The garden/orchard opposite was sold to the Wilson family to build Hawthorns (No. 62) in 1962.

The main property was conveyed on 1 September 1966 from J F Johnson to Wynne and Beatrice Jones. Beatrice was elected to the District Council for 1976-79 representing CRAG – the Chester Residents' Action Group.

On 27 February 1981 The Limes passed from Mr and Mrs Jones to Paul and Jenny Jennings.

The Limes has been the home of Kevin and Annemarie Asbridge since the late 1990s. They have carried out considerable refurbishment, very much retaining the period style of the property. The front porch has been enhanced and the second floor extended out over it.

No. 62 Upton Park
Known as Hawthorns

Bill Wilson had the house built in 1962 using builders J C Parkers, after acquiring the garden grounds of The Limes (No. 25), opposite. The Wilson family moved from Hawthorn Villa (No 21), and took the Hawthorn name with them when they moved.

Built in the style of the times, the house has under-floor ducted hot air central heating.

Bill Wilson is featured in Chapter 7.

No. 60 Upton Park
Known as Fosse Way

Ken Starkie of Parkstone (No. 19) had Fosse Way built for his use in 1967 after acquiring the garden plot from Harold Sabine of No. 23.

Ken served many years on the committee. He held the posts of Treasurer and 'Roads Advisor' as well as serving on sub-committees. He had highways experience, becoming Assistant County Surveyor with Cheshire County Council (as was his father from 1930-35). He moved out of the Park c1997 after 40 years.

Fosse Way was then acquired by David and Mary Hogg and family, who moved up to the area from Sussex. They extended the property to the rear.

Section D: Plot 1

**House numbers
56 and 58 built c1870**

When Pitt, Shone and Wood took up individual ownership of the building plots, this plot 1 went to Shone but was quickly sold to Griffiths (No. 56) and Foulkes (No. 58). The double property is shown on the 1872 OS survey. The 1871 census does not record occupied dwellings that would appear to be this property. It does however note several that were unoccupied and from the architecture the suggested build date is around 1870.

The house name Fern Bank is first used in the 1891 census and appears to be for the double property.

The double property has the distinction of having beeen included within the city boundary before the rest of the Park.

The 1872 OS survey and early Upton Park estate plans show a pond to the southeast of plot 1. The precise location of this pond varies on each early map suggesting that it was very variable with climatic conditions and the timing of the survey. Indications suggest that the pond took in the southeast corner of No. 58's garden as well as part of the Avenue immediately to the east of No. 58 and also land to the south now within the grounds of new property outside the Park. The pond is not shown from the 1898 survey onwards, however memories from around the 1950s recall pond plants and garden waste being dumped as landfill.

From the road with No. 58 on the left. The gable-end was added in the 1990s, considerably increasing the size of the property.

No. 56 Upton Park
Known as Fern Bank

As seen from the side garden after extensions made by the current owners

The property has been significantly enlarged since its first build with a major extension carried out by the current owners in the 1990s as seen in this photograph.

Indications are that Griffiths may not have lived here but was the landlord. The 1881 census names the Pugh and Wess households for the double property and then by 1891, Margaret Lewis with her daughters and a gentleman boarder are all recorded for No. 56. By 1901 the landlord has changed to Peter Cole of Halifax.

The Park accounts ledger implies that Miss Helen Dean (of the Mill owner family) owned the property from before 1921 until 1952. After her brother's death she also became the named ratepayer for Parkstone but where she actually lived is not clear. Post-WW2 her address is recorded as in Anglesey. During her ownership H E Crane was an early tenant and then, by 1927, Mrs M Davies.

From 1953 Mr W Fletcher is recorded as the ratepayer and by 1958 Mr D G Myles. From the early 1960s until 1993 Mrs Mitchell was the occupant.

In 1993 Fern Bank was bought by Charles and Marianne Buck who moved in with their two sons, Surya and Joe. With their strong interest in oriental medicine they have embarked on a plan to establish a botanical collection of oriental medicinal plants.

No. 58 Upton Park
Now known as Emanuel
formerly Lowther and Mona Villa but originally Fern Bank (as No. 56)

There is no evidence that Foulkes actually lived in the house; it is likely that he was the landlord. The 1881 census records the Pugh and Wess households in the double property. Edward Pugh as Chief Railway Clerk was the most likely for No. 58 since there are many indications of the house's association with the railway. By 1891 the occupier is recorded as railway clerk Owen Robinson who is still named by 1911. By 1901 the house-name had become Mona Villa.

The 1921 Park accounts ledger records the name as Mona Villa with an area of 1230 sq yds and the rate payer as Mrs Whaley.

In 1956, builder Mr D Jones of Upton Heath applied to build a bungalow in the grounds. The application contravened the restrictive covenant and was withdrawn, with the land being returned to the owner of Mona Villa.

Plans for a glass house in the grounds were presented to the UPPA committee in 1965 and approved.

The house was owned by Mr Spruce in the 1970s. In 1973 he submitted a planning application to build a property in his grounds.

The current owners, Paul and Eileen Howard, bought the house in 1991-2 from Mr Spruce.

Section E: Plot 23

**House numbers
19 and 21 built c1870**

Plot 23 was acquired by William Pitt when Pitt, Shone and Wood divided the Park up for their individual ownership. By August 1857 he had sold half the plot to George Holland, also a railway clerk of similar age. It is likely that they both then built. Although the properties are not named the two families are recorded in the 1871 census and the 1872 OS survey records the name Hawthorn Villas. The style is classic Victorian double villa of the time and both had stable/coach-houses.

Nicola Quartermaine retaining the Park tradition for vintage cars. Seen outside the stable block of No. 19.

No.19 Upton Park
Now known as Parkstone
was Hawthorne Villa until the mid-1920s

Showing the side of No. 19 and front elevations of Nos. 19 and 21

It is most likely that William Pitt and family lived in No. 19 during the early 1870s after moving from No. 84. By 1881, the occupier was Fanny Wannop - possibly the mother of William in No. 9. It is likely that she was a tenant of Pitt's. By 1891 only William Fitch is named for the double property of Hawthorne Villa.

Charles Dean, born 1880 into the Mill owner's family, eventually acquired Parkstone which then passed c1920 to his sister Miss Helen Dean (b1878) until c1950. The next owner was Mrs.Dobie, wife of solicitor Cyril Dobie - Douglas Dobie owned Upton House in 1911 but a relationship has not been established.

The property was acquired by Ken and Margaret Starkie around 1956. The Starkie family stayed until they built Fosse Way (No. 60) and moved there in 1967.

After David and Kay Grant, Paul and Gill Stevenson then owned the house from 1975 to 1985. They built the extension as seen central in the photograph.

Parkstone is now the home of Nicola Quartermaine and her family.

No. 21 Upton Park
Now known as Norland House
previously Hawthorne Villa, the name being taken when the current owners built No. 62 and moved to it.

The 1871 census records show George T Holland as head of household, with a family. By 1881 he has progressed from a railway clerk to being a coal merchant and agent, with only his youngest son still at home.

By the 1891 census the owner is William Fitch, a retired hair dresser. He is also named in the 1901 electoral roll but not in the 1911. Advertisements for his hairdressing and perfumery business at 11 Bridge Street Row can be seen in copies of the *Chester Chronicle* dated November 1859. He was an active member of the Proprietors during the early 1900s.

The earliest Park accounts show the owner as Mrs Margaret Davies of Rossett, near Wrexham. The occupier, if any, is not known. The square yardage is given as 1084. By 1937, Mrs M Davies is still shown as the owner but the rates are being handled by an agent, W E Brown & Son of Pepper Street, Chester. By 1945 the accounts show Mr Craig as ratepayer. Mrs McClellan was there until 1952. C W Wilson and family lived at the house from 1952 to 1962, when they moved to their new Hawthorns (No. 62).

When Major Brunton acquired the property he established the name of Norland House. The 1976 Park Newsletter shows the occupiers as Rea, Holland, Hardy & Cheales. This is interesting in that Hollands were the first family to own the house.

Section F: Plots 24, 25

House numbers
9, 11 built c1859
15, 17 built c1884
11 evolved over a period

By Febrary 1857, Pitt, Shone and Wood had already sold these two plots – plot 24 to Hill and plot 25 to Richard Wyatt. Thomas Wood at this time held plots 5-9 but by the August of the same year he had sold these to Dicksons, and bought plot 24 from Hill and half of plot 25 from Wyatt.

Thomas Wood and Richard Wyatt, who at 34 years old was managing a telegraphic office, then built one of the first properties (Nos. 9 and 13) and were occupying them by the 1861 census. In the 1872 OS survey they are known as Laburnum Villas. Certain architectural features such as the gothic-style doors are early Victorian and do not occur elsewhere in the Park. The 1871 OS survey shows Wood using plot 24 as his garden with his two-storey coach-house/stables at the far end. Wyatt had only the half plot but his stable block, which was also two storey, was situated at the rear. Nearly a century later it was extended to create No. 11.

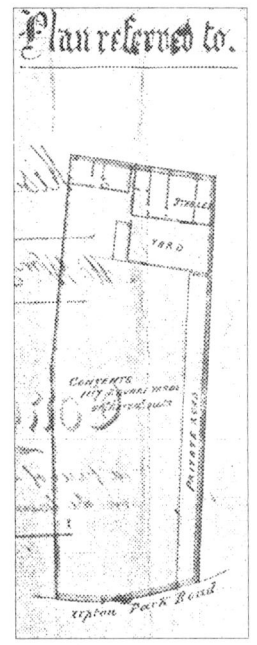

An indenture dated 25 March 1882 conveyed Wood's stable block on plot 24 as part of a 1117 sq yd subplot from Miss Sarah Thomas to Mr William H Finchett. It is assumed that the other half of plot 24 was also sold and that the double property (Nos. 15 and 17) was then built, completing the development of the plots on the inner circle. By now Upton Park had become established and desirable and this property was one of the grandest, reflecting the Chester late Victorian vogue for mock-Tudor half-timbered architecture.

Thomas Wood's widow Sarah, now 67 years old, was still living in No. 13, presumably selling off the large garden. Could she be the Miss Sarah Thomas of the conveyance?

No. 9 Upton Park
Now known as Laburnum Cottage

- Richard Wyatt and family had only a brief stay, and then George Roberts acquired No. 9 in 1861 with a mortgage from Thomas Kerfoot. Roberts, a draper, resided there for the 1871 census but then moved to the newly built Spring Villa (No. 29).

For the next 100 years (nearly) the dwelling stayed 'in the family' (see Chapter 7).

- From indentures, William Wannop, a railway cashier aged 34, bought the property with its 1074 sq yd land on 25 March 1873 for £360, from Thomas Kerfoot (£250) and George Roberts (£110).

On 14 September 1878 William Wannop took out a mortgage with the North Wales Permanent Investment Benefit Building Society to extend the property. The 1881 census records the Wannop family sharing the dwelling with another railway family. By the 1891 census the occupants are a different railway family and in the 1901 electoral roll Wannop is named as an absent landlord living in Stockport. By 1911 Wannop is shown as again living at No. 9 where he died on 30 January 1915, aged 76 yrs.

- His daughter Mrs Ann Eliza Trant then inherited the property and lived there with her husband Alfred, who was a sea captain.

The earliest Park accounts show Laburnum Villa as 1074 sq yds. In 1927 the accounts then show the Trants as acquiring land of 1412 sq yds, believed to be from Dicksons, plot 10 – the as yet undeveloped plot opposite which was later the site of Treehaven No. 44.

• From 1934 Captain Trant's name leaves the ledger and Mrs Ann Eliza Trant is named until 1946. The Trant daughters, Mary Vincent Trant and Margaret Patricia then inherited Laburnum Cottage and initially lived there using the coach-house/stables at the rear to house a weaving loom. J C Parkers converted the coach-house/stables into accommodation for the Trant sisters who were then able to rent out the main house.

• Around 1970, presumably following the death of the last Trant sister, it was briefly in the hands of Bollands Court Nominees Ltd. On 8 April 1971 they sold to the sitting tenants, Anthony David Ward (a bus driver) and his wife Annick Clare Helena Ward, for £3,500.

• On 2 May 1974 they sold to James Parker and Son Ltd of 1 West Street, Hoole for £10,750. By this time the land was reduced to 378 sq yds after separating off Loft Cottage (No. 11). Parkers rented the house, which had now not only lost its stables/coach-house, incorporated into No. 11, but also the back part of the house was not in use, reducing No. 9 to a '2½ up /2½' down. Mrs Fletcher was a tenant during this time.

• Gareth and Hilary Williams and family then bought the property and brought the back portion back into use as a kitchen. Hilary was UPPA Vice Chairman in the late 1980s and Gareth was Chairman in the 1990s.

• Pat and Janet Walsh and family acquired the property and moved in on 7 March 1995. Pat carried out some good Victorian architectural restoration. The end two chimney stacks had been taken down below roof level and canteen-style tubular steel flues installed. Pat had the stacks rebuilt and pots instated of the common Upton Park style – yellow square. Reinstatement of classic Victorian fires was completed with two cast iron fireplaces.

• Simon and Annette Lilley, with their son James and baby daughter Grace, acquired the property in January 2001, returning from several years living in Germany.

No. 11 Upton Park
Known as Loft Cottage previously Loft House

Loft Cottage has evolved out of Laburnum Villa (No. 9). The original part of No. 11 was converted from the stable and coach-house of No. 9 in 1953-4. The 1954 Park ledger shows it having a council rateable value of £14 and reducing No. 9 from £32 to £29. Interestingly the 1950s OS survey records the name Loft House not stating Laburnum Villa (No. 9) even though all other house names are shown. The 1959 UPPA Minutes note the erection of two garages. During the early 1970s the property was extended to how it is today.

From the age of the horse and carriage through until after WW2 it appears that the stable and coach-house fell into disuse. Miss Trant, on returning from war service took up weaving as a source of income and installed her loom in the coach-house. As she aged this became impractical and the Trant sisters were faced with a more extensive property than they needed and yet with little source of income. The idea was mooted that builders J C Parkers could modify the stable/coachhouse into a 'two-up two-down' house for the Trant sisters and they could rent out the No. 9 as a source of income. Clearly this was seen by some Park stalwarts as a covenant infringement making the building into a triple rather than a double. Others saw it differently with plenty of early precedents – many single and semi properties in fact had two households. It is reported by Robin Parker that Bill Wilson, a key guardian of the covenant, in fact strongly supported this idea as the only practical way for the Trant sisters to remain in the Park. Miss Trant was involved with the running of the Park, serving as Chairman after the first Bill Wilson chairmanship.

When the last Trant sister died in the early 1970s, J C Parkers acquired the full dwelling of Nos. 9 and 11 and carried out the extensions on what is now No. 11. Elsie Parker and her daughter Wendy moved in, and a drive was established, hedged from the side garden of No. 9, which was rented out. In 1983 the property was bought by Barry and Christina Graham who were still based in Saudi Arabia. Elsie and Wendy later moved to No. 7 after its conversion to flats and the Graham family with children Peter and Catherine returned from working abroad in 1988 and took up residence.

No. 13 Upton Park
Known as Lyndale since 1925 but previously:
Ivy Cottage, Laburnum Bank,
originally part of Laburnum Villas

The frontage pre-WW1

Thomas Wood's widow lived in the house alone in 1891, aged 76 years. It is not known when she died, or who subsequently owned and occupied the house until 1908, when Walter Cockram and family arrived – possibly as tenants initially, but the 1911 electoral roll implies that they were owner-occupiers. They stayed until c1920 and took many photographs around the Park and their home. Walter's great granddaughter, Janet Walsh, later lived at No. 9 and several of the photographs now in her possession have been reproduced in this history.

The 1921 electoral roll lists only the Furleys – A W S and Daisy Rebecca – who acquired other Upton Park property at that time.

The 1925 Park accounts ledger shows the rate-payer changing from Furley to Mr. E W Hylton Stewart of Queens Park, Chester. The 1929 electoral roll records Eric and Miriam Hylton Stewart but by 1939 they have returned to Queens Park and have rented Lyndale to Raymond and Elsie Musgrave, who were still there in 1945. From 1950 the account is shown as with Mrs Hylton Stewart,

UPTON PARK, CHESTER

Relaxing in back garden pre-WW1

Working the back garden. Note the livestock!

Damaged damson trees following the heavy snow in the winter of 1912. Note the privy.

and then from 1954-1962 the property is under the name Mrs Good.

From 1962 to the late 1970s the occupiers were the Sowerby family – Tom and Megan with their children Janet, Roland and Peter. Tom was a self-employed painter and decorator and he is recalled as being the one who always wanted to light the fireworks for the annual Park November 5th celebrations. Janet recounts how her father told of business picking up after moving into the Park. Janet and Peter still live locally but Roland now lives in Australia and has contributed to the website 'guestbook'.

Ian Pillow and family owned the property late 1970s and early 1980s. Ian was a violinist with the Liverpool Philharmonic. They were followed by the Formstone family.

From the mid-1980s to the mid-1990s the Bye family owned Lyndale. Richard Bye was UPPA chairman during the early 1990s.

No. 15 Upton Park
Now known as Carden Bank
Initially named Norton Villa

Like Holly Bank (No. 17) next door, the property had a well and a hand-pump to pump water up to the loft. The gauge on the wall outside then showed the water level.

Carden Bank must be the last house in the Park to have had a stable built. During the 1970s the Parkers demolished the back yard with its outside toilet and the disused Scout hut, building a workshop and by 1980 constructing a stable.

* The 1891 census shows lead works manager William Morris and family in residence.
* By 1921 the Park accounts show owner as Mr Anderson possibly taking over from Mr A Weaver (unless he was the tenant?) and the square yardage as 927. Anderson changed the name to Carden Bank in the early 1920s.
* Brigadier and Mrs Stewart lived there from 1950 until the widowed Mrs Stewart moved to No. 102.
* Robin and Gweneth Parker and family were the owners from December 1968. The Parkers created the lawn, removing the mass of raspberry canes and other growth. The main front bedroom acquired a lock retrieved from Eaton Hall where J C Parkers were engaged in demolition work.

No. 17 Upton Park & stable block
known as Holly Bank

The 1872 OS survey shows the two storey coach-house / stable block which, though becoming derelict, was still in place in 1950. On the right are the great entrance doors for the carriage, to the side of this a double stable with a partition for two horses, and at the extreme left, the tack room with a fireplace. Upstairs, which was approached by a draw ladder, was a hayloft where bales of hay still lay in 1950 but by this time the floor of the upper storey was wholly unstable and had to be demolished. None of the 19th century census records show a coachman living there. The site of the coach-house/stable block is now a double garage but the original flooring clearly shows its usage with a cambered floor and drainage in the stable area. The tack room is still evident with its fireplace.

OS survey maps right through to the 1932 revision suggest that the coach-house and its access drive were separate from Holly Bank's grounds.

The wash-house block, which has been retained as a utility room, would appear to have been built at the same time as the house. There was a well with a hand-pump to take water up to a tank in the loft. The level gauge still exists on the outside wall. Its life must have been fairly short since mains water came to the park in 1890.

There is a boundary shown in the OS surveys up to 1932, crossing the current lawn. This tallies with suspicion of wall foundation noted by the current owners.

Owners

• The 1891 census records the residence in Holly Bank of widow Mary Beaumont (60yrs), living on investments, daughters Mary (34yrs), Florence (27yrs) and son James (19yrs) theology student.

• The property was acquired by William Shone of Oaklea (No. 68) in 1896 presumably as landlord. It appears that he used a mortgage from a John Griffiths. Then mortgaged at £2011 to his son William in 1908 again as landlord. Tenants during this time were Mr Warner, followed byMajor Fanshawe and then Mrs Gladys Taylor.

Water-level gauge

• Conveyed in 1918 for £830 by Horace Pritchard as Attorney on behalf of William Shone (grandson of founding father William Shone), who was on war service, to Henry Speed recorded as 'a Gentleman' and no stated occupation. The earliest Park account records in 1921 show Henry Speed as the departing owner. The ground area is now shown as 1222sq yds which corresponds with the current area and being greater than the 1882 conveyence.

• References in a conveyance of 4 May 1944 relate an earlier conveyance dated 5 April 1923 showing William, Edwin, Arthur and Emily Griffiths as joint tenants.

• From 1921 until 1940 the Park accounts name farmers Messrs Griffiths (W E & A) although from 1937 just A Griffiths. The 1939 Electoral role records Edwin and Arthur as the sole occupants of voting age. Edwin is known to have died on 23 January 1944 while still resident of Holly Bank. The three Griffiths brothers are remembered very much in their roles. One the businessman in winged collars, one the shopkeeper and one at home as the housekeeper.

(From 1925 Spring Villa, No. 29, was owned by a John W Griffiths and family. Spring Villa backs onto Holly Bank and there are suggestions that a route through the boundary may once have existed. May these Griffiths have been related?)

- Conveyed 4 May 1945 to butcher Mr Arthur Astle of Stanton Drive, Upton from Farmer Arthur Griffiths, as the sole survivor, for £1400.
- Furtther conveyances were on 17 January 1947 to Major Charles Humphrey Rochfort Hyde and on 23 December 1948 to Henry Armitage Darby Wade for £3400.
- Conveyed 20 March 1950 to Egryn Kenneth Davies, (known as Kenneth) who came to Chester to take up his appointment as Area Secretary of the Chester and North Wales Law Society, at the founding of the Legal Aid scheme in England and Wales. He had previously worked for the Treasury Solicitor's Department in London, but being bilingual, with elderly parents still living in North Wales, this appointment had the advantage of bringing him back to the area of his pre-war practice. As a lawyer, he was frequently called upon to advise UPPA on legal matters pertaining to the Park. Kenneth was also known as an accomplished musician and was an organist at City road.

Kenneth took up residence with his wife Lena and their young family – Howard, Rhoderick and John. Elizabeth was born while they lived in the Park. Rhoderick recalls many happy memories of his childhood years in the Park.

During the Davies era many of the derelict outbuildings had to be made safe for raising a young family. They demolished the great greenhouse that had obviously enabled the previous occupants to supplement their rations during and after the war when half the rear garden was given over to vegetables and fruit trees. It lay almost the full length of the far wall backing onto Mrs Griffiths' garden (No. 29), and was very dangerous. The old coach house, so tempting to adventurous children, was similarly partly demolished. In the walled area in front of the coach house was a chicken coop. In the surviving greenhouse adjoining the wash-house was an old vine, which was lovingly tended for its occasional grapes. As regards the house, the large family kitchen with its range was still in place as was the separate walk-in larder. Today the modern kitchen is in the old scullery and the back door, rather than

UPTON PARK, CHESTER

A snowy day early in the Davies era showing the stable/coachhouse block and Spring Villa (No. 29) in the background left.

entering the large family kitchen, now enters a passageway with two side rooms.

The Davies family left in July 1964.

• The next owner-occupier from September 1966 until July 1976 was Brigadier Rigby and family. During this period Anthony Wedgwood Benn MP was in the area and stayed overnight between engagements in Chester and Aberystwyth.

• Briefly, until May 1979, the residents as tenants were then Roy and Sarah Darwen – an American family who are understood to have removed many of the downstairs doors to obtain the then fashionable more open plan style. These doors have now been reinstated. The property had been bought by the Cabot Carbon company for the Darwens' use. The family have reflected that this was their favourite of all their homes.

• William and Beryl Fieldhouse family from May 1979.

• The Evans family from July 1982.

Section G: Plot 26

House numbers
5 & 7 probably built c1868

This property appears to slightly predate next door (Nos. 1 and 3) and to have been built in the mid to late 1860s. On the left side No. 5, named Portland Villa, for schoolmaster Edwin Wilkins and on the right side No. 7 named Lily Villa. Records show Wilkins already owning the half-plot of plot 26 by 1857 but the 1861 census shows no occupation. Wilkins also owned the next two plots 27 and 28 but indications are that he died in the early 1870s and his widow moved to Birmingham, selling on his estate.

The 1872 OS survey plan shows the double property much as it is today but for the garages first added in the 1930s. Unlike many of the other early properties there is no indication of stable/coachhouse blocks.

No. 7 is known to have had a well.

No. 5 Upton Park
Now known as Ravensworth
but originally Portland Villa

The OS surveys from the 1872 survey show No. 5 to be a smaller half than No. 7 and the property has been enlarged gradually over the years. Originally it appears to have had an enclosed yard over which there has been some house extension. The back bay appears to have been added to convert the back kitchen into a lounge while a new kitchen and subsequently a bathroom above occupy some of the former back yard.

- An indenture dated 19 July 1870 conveyed the property to Mr Whitworth, possibly as an absent landlord. The 1871 census records Miss Hilton as head of household.
- By 1881 census the Bate family are recorded; they are still there in 1891.
- The 1921 accounts show Mr Thomas Edwards and a sq yardage of 861.
- During the period between 1935 and 1953, Mr S Moore is named as ratepayer, however it is understood that he was an absent landlord.
- By 1958 Mrs Jackson is known to have lived in the house.
- Ravensworth was conveyed on 9 September 1959 from

Katherine Jackson to Julia (known as Jean) Birchall, who was of Belgian extraction. Jean was a buyer at Browns and her husband Willy was a bookie who had the Duke of Westminster as one of his clients. Carpets and curtains came from the Old Eaton Hall. In 1967, after Willy's death in 1966, Julia Birchall had the house converted into two flats.

- The first floor flat was then sold to William Dunstan Wilcox and Mary Parry Wilcox on 24 August 1968. Julia continued to live in the ground floor until her death on 6 July 1972. Dalzie Comyns was her executor.
- The ground floor flat was on the market for many months until a chance remark from Ron Lloyd of No. 28 to a teacher colleague at Ellesmere Port Boys Grammar that the house was a good buy. So it was conveyed on 30 April 1973 to Biology teacher Ellis Gareth Jones – later Deputy Head at the same school.
- William Wilcox died in December 1971 and Mary in March 1986. Gareth then bought the first floor flat on 14 July 1986 from their estate and sold the property as a whole in 1997 to the current occupants. So ended the 20-plus year era of seeing various MGBGT and other sports cars parked in the drive.
- Ravensworth has been the home of Andrew and Susan Creeth and family (Josie and David) since December 1997.

No. 7 Upton Park
Known as White Cottage
but originally Lily Villa

Owners

- The 1871 and 1881 census records show Miss Evans, an artist in watercolours, as householder and the house name change to Lilley House.
- By the 1891 census the Ballance household is living there, and is still recorded on the 1901 electoral roll.

The earliest records of the name "White Cottage" appear in the first Park accounts ledger of 1921.

- The 1921 accounts show the owner as Mr Albert Dean (the Dean family owned the Mill). The sq yardage is shown as 861 – exactly the same as the other half of the semi (No. 5).
- In 1925 the accounts records show the property passing to Willian Jeffs. By 1935 he is shown as absent and the account going via Swetenham & Whitehouse of Abbey Green until 1937.
- The property was acquired by Mr James Cecil Parker and Mrs Elsie May Parker in 1937 and remained with the Parker family for many decades. Cecil Parker was an active Park committee member during the middle years of the 20th century.

'Cec' is seen here in his garden with No. 9 in the background. The framework is believed to be the handiwork of organmaker Mr Brocklebank of No. 31.

For more on the Parker family see under 'People'.

'Cec', as he was known, died in 1970 while still at No. 7. He loved old cars and the garden was still full of them.

During the Parker era the enclosed back yard was demolished, enabling the enlargement of the kitchen.

After the death of Cec his son Robin, having taken on J C Parkers (builders), converted the dwelling into two flats.

The lower floor had a number of occupiers during the 1970s and 1980s including Jones and McInerney. The top floor was initially let but was then used by Elsie Parker and Wendy when Loft Cottage (No. 11) was needed by the returning owners.

The Jordans owned White Cottage during the 1990s returning it to a two-storey dwelling.

The current owners from April 2001 are Peter and Judith Barry with their small daughters Kiera and Ellen. They have carried out a number of modifications including building a wall edging the side garden.

Section H: Plots 27, 28

House numbers
1 & 3 built c1870
31 & 33 built c1877

The 1857 plot allocation plan shows both plots under the name Wilkins, however, indentures dated 26 December 1871 record Shone selling plot 27 with its property and the vacant plot 28 to Edward Wilkin – schoolmaster (who also seemed to own house No. 5). The 1871 census does not record occupied property that can be identified as Nos. 1 and 3 but the census does note a number of unoccupied properties. The 1872 OS survey shows the unnamed property (Nos. 1 and 3) with a plan-view much as today but without their garages.

Indentures dated 12 June 1873 show Mrs Louisa Wilkins, formerly of Upton Park and now living in Birmingham, presumably after the death of her husband Edwin, conveying the double property to James Wilkins, a Stafford bookseller, on a £400 mortgage.

Also in 1873 the vacant plot 28 (as land 2172 sq yds, plus half of road 166 sq yds) was sold to Thomas Maddock but with a modified plot boundary giving house No. 1 less ground but No. 3 more. Whether Maddock then built is not yet resolved but the property (Nos. 31 and 33) exists on the 1898 OS survey.

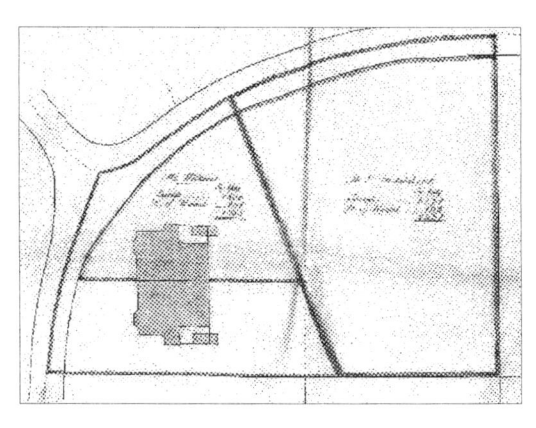

Early days of the double property Nos. 1 & 3

Nos. 1 and 3, with No. 1 on the left

Until the last 50 years or so, the double property (Nos. 1 and 3) has mainly been owned by remote landlords with tenant occupants. In the early days these frequently were members of the church – was The Hollies house-name (many Upton Park house-names are trees) based on "The Holies"?

Indentures dated 20 September 1876 show the double property conveyed to John Davies and then briefly in 1881 to John Davies, William Hughes and John Griffiths, before passing only three months later on 31 March 1881 to Elizabeth Cox, Harriett Cox and Charlotte Hollis Cox.

Although the double property appears to be vacant for the 1881 census, the 1891 census records a Thomas Cox, a retired clerk of holy orders. Thomas Cox is on the 1901 electoral roll. The 1891 census record is the first noting of the house name The Hollies.

An indenture dated 5 May 1903 shows the Rev James Richardson of East London, a South Africa missionary of the London Missionary Society, mortgaging for £600 the double property to widow Mrs Eliza Davies of Burland, near Nantwich and farmer Robert Davies of Faddiley, near Nantwich. At this time the tenants were Robert Johnson and John Griffiths.

Mrs Eliza Davies died on 9 August 1908 and on 27 October 1909 the mortgage transferred into the names of farmer Robert Davies still of Nantwich and John Davies of 41 Liverpool Road, Chester.

An indenture dated 4 July 1918 then conveyed the double property at £840 from farmer Robert Davies still of Cooks Pit, Faddiley, near Nantwich, to Samuel Ollerhead, another farmer from Malpas. At this point the £600 mortgage with the Rev James Richardson was paid off. By this time the Rev James Richardson is recorded as being of 26 Park Road, Lytham, Lancashire – a minister of religion. The indentures record previous occupants as the Rev James Richardson and also the Rev Miles Towers of Upton parish church. Later G Caine? and the Rev W Fairy? Williams.

Samuel Ollerhead died in May 1933. The Park accounts then show the Park rate being settled for a few years by Mrs F Ollerhead for both The Hollies and The Anchorage. The Park rate was then paid by Mrs Griffiths for The Hollies (a Mrs Griffiths owned Spring Villa, No. 29) and Mr W Jones for No. 3, now known as Derrymore. On Mrs Ollerhead's death it appears that the double property was inherited by her son, John Blake Ollerhead, who sold the two halves of the property independently, apparently prior to emigrating to New Zealand.

No. 1 Upton Park
Known as The Hollies
briefly Eardsley in late 1950s and early '60s

In the 1950s, Mrs Dolly Hinde, aunt to Graham Hinde of No. 3, who was possibly already a tenant, bought the house from the landlord, Mr Ollerhead.

During the 1980s the house was acquired by the Borman family with five boys. Mr Borman was a building inspector and carried out significant refurbishment of the property.

It is currently the home of Dr Steve and Dr Paula Kaye with their children George and Claire.

No. 3 Upton Park
Now known as Derrymore
previously Vron Deg and then The Anchorage

The home since January 1960 of Graham and Megan Hinde with their family, Simon and Kathryn.

No. 31 Upton Park
Known as Mayfield

Mayfield is named in both the 1881 and 1891 census returns with occupants brother and sister James and Mary Clark.

The earliest Park accounts ledger of 8 April 1921 record Mayfield at 1074 sq yds owned by representatives of F Maddock. This suggests that the house had stayed with the Maddock family since being built. The 1921 electoral roll lists two tenants, Stanley Maddocks and Thomas Harold Davies.

It was owned by organmaker Mr Robert Gardner Brocklebank from c1933 from the estate of Mr Maddock. Mrs Marjorie

Mayfield's front garden pictured in the summer of 1913.

*Mayfield and Belmont (No. 33) shared a well
built on their boundary in the back garden.*

Brocklebank operated a nursery school from Mayfield. This had about ten young children including Robin and David Parker and others from the Park. Robert made swings for the children from spare pipework.

Probably after her husband's death, by 1947 Mrs R C Brocklebank of Halkyn Road, Newton is shown as owner into the mid-late 1950s.

The UPPA Minutes for January 1959 record Mr Hunt proposing to divide Mayfield into flats having been told by his solicitor that no restrictive covenants affected Mayfield.

Blackwell is then shown in the records from early 1960s. By 1976 Margaret Rowlands and her family have moved in and by 1980 the Rogers family are recorded.

Mayfield is currently the home of the Gifford family – Malcolm and Judy and their four sons.

No. 33 Upton Park
Known as Belmont

Belmont is not mentioned in the 1881 or 1891 census returns although one unnamed dwelling recorded in 1881 could be Belmont with occupants widow Diana Burnett and her three spinster daughters.

The 1921 Park accounts ledger records Belmont owned by Major Whitley. From 1936 Mrs Whitley is recorded.

In 1946 the house was acquired by the Adams family who had now outgrown their Selkirk Road home after the return from WW2 of daughter Mary Evans with her family. Mary was married to Group Captain Thomas Evans and had two sons, David and John.

Marjorie and Phyllis Adams were both teachers in Chester schools.

Group Captain Tommy Evans was renowned for his sports cars which he initially garaged at No. 6 and he subsequently built a very large garage complete with a service pit. Belmont remained the Evans family home until 1988 when it was acquired by the Hedley family, Colin and Joan with children Ruth and Laura.

The garage was subsequently demolished and was a pile of bricks when acquired by the Hedleys. Colin Hedley then cleared the site in the late 1990s and built a new double garage.

The old garage once was the venue for an UPPA AGM – see 'Yarns'.

During the late 1990s Belmont has been extended, very much in keeping with the existing building.

Section I: Plot 29

House numbers
29 built c1873
27 built 1964

William Jones is shown on the 1857 estate plans as owning plot 29. Whether he built the property for George Roberts of No. 9 or just sold him the plot is not known. George Roberts sold No. 9 in 1873 implying that he then moved into the newly built No. 29 which is not featured in the 1872 OS survey.

No. 29 Upton Park
Known as Spring Villa since it was built
although the current owners adopted the name 'Woodbriar' after the name of the family tea plantation

This is the only single (detached) Victorian villa built on the inner circle, on plot 29, and was built a few years later than most of the others. The property is first featured and named as Spring Villa in the 1881 census.

The house is of classic 'double fronted' style, i.e. a central door with a bay window each side. The Spring Villa on nearby Liverpool Road is to a similar style.

Owners

• Tailor and draper George Roberts first lived in the Park at No. 9 – one of the very first Park properties. His family is recorded there in the 1871 census and then selling in 1873. Eventually with a family of eight children and presumably a successful business they moved to the new single property on plot 29, presumably after selling No. 9, which provides a build date of 1873. By the 1891 census George Roberts was still aged only 52, with their youngest child 14, but he is not named on the 1901 electoral roll.

- The earliest Park accounts ledger of 1921 records the name of Mr. S Davies and a plot size of 2149 sq yds.
- John Griffiths who transferred from South Wales with Pearl Assurance is named as living in Upton Park in the 1911 and 1921 electoral rolls. He is not named in the UPPA accounts from 1925 – possibly on buying the property from his previous tenancy. John Griffiths was Park chairman from 1926 through 1934. In 1932 he was appointed Chairman, Hon Secretary, Hon Treasurer and sole signatory. The Griffiths had four daughters and a son John. Other Griffiths – no relation – lived at Holly Bank during this period and a John Griffiths is named as being the mortgagor. Whether this is the same John Griffiths has not been established but the two families did appear to have an interconnecting gate between their two premises.
- John Snr is not named in the 1945 electoral roll and by 1950 Mrs Clara Griffiths is named as Park rate payer, presumably after John's death. Mrs Griffiths' death in 1956 is noted in the UPPA Minutes with recognition of the very long time in which she had resided in the Park. From 1956 the accounts record daughter Dalzie Comyn. In the early 1960s it is believed that Dalzie's brother John had the new detached property (No. 27) built alongside Spring Villa and Dalzie moved into that, subsequently selling Spring Villa.
- The next owner was D I Twine and subsequently the Smith family. They considered adapting the property to a guesthouse – a plan that was fiercely contested by fellow residents and was eventually dropped.

No. 27 Upton Park
Known as Rosina

The property was built in the side grounds of Spring Villa in the early 1960s for Mrs Dalzie Comyn. Dalzie, who had grown up in Spring Villa (No. 29), then moved across for the last 20 years of her life. She was the king-pin of the Christmas round of cocktail parties in the 1960-70s. She died on 29 January 1982, and at the time she was considered to be the resident with most years in the Park.

After her death the house was vacant for a while and was then bought by Pauline Rourke who subsequently became Chairman of UPPA.

Section J: Plots 2 – 7

Never developed and taken out of the Park in 1950s

When the Park was originally carved up for individual ownership by each of the three founding fathers, Pitt acquired plots 2, 3 and 4 and Wood acquired plots 5, 6 and 7. Presumably due to the difficulties in selling plots for development over the first ten years, these six plots were sold to Dickson who owned the surrounding land as his nursery business. Another possibility is that the land was deemed too wet for housing, although the site surveyor had laid out plans for housing on these plots in the mid-1850s. A conveyence dated 29 September 1870, shows Pitt selling plots 2, 3 and much of 4 to Mrs Selina Dickson. The plan of this conveyance shows the remainder of plots 2-7 (and possibly part of plot 8) at 12122 sq yds and not with plot allocations – maybe suggesting that Dicksons may have already acquired this from Wood.

The earliest Park accounts ledger shows Dicksons owning 11260 sq yds of covenanted Park land and being charged at the same sq yd rate as the developed plots. It appears that they were not actually paying this full amount and then in 1928 the Park rate went over to being based on Council Rateable Value which brought their charges down significantly to a level which they did honour.

As a result of the housing development after WW2, property was encroaching on the Park on this side. In 1953 UPPA decided to close the gateway into what had been Dicksons Nursery. The track ran between plots 2, 3 and 4 on one side and 5, 6 and 7 on the other. When Dicksons sold out it appears that Pritchard and Shone had acquired plots 2 through 7, and in 1957 UPPA was informed that Letts were seeking to build on these plots. Finally a Land Tribunal met on 30 January 1958 under Mr J R Laird TD FRICS FAI and made a ruling as reported in 'The Estates Gazette, 22 March 1958'.

He ruled that "he was not satisfied that the covenant is entirely obsolete", however with the plots having no access to the Park, the Park properties would suffer no injury from the proposed development.

The plots duly left the Park and Finer Homes, who had submitted the application, began housing development.

Section K: Plots 8, 9, 10

House numbers
48 built 1930
44 built 1947
54 built 1953
50 & 52 built 1965

The February 1857 plot allocation plan shows plots 8 & 9 with Thomas Wood. By August 1857 plots 8,9 & 10 were allocated to the Dickson family and possibly incorporated into their nursery.

At some point it appears that these plots became part of the estate of the Rev Algernon Ernest Grimes who owned Upton House, to the west of Upton Park. By this time the land does not appear to have been used as nursery land but rather as paddock with occasional use by horses.

In 1925 the Park accounts ledger shows him paying the full Park rate for his 6222 sq yds of land. By 1927 this had reduced to 4813 sq yds by selling land that was substantially plot 10 to Captain Trant of No. 9. Trant did not develop this land but used it as an allotment. It appears his daughters sold it post-WW2 for building development (No. 44).

In August 1929 a plot of 700 sq yards, mainly within plot 9 but with some land beyond the covenanted area, was conveyed to Ernest Herbert Hardy for the building of No. 48. Later that year a further 142 sq yards to the south was acquired from Grimes.

Builders Capstick & Owen had bought up land in the Upton area during the 1930s and built extensively in the Upton and Hoole area both pre-WW2 and post war. They acquired much of the former Grimes estate to the west of the circle and developed the Orchard Close and The Croft.

On 6 January 1955 Capstick & Owen conveyed to Hardy for £75 a further 23ft of Upton Park frontage and land bordering onto No. 44 which was within the covenanted area.

In 1953 William Capstick built a home for himself and his family on plot 8. Land he owned adjacent to Redlands (No. 54) was used for some vegetable growing but was largely rough ground and used for November 5th bonfire and fireworks

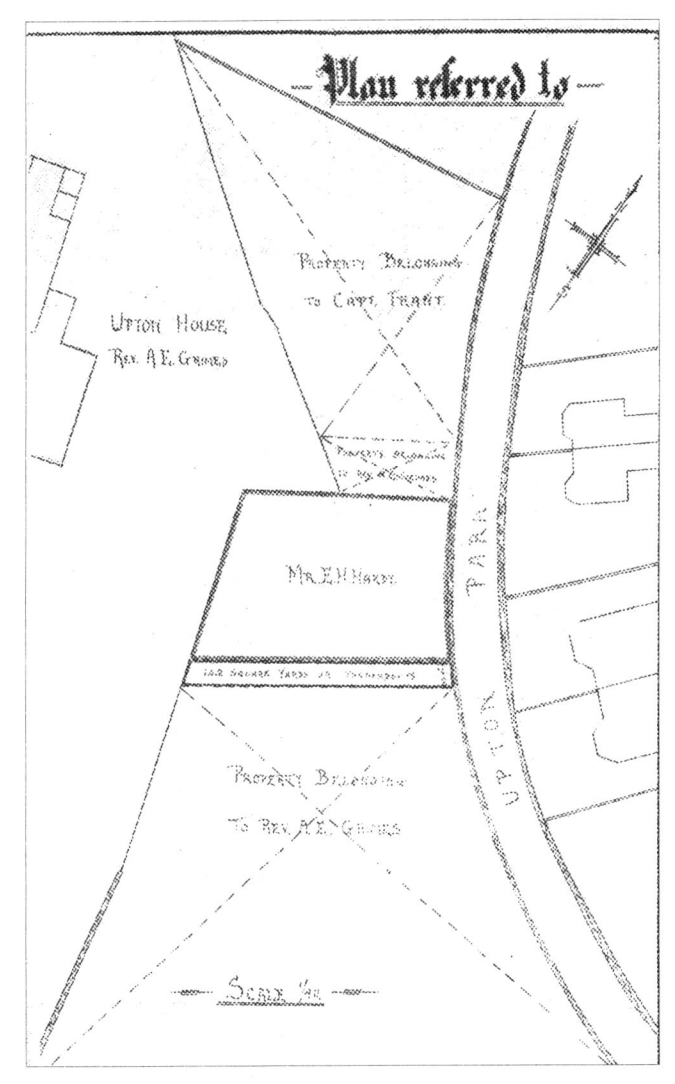

*Plan from the 1929 conveyance from Grimes
to E H Hardy for No. 48*

Finally winding up the business in mid-1960s, William Capstick auctioned land straddling plots 8 & 9. It was bought by another builder Dentith who built Nos. 50 & 52 in 1965.

No. 48 Upton Park
Known as Lindum

Ernest Herbert Hardy, an accountant from Ellesmere Port, used J C Parkers to build Lindum as his new home. In January 1955 he was able to acquire more land following Capstick & Owen's building development behind them (see plan below).

After the death of his wife, Mr Hardy took on a housekeeper who kept the property in prime condition even after his death and with the property on the market.

Jim and Pat Feakins then bought the property in 1967 settling with their family of Michael and Helen. They have added two extensions.

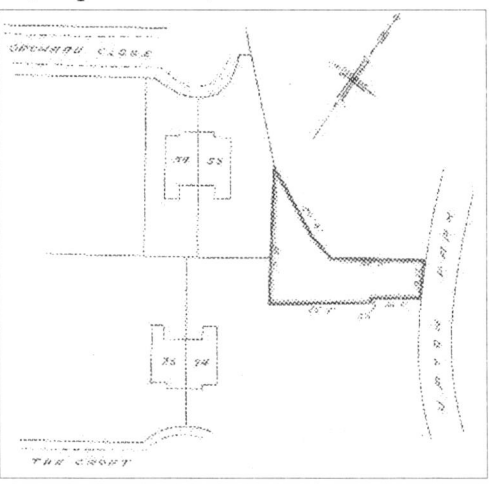

Yes - the old cast iron lamp post was leaning at the time of the photograph...this now rectified.

No. 44 Upton Park
Known as Treehaven

The house is now much enlarged since the original which was restricted by post-war building regulations to a £1200 value.

It was built by Mr Frederick Oldham, who was living with his mother-in-law Mrs Annie Carbutt in No. 18. As the family grew they moved to a bigger house in Church Lane, Upton which they also named Treehaven.

The next residents, Tommy Trelfa and family, developed the gardens – very much a feature of No. 44.

The current residents, John and Christine Browne and their daughter Claire, moved in 1978 and carried out a major extension around 1981. Christine, a keen horticulturist, has further developed the gardens and attained local horticultural prizes.

(In 1978 another family had the house, but only for six months in between the Trelfas and the Brownes).

No. 54 Upton Park
Known as Redlands

Redlands was built in 1953 by Capstick & Owen Ltd. Bill and Joan Capstick moved into Redlands with their two sons David and Richard. The house was built to a similar pattern to their previous home in Woolton which Bill had built in 1938. They named the house Redlands after the Redland district of Bristol, the home of Joan Capstick.

The UPPA Minute Book records the committee viewing of the building plans and the welcome extended to prospective new proprietor Mr Capstick who then joined the UPPA committee in 1954 continuing through into the 1960s.

The house was bought in October 1973 by the current owners, David and Barbara Capstick who moved in with their two children, Joanna and Anthony. David was also active in the running of UPPA, serving as Secretary and producing an UPPA newsletter for several years.

No. 50 Upton Park
Known as Kyleakin

Peter and Margaret Measures moved in December 1965 with their three children, Susan, Richard and Kathryn who were all raised at Kyleakin and have subsequently flown the nest. Peter and Margaret are still in residence.

The house is basically as built but with a back sun-lounge added after some five years.

At the back of the house stands a large cedar tree being the only remaining one of the original three.

Nos. 50 and 52 nestle amongst the trees

No. 52 Upton Park
Known as Canonbury

Built in 1965 and originally the home of Mark and Jenny Rogers with their family, Justin and Sebastian.

After the Rogers left, the house was let for a few years and then sold to the current owners.

The Rogers carried out some extensions and Canonbury is now a five-bedroom house.

Section L: Plots 11 & 12

House numbers
40 & 42 built late 1860s
36 built 1974

No records have been uncovered prior to the 1857 plot allocation plan which shows Haswell owning the half of plot 11 closest to plot 10. Denson is shown as owning the other half of plot 11 along with plot 12. The double property is shown on the 1872 OS survey named as Grafton Villas. No residents are recorded in the 1871 census but the 1881 census records three separate heads of household as well as a boarder, a lodger and two servants. One is Denson but Haswell appears to have been an absentee landlord.

No. 40 had a stable/coach-house block and for many years plot 12 served as the paddock. Post WW2 the plot 12 paddock was used for many Guy Fawkes night celebrations when the Park residents and friends had a bonfire, fireworks and hearty refreshments (see Chapter 6). After the death of the last Miss Crosby in the early 1970s, the plot was sold and a new detached house built.

No. 40 Upton Park
Known as Grafton Villa from its origin
as one of the earliest Park properties

The 1872 OS survey shows the ground plan much as it is today although it is believed that builder Mr Little, the owner in the 1980s, significantly refurbished the back outhouse area, incorporating it into the house.

The first recorded resident from the 1881 census was Joseph Denson – at that time a 67-year-old widower and retired chemist /druggist with two servants. It is believed he was already resident in 1874. New names are recorded in the 1891 census. The 1911 electoral roll shows the occupier as Mrs Mary Crane with (presumably) her two sons George and Percy as paying lodgers.

The earliest Park accounts for 1921 show Grafton Villa owned by John Crosby, with 2835 sq yds including the paddock on plot 12.

After the death of John Crosby in 1939, the property stayed with the Crosby family through into the 1970s. Miss Eugene Nettie Crosby became the named proprietor, by which time they also owned The Nook next door (No. 42). Prior to her death she was believed to have clocked up the most years in the Park for all the current residents.

The property was then acquired, without the plot of No. 36, by builder Mr Little who lived there but also carried out major renovation.

It has been the home of Dan and Mary Carbery since 1991, when they bought it from Dr. Irvine.

No. 42 Upton Park
Known originally as Grafton Villas (with No. 40)
but later No. 42 became **The Nook**

For its first 100 years this dwelling was owned by an absentee landlord. From build this was W Haswell but by 1929 the Crosby family living next door in No. 42. Tenants are named in the census records and electoral rolls. The Wynne family were tenants during the 1920s and the Mrs Dorothy Loveday Blagden, there in 1945, is believed to have been the daughter of Mrs Martyn from No. 32.

While owned by Miss Crosby of No. 40, the property was initially rented in 1952 and later bought by the Jackson family. They stayed until Mr Jackson's death in the mid-1980s. (NB these Jacksons were no relation to the Jacksons of No. 32). Their son Leo, still living in Chester, recalls other boys of similar age in the Park during the 1950s and 1960s.

No. 36 Upton Park
Now known as Skellig
previously Fox Covet when built in 1974

The house as newly-completed around 1975

No. 36 was constructed as a self-build by former Chester City footballer, and plumber by trade, Norman F Bullock of Laverstock (No. 14).

UPTON PARK, CHESTER

Norman recalls paying what he believed to be a local record price for the building plot – some £9000. He then built the house with the front elevation as it is today. They named the new house "Fox Covet".

Now launching into his own building business, Norman sold in 1976 to Mr and Mrs Bowitz – a German helicopter pilot and his English wife. They renamed the house as Skellig.

Later the house became the home of the Ken and Isobel Curry and family until the late 1990s.

From the garden of No. 36 showing No. 42 prior to refurbishment.

Section M: Plot 13 and land to its rear

House numbers
32 built c1893
34 built 1960
32A built 1979

The 1857 plot allocation plan shows Woodward owning both plots 13 and 14 and these are still shown as orchard in the 1872 OS survey.

The 1898 OS survey shows the single late Victorian property on plot 13 to a ground plan very similar to today but without the side garage. As built the house had the full 2230sq yds of plot 13 as its grounds. The house had a stable/coach-house block to its rear. Rock Cottage is not named in the 1891 census and the implication is that the house was built around the mid 1890s.

Dicksons nurseries owned the land behind plot 13 and eventually the nurseries closed down. As the post WW2 housing development escalated the land immediately to the rear of No. 32 became landlocked. Towards the end of the 1950s the then Chairman of Upton Park and owner of No. 32, Dr Sconce, took the opportunity of using a boundary slice of his land to gain access to some of this land. While this raised emotions within some members of the Association the property (No. 34) was built and with its drive within the covenanted area it became part of Upton Park.

Some years later in the late 1970s the then owner of No. 32, Jim Irvin, repeated the exercise to access more land to the rear. Unable to gain consent from the owner of No. 34 to share their drive, another parallel drive was cut through the side garden of No. 32 to gain access for another property (No. 32A) which also joined the Park. Since both these two later properties were outside the covenanted area they were not challenged as regards the covenant.

No. 32 Upton Park

Now known as Levens House
but originally Rock Cottage

The 1911 electoral roll names ownership with Henry William Thorn as an absent landlord living in Mold.

The earliest Park accounts dated 8 April 1921 show Rock Cottage at 2230sq yds owned by Mrs Martyn but the account was settled by Mr G S Martyn (presumably her son), c/o Potts Potts & Gardner of Northgate Street. By 1935 the name is solicitor Mr Gerald S Martyn (presumably following his mother's death). Mr G S Martyn was chairman in 1935 for just one year preceding the 20-year reign of Harold Sabine. Martyn remained active as a committee member. The Martyns kept horses within their fairly extensive grounds and Mrs Martyn was often seen in her pony and trap. She also kept chickens and would take neighbours gifts of eggs when she thought it appropriate.

Martyn sold in 1950 to Mr Thomas.

Dr Ken Sconce (son of Councillor Charlie Sconce) bought the

house in 1951 changing the name from Rock Cottage to Levens House, reputedly after Levens in Cumbria, his birthplace. He was a GP. His son Jonathan is believed to have become a doctor as well. Dr Sconce was Park Chairman after the resignation of Harold Sabine and is remembered as driving a Bentley. At the time of the early 1950s before new post-WW2 houses were built, Levens House was by far the highest council-rated Park property at £68. The flat roofed adjoined side double garage was added by the mid 1950s and it appears that the corner around the front door is an extension.

Mrs Jackson then acquired the house around the late 1960s and she has reminisced how she planted the laurel hedge to provide some sunbathing privacy for her daughter. Mrs Jackson also recalls a door in the middle of the large front bay window.

Jim and Margaret Irvin then owned the house through to the late 1970s during which they hosted the evening celebrations for the Queen's Silver Jubilee which were held in the Park.

In the late 1970s Jim Irvin built the bungalow No. 32A and following ill-health the Irvins then moved into the bungalow and sold Levens House to the Hinsleys who only stayed about 18 months.

It has been the home of Art and Bep Le Miere and family since June 1980. Their children Julian, Suzanne and Christian were raised here and have subsequently flown the nest.

No. 34 Upton Park
Known as Barn Hey

View looking down the drive from Barn Hey towards the circle. Levens House (No. 32) can be seen to the left and No. 36 to the right.

Built in 1960, and initially the home of local bank manager Mr Brindley and his family, Barn Hey was then acquired by retired farmer Mr Sherwin and his wife.

No. 32A Upton Park

Right: showing the drive off the Circle

No. 32A was built in 1979 for the Irvins who then moved in from No. 32. The property later belonged to the Carr family and has been the home of Kathleen and Joe Anderton since 13 October 1990.

Section N: Plots 14, 15

House numbers
28 built c1893
24 & 26 built 1967
30 built 1985.

Most people recall this double plot as being Garden House (No. 28) with its large garden and orchard. In fact although No. 28 was built c1893 it appears to have only acquired plot 15 (the orchard) around the 1930s or even later. The 1872 OS survey shows trees but no building on plot 14, while plot 15 is not shown to have trees until the post-1936 OS survey.

The 1857 plot allocations plan shows both plots 13 and 14 under the name Woodward. William Pitt originally owned plot 15 in 1857 and conveyed the plot to Margaret Anne Higginson, a widow of Chester, on 25 January 1873. The plot was still undeveloped over the next 60 years and ownership is not known until it was acquired for an orchard by Miss Longworth Dames, the owner of No. 28.

On the death of Miss Longworth Dames in 1961, the orchard plot was auctioned separately and in 1967 Nos. 26 and 24 were built on the 2337 sq yds plot. Planning permission had been granted for three properties but the Land Tribunal ruled in favour of the Covenant and only two properties were built. Despite further attempts to develop the remaining third plot it continues to be a natural wooded sanctuary amongst the tended gardens of the surrounding households.

No. 30 was the last house to be built in Upton Park. Constructed in the grounds of No. 28, both properties are home to the Lloyd family and no boundary line is physically in place.

No. 28 Upton Park
Now known as Garden House
formerly Sycamore Cottage and then The Briars

The build date has not yet been established but the use of engineering red and blue Westminster brick (characteristic interleaved W M) suggests that it may have been built in the 1890s. The two side wings and the frontage are later extensions.

The house, probably as first built, is shown on the 1898 OS survey.

Under the name of Sycamore Cottage and probably with the house as originally built, the property was bought by R S Johnson around 1905 and its history in that era known from the recollections of Grace Johnson. The Johnsons extended the property with side wings and renamed the house The Briars.

The earliest Park accounts in 1921 coincide with the ownership change to Miss Longworth Dames and give the total area as 2582 sq yds. Miss Dames changed the house name to The Garden House and lived in the Park for 40 years. She was a strong character and is well-remembered. She was reputedly a refugee 'from the Irish troubles' and was infamous for her strictness – she would walk around with a stick ordering residents to get their hedges trimmed, drive slowly, etc. When she died her live-in uniformed maid Eva was taken on by Mrs Carbutt of No. 18.

Following her death in 1961, the estate was inherited by her niece from Ireland who sold Garden House and the orchard plot separately at auction.

Ron and Betty Lloyd bought Garden House, moving in December 1962. In 'Reminiscences' (Chapter 8) Betty relates her dream that clearly meant they were destined to live there. Ron had the frontage extended out and demolished the lean-to greenhouse on the house side as featured in the 1898 OS survey.

In 1984 they decided to build a house in the grounds and in 1985 Betty and her daughter Shirley moved into No. 30. Son Jeremy with his wife Jenny and their sons Nicholas and Simon moved into No. 28. Without any boundary fence between the two, the shared lawn has been useful to the two boys growing up.

The Lloyds have been active within UPPA, with Ron serving as Chairman and Vice Chairman while Jenny is currently Secretary.

No. 30 Upton Park

Built in 1984-5 by builders John Goode in the garden of No. 28, this became the home of Betty Lloyd and her daughter Shirley when they moved from No. 28. The design was based on the sketched requirements of Betty and allowed her to have 'the right house for them now' while staying in the Park with its small village-like community.

No. 26 Upton Park

No. 26 was built by a developer in 1967 as one of two houses on plot 15 – known as the orchard plot.

It was known previously as Laurlands and owned by Bill Fieldhouse and family. In 1974 they carried out a small single storey extension at the rear. It was then briefly home to the Holmes family. French Mrs Chantelle Holmes, gave the house a French name (Brisant) and she gave birth to baby Oliver.

It has been the home of the Mason family since August 1984. The house had been empty for almost a year and the garden had that 'jungle' look. Major modification was carried out in 1997. Phil Mason has provided the technical management of Park roads for several years, having formalised the process by introducing a schedule of rates.

No. 24 Upton Park

No. 24 was also built in 1967 on the orchard plot. Initially owned by the Bennett family it was named the Wolery. It has been the home of the Bailey family since 1985, when the Bennetts moved to York.

Section O: First development along the south side of the Mill arm

House numbers
12, 14, 16, 18 built 1904-5
20 built 1955

This land belonged to Dicksons Nurseries and it appears that by the early 1900s the Park was sufficiently established and successful that a building developer managed to buy a plot of land – some 1440sq yds – and build these two pairs of semis in 1904-5, immediately adjacent to the boundary of the covenanted area of Upton Park. As built they each had a 360 sq yd plot and featured the hard red engineering brick, Ruabon Red, which is not featured in most of the Park predating this period.

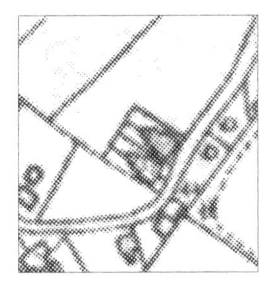

Above: 1908 OS survey

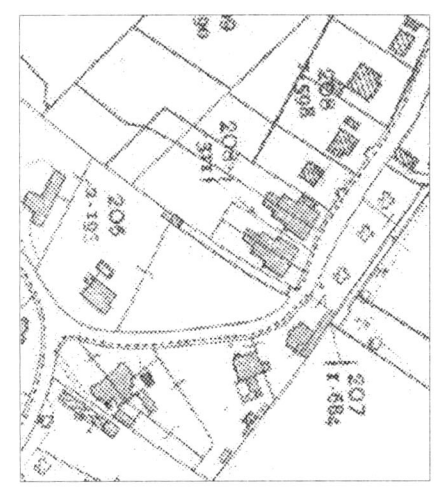

Right: by the 1932 OS survey

Post WW1 Dicksons must have sold valuable building land along the roadside of Mill Lane and the Upton Park arm to the Mill. Probably while selling the land for house numbers 2-10, these semis were able to acquire more land to their rear. The owners of Willowdene (No. 12) extended theirs out in line with their boundary but the owners of Laverstock (No. 14) acquired the land stretching back behind themselves and the other two (Nos. 16 and 18) giving them 1460 sq yds prior to the Park accounts ledger of

113

Major Frederick Matthews and his son Peter of Laverstock (No. 14) during the 1940s.

1921. Also, prior to the 1932 OS survey Laverstock had managed to acquire some of covenanted plot 15 to enable a drive and garage to be constructed.

Now with a sizeable plot to their rear and an access drive it was only a matter of time before this was developed. That occurred post WW2 in the early 1950s when the owner of Laverstock, living in Bulawayo, Rhodesia built a new bungalow in the grounds, returning Laverstock to its original 360sq yd plot.

For much of the first 50 years or so these four semis were owned by various absent landlords who let them, in several cases, to tenants who stayed for many years. In the 1920s it appears that Miss Clarke and Mr Woodward swapped ownership of Nos. 16 and 18.

No. 12 Upton Park
Known as Willowdene

Believed to have been built in 1905, by 1911 Willowdene was home to James Henry Haselden who was Chester's Sheriff in 1932.

From the Sheriffs' roll of honour board Town Hall Chester

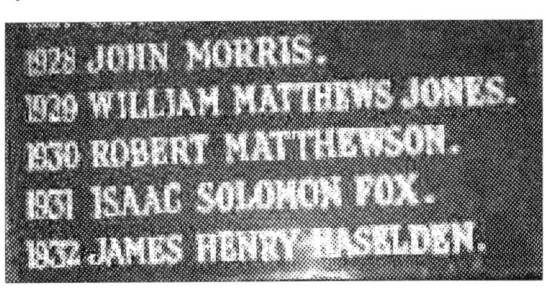

1928 JOHN MORRIS.
1929 WILLIAM MATTHEWS JONES.
1930 ROBERT MATTHEWSON.
1931 ISAAC SOLOMON FOX.
1932 JAMES HENRY HASELDEN.

By 1939 only his wife Sophie is recorded along with Edith Matterlead.

By 1945 it was the home of Oscar Davies, a Registrar of Births and Deaths.

By the mid-1950s Willowdene was owned by Harry Rothwell, believed to have been a representative with Chester Farmers. His wife was Austrian and they lived abroad a lot, renting out the house for many years before returning c1972.

The owner-occupiers were then the Leadbetter family for a few years before the current owners Clive and Sylvia Clarke.

No. 14 Upton Park
Known as Laverstock

Laverstock was built in 1905 and the 1921 Park accounts show the name L Nicholson and transfer to Shearer. The tenants in 1921 were Alfred and Effie Jones. B F Shearer is named until 1927 and then Austin Jones acquired the property in 1928 remaining until 1952. He also let the property with Florence Kellett recorded in 1929 and William and Mildred Jones in 1939.

During WW2 and the immediate post-war period the property was rented to Major (later Lt Col.) Frederick Matthews and family. Major Matthews was a Quartermaster and based at The Firs prior to posting to Liverpool with searchlight responsibilities. Subsequently he was posted to Germany at the end of the war. Son Peter lived here between the ages of 2 and 11.

By 1952 Laverstock was owned by Mr Lloyd who lived in Rhodesia and had Bulawayo (No. 20) built in the grounds gaining access via the garage drive. In 1957 Chester City footballer Norman Bullock wished to buy Laverstock but as a professional footballer was unable to get a mortgage through the normal channels. He resorted to writing to Mr Lloyd in Rhodesia who turned out to be a Chester football supporter, following the team weekly via the *Chronicle*. Feeling that he already knew Norman through his exploits, a private mortgage was arranged and Norman and Dorothy moved into Laverstock in 1957. In 1971 Norman Bullock acquired plot 12, built No. 36 and moved there in 1974. They sold Laverstock to the Lewis family who stayed until c1980.

It is currently the home of Dr Robin and Karen Davies with their family Sarah and Ben. Karen was UPPA Secretary in the 1990s and is currently Vice Chairman.

No. 16 Upton Park
Known as Fairfield

Fairfield (No. 16) on the right with Ranmere (No. 18) on the left

With no records for the first 15 years, the house was rental property until 1954. Throughout most of this period it was the home of William and Mary Singleton and in the early 1920s Arthur and William – presumably their grown-up sons.

The earliest Park accounts of 1921 record Fairfield as owned by Mr H Woodward. By 1927 ownership was with Miss Edith Clarke of Balham having swapped with No. 18. From 1936 the accounts show Miss H G Clark of Eastham. Briefly after WW2 accounts show Mrs Schofield of Guernsey but then Miss H G Clark is named for both Nos. 16 and 18 until 1954.

In 1954 Fairfield was acquired by Thomas Gerald Michael Scally. Thomas and Suzanne Scally (see 'People', Chapter 7) and their family of nine children lived in Fairfield for 15 years and were well known within the Park. Like many other Park residents, Tom was a collector of old cars and the front garden was a parking lot. The back garden became a yard in the true sense with not a blade of grass growing due to so many young children, a Persian cat (that got run over outside the house) and an English bulldog which scared most visitors when not tethered on a large chain on a steel wire that spanned the back yard. In 1969 Tom retired and moved with his family to the Isle of Man. Fairfield remained empty for almost two years as it became in need of refurbishment before being sold.

The current owners, themselves with a large family, have extended the property and it now has six bedrooms.

No. 18 Upton Park
Known as Ranmere

The 1911 electoral roll records ownership with Henry Woodward, an absent landlord living in London.

The earliest Park accounts of 8 April 1921 record Ranmere owned by Miss Edith Clarke who then swapped Fairfield with Henry Woodward. For the 1920s and 1930s the tenants were Edward Twist Jones, his wife Henrietta and their family.

By 1945 the tenants were Mrs Annie Carbutt with daughter Betty and son-in-law Frederick Oldham who post-WW2 built No. 44. Annie Carbutt had owned The Limes (No. 25) in the early 1920s. Annie Carbutt took on Eva Roberts as her live-in housekeeper after the death of Miss Longworth Dames and the subsequent sale of The Garden House (No. 28).

Ranmere was home to the Pye family from the mid 1960s until the late 1980s. Mr Pye served on the UPPA committee for much of their period of residence.

No. 20 Upton Park
Originally named Bulawayo
Later called Orchard Close although that name is no longer used

No. 20 was built c1955 for Mr Lloyd who owned the land as part of Laverstock (No. 14). He had served with the Rhodesian Police and wrote a book on his experiences there during the Roy Walenski era. Back in the UK he was involved in security on the Eaton estate. The bungalow was built with most of its garden grounds to its front. A double garage has been added and the original garage of Laverstock demolished. In 1956 this property had the second highest rateable value at £58 and the accounts were being settled by the Chester estate agents Swetenham, with Lloyd still in Rhodesia.

By 1963 the RV was still the second highest at £202 and with the owner noted in Park accounts records as C H Band. The bungalow was acquired by Karl and Jennifer Giffin and their family.

Currently the home of Jim and Doreen Judge who raised their family of three daughters there. Jim was a GP in Chester and Doreen taught at the Queens Prep school. They bought the house in 1972 at auction, securing the purchase at less cost then they had earlier offered.

The much smaller property (right) sometimes mistaken for No. 20 can be found at the beginning of the drive but as yet no-one has ever been found in...

Section P: 1920s developments opposite the Mill

House numbers
2, 4, 6, 8 all built 1923-4
10 built 1930

The 1932 survey revision of the OS shows all five of these properties opposite the Mill although at that date only a few houses had been developed along Mill Lane. The land, outside the covenanted area, was formerly part of Dicksons nursery. Although four of the properties date from the same year or two the assumption is that individual builders were engaged to meet the requirements of each first house owner, for the properties all have very different styles.

No. 2 Upton Park
Known as The Westing

The house fronts onto Mill Lane but with its side entrance drive onto Upton Park. Facing west the house probably had a clear westerly view when first built although property was developed opposite in the 1930s. The Park accounts ledger first records The Westing at 840 sq yds in 1925. It appears that the first owners were Frank and Phylis Randles who lived there until c1934.

Ownership then transferred to J H Lightfoot of The Gables in Upton. The property was rented out with Garfield and Dorothy Cox as tenants during the WW2-period.

From 1955 until after 1962, Park accounts name Mr E E Winter as the ratepayer.

By the 1970s the owner-occupiers were the Osborne family, who stayed into the 1990s.

No. 4 Upton Park
Known as **Rhossili** since being built in 1923

This property was built on a 720 sq yd plot for Charles Hartwell Compston, an engineer in the steel trade. The builder went bankrupt during the construction period and Charles Compston had to complete the building himself.

His daughter Joan recalls the house: *"The exterior was grey pebbledash, which was very popular in the 1920s. As originally built there was no dormer window. The roof tiles were especially shipped from Marseilles reflecting Charles' affectionate memories of visits to France in 1900. The house was well built. Internally, there were parquet suspended floors and electricity was installed in 1923 but as it was so very new Charles had gas put in as well, so we had the choice. The electric switches went sideways for on/off. The garage, later demolished, was built in brick and pebbledashed, and with the Marseilles tiles all matching the house. It had an inspection pit and was used by Charles and later by Geoffrey to carry out their own car servicing."*

• Charles Compston with his wife Margaret Penny and children Kathleen, Joan and Geoffrey were lodging at Fernbank (No. 56) at the time but were forced to leave there and take up occupation before the house was completed during their son's illness. For Joan's happy memories see 'Reminiscences', Chapter 8. They named the house after the venue of their holidays spent on the

Gower.
- By 1940 Margaret Compston had moved to Birmingham, renting out Rhossili.
- Mr and Mrs Harold Sumption moved in during 1939, initially as tenants and eventually buying. After Harold's death, Jessie Sumption continued to live in No. 4 for many years. She moved into a nursing home during the 1980s and died in the 1990s. It is reputed that her dog Pepe was shut in the kitchen during the Blaster Bates demolition of the mill chimney and then refused ever to go in the kitchen again. When the house was sold, after her death, it had escaped much of the 'modernisation' of the post-WW2 decades. Electric lighting was used but the gas lighting remained. All fireplaces were intact including in all the bedrooms.
- The current owner, Dr Anthony Kaufman, has taken care to retain many of these preserved features while refurbishing the property.

No. 6 Upton Park
Known as Woodcroft
Often referred to as The Bungalow

The property was built in 1923 and is first shown in the accounts ledger for 1924, on a plot of 1505 sq yards, under the ownership of Mrs E Pinnington. In 1930 it was inherited by plumber Mr R Pinnington who appears to have rented it out to J Breward from 1931-3 and then to Mr Hough for 1934.

Around 1936 the property was bought by Mrs Loadman of No. 10. She relocated to the bungalow letting out No. 10.

Around 1964 the property was acquired by Dill, transferring to Millikin in the 1970s and then Pond through the 1980s into the 1990s.

UPTON PARK, CHESTER

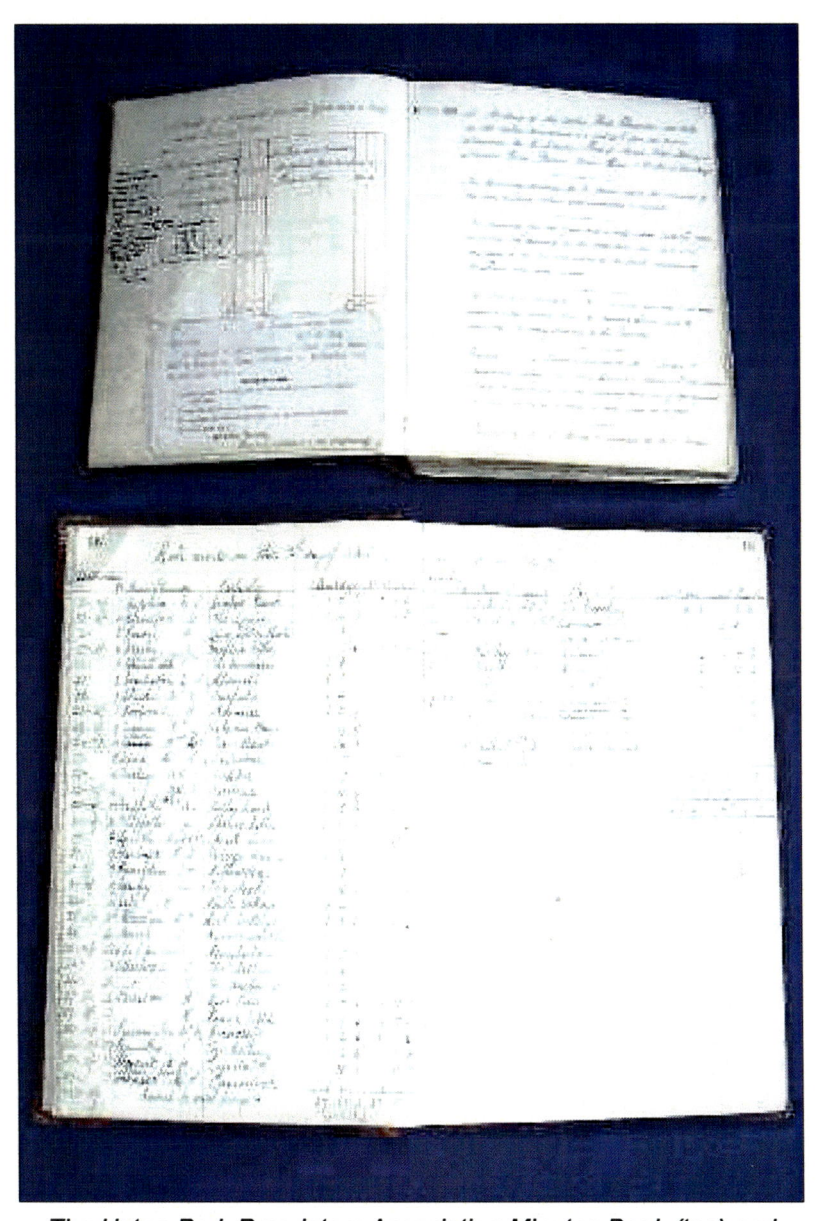

The Upton Park Proprietors Association Minutes Book (top) and Accounts Ledger (below)

UPTON PARK, CHESTER

Left: the Avenue in winter
Below: the Avenue in summer
Both pictures taken in 1912

UPTON PARK, CHESTER

The Circle pictured in 1912

UPTON PARK, CHESTER

Aerial photograph of the north end of Upton Park

UPTON PARK, CHESTER

Aerial photograph of the south end of Upton Park

UPTON PARK, CHESTER

Year 2000 record of the Upton Park households

6

UPTON PARK, CHESTER

Year 2000 record of the Upton Park households

UPTON PARK, CHESTER

Year 2000 record of the Upton Park households

No. 8 Upton Park
Known as Heatherlea

Built in 1924 and first recorded in the Park accounts for 1925, the ground area is shown as 740 sq. yards. It appears that Heatherlea extended its back garden when Dicksons nurseries was finally sold up for housing development and Delvine Drive was built.

The 1925 ledger names the owner as B J Willis until 1934 when it passed to Albert and Maude Warner and daughter Phillipa. Albert Warner was the managing director of the photographic business Will R Rose. He became Chief of the local Air Warden Service during WW2 and also became an UPPA Vice Chairman until he died in 1954. Maude Warner remained in the house for a number of years and then sold to the Eggitt family who had three daughters. Another family then lived there for a short period before it became the home of Dr. and Mrs. Wakefield and their two children. Dr. Wakefield was an ICI chemist and became UPPA Chairman in the early 1970s. For a period of a few years they let the house to an Australian family – Ieva and Keith Lidgerwood.

The Wakefields then sold to the Ireson family. The Iresons hosted the 1977 Queen's Silver Jubilee children's party.

Heatherlea is currently the home of Brian and Claire Heald with their sons, Jeremy and Simon.

No. 10 Upton Park
Known as 'The Garth' (garth being a word for 'yard')
formerly Morcove

Built in 1930, the original owner was Mr J H Jones, a bookseller in Werburgh Street, Chester. Mrs M C Loadman (Mrs Lees' mother) bought it in 1934. Her husband, W A Loadman, had been a greengrocer in Chester's Watergate Street. Unnamed originally she called it Morcove – the name reputedly coming from a girls' magazine about a girls' school.

Mrs Loadman then bought the bungalow (No. 6) and moved there in 1936-7. No. 10 was then let to tenants. Her son James C Loadman lived at No. 10 from 1946-50 before moving to Kenya

The Garth has been the home of Mr and Mrs Lees and family since 1950, although Mrs Lees grew up in Nos. 10 and 6. Their daughters Valerie and Helen grew up in No. 10 and have now flown the nest. Andy Lees has audited the Park accounts since 1959 (see 'People', Chapter 7).

Section Q: Upton Mill and its former grounds

Upton Mill House, which predates Upton Park, became a member of the Proprietors Association from its inauguration but left when it was no longer inhabited. The Mill grounds were developed for housing in phases during the 1960s and although they first had a different postal address, those fronting onto Upton Park acquired Upton Park addresses (Nos. 86, 88, 90, 92, 94, 96, 98, 100, 102 and 104) in 1966 and became members of UPPA. When the Mill itself was converted to residential property it did not have access from the Park and did not join the association.

The restored Mill and the 1960s housing photographed in 2001

It appears that during the late 1920s an access road was cut between the Mill yard and its orchard grounds. This is recorded as giving access to Government House and the Army Pay Office paid five shillings annual Park rate for the privilege. By 1950 this was used more extensively with more army property and the rate increased to £1. The accounts record no further payments after 1957.

Residents recall air raid shelters on the site of the Mill orchard grounds. These were the mound-type above ground and with a conning tower. After the war the doors were locked, much to the disgust of the local children. The other attraction on the Mill

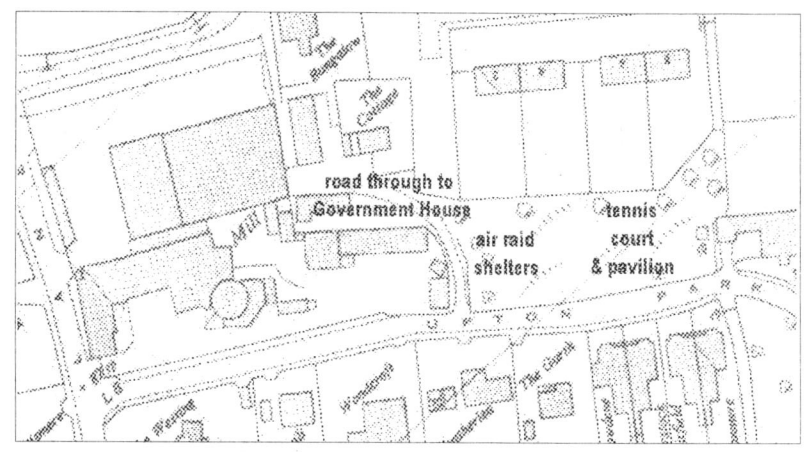

Section of the 1957 OS survey overprinted to show where it understood that the shelters and tennis court were located. Also noting the road through to Government House.

orchard grounds was the tennis courts and pavilion. These had been used in the between-the-wars period as a very exclusive tennis club, mainly for the ladies of the Park, with strictly no children allowed.

The UPPA minutes (see Reference section) record much of the phased development of the new housing during the 1960s. Nos. 86-96 seem to have been built by Austins and Nos. 98-104 by Pringle.

The land between the new houses and Millside (No. 84) has an electrical sub-station, a set of six garages and small parcels of land. These garages and the parcels of land are largely owned by the Edwardian properties opposite. When they acquired this land in the late 1960s or early 1970s, Park residents lost their quick easy access through to the library.

From the Mill end:

No. 104 built 1967: Tom & Kathleen Griffiths were the first owners moving in during January 1968. When Tom came out of the fleet Air Arm after WW2, he returned to his career in Custom & Excise based at Ellesmere Port.

No. 102 built 1967: Nora Stewart was the first owner moving in during 1968 from Carden Bank (No. 15) after the death of

Brigadier Stewart.

No. 100 built 1967: Originally Mrs Walker who then moved into one of the flats.

No. 98 built 1967: Originally owned by Mrs Searle - daughter of Mrs Walker. Then Michelck and currently John and June Dodds since c1980.

Nos. 90, 92, 94 and **96** are flats mainly rented out by absent landlords.

Nos. 86 and **88** are believed to have been built first in the early 1960s. As built they both had integral central garages but both dwellings have now given up their garages as part of extending their properties.

No. 86 was bought by a retired nurse Sister Cairns, and No. 88 by Doris Aethwy-Jones. No. 88 then passed onto Doris's sister and her husband Professor Robert Roaf.

Looking towards the Mill Lane entrance after the Mill conversion - sketched by Arthur Garrod on 27 February 1988

The working mill and its demise

Built in 1775, Upton Mill was a full working flour mill with outhouses, yard and orchard stretching up to the boundary of the covenanted area. It lost its sails in the early 1920s, by which time it was presumably powered by electricity. Many Park residents from the first half of the 20th century recall purchasing bread and cakes directly from the Mill as a working bakery. It closed down, becoming uninhabited in 1953.

The mill around the time of WW1 viewed from behind – the site of Old Mill Court.

The projected site plan for Upton Park in the 1850s shows the Mill and its yard having two gated entrances – one at each end of the lane passing through it.

The Mill entrance at its junction onto Mill Lane, photographed in 1918 for a postcard.

Only the base of the left pillar remains as does the Victorian letterbox.

At the time of establishing the Park the Mill owner was William Carter. Pitt, Shone and Wood had to negotiate access with him. He is still named in the 1871 census but by 1881 his son-in-law Edward Dean is named as head of household. His son was also named Edward and the UPPA Minute book for the early 1900s records Edward Dean Jnr as Hon Secretary with committee meetings taking place at Upton Mill House.

Other members of the Dean family acquired various houses within the Park during its first few decades.

Reference to the OS maps shows significant expansion by the 1930s, behind the original Mill buildings and an access road from the Park roadway. This may have been part of their expansion into bakery. From being Dean's bakery they traded under the name of Country Maid Bakeries and were highly respected for their packaged sliced bread as an innovation of the day. In 1954 it appears that they considered demolishing the Mill as part of modernisation plans for the site and the business. The demolition of the disused shell of the Mill was opposed by Upton Park residents and other locals. Eventually, they transferred their operation to Saltney, became part of Sunblest and what is now Allied Bakeries.

The Mill viewed from across the fields (pre WW1)

After the Mill closure there were various proposals for its use but the only actual use that can be recalled was by T Houlbrook & Sons Wholesale Vegetable Merchants during the early 1960s. Their use provoked considerable local concern with the local MP, J M Temple, becoming involved. They moved out and soon demolition and clearance for housing was seen as the only solution. The chimney – presumably for the ovens – was reputedly felled by Blaster Bates as part of the demolition process.

In 1979 the Mill was put on the market as suitable for conversion to a private residence. Bought and restored by Michael Field for his own use, the boundary wall was rebuilt and with no access to the Park the new dwelling did not become part of Upton Park and its Association.

As seen from Mill Lane (c1912)

A 1979 photograph of the Mill with No. 104 in the foreground.

Upton Park's house-style

Walking around the Park, a clearly evident house-style is the frequent use of high holly hedges bordering the frontage to the roadway. Early UPPA minutes comment on hedges being too high for the safety of traffic and pedestrians which suggests that they are a long-established feature of the Park. Hawthorn was also common and some of today's front hedges are a holly/hawthorn mix.

As for housing, the Park has developed for over a century and so, like many small villages, the housing is to customised designs and built to the style of the day. No property has been built in the style of yesterday although most house extensions have preserved the period of their original.

One of the first houses, Thomas Wood's (Nos. 9 and 13) does feature the gothic-style doors of the early Victorian period and many of the Victorian houses still have their original robust front doors and sash windows. While no record of the builders used for these Victorian houses has been identified, it is clear that some of them either used the same builder, or at least followed similar styles and use of materials. Numbers 80, 56/58, 40/42 and others use similar window frames and brickwork. Around this 1870 period no hard engineering bricks seem to have been used but soft yellow bricks have provided ribboning in the front elevation brickwork. Interestingly No. 84, built in the late 1850s, imitated this style many years ago by painting on its yellow ribboning.

Further into the 1870s, the houses become grander in style and blue engineering bricks are used at damp-course level and for ribboning. Hard Ruabon red engineering bricks, at least for the full house frontage, were not used until the 1890s and early 1900s. One house – No. 28 – not only uses these but features the WM brickwork patterning associated with Westminster property. The popular Chester city Victorian styling of mock-Tudor is used only once on the last vacant plot in the inner circle. Nos. 15/17 have their top half black and white timber framed.

Sandstone, probably from local quarries, is commonly used for window sills and for gate posts. With many of the gate posts now gone, several gardens feature re-used sandstone blocks. Although the lane to the Mill does not feature holly hedges, nevertheless there is a common style of using sandstone blocks probably salvaged from the demolition of the Mill grounds.

As for trees, the Park has a good variety of deciduous and evergreen trees, many of which are very mature. However, the tradition of tree planting has continued and so the Park atmosphere is destined to remain into the future.

Finally, the chimney pots. While various styles are to be seen on the older properties, nevertheless one style is predominant – the square yellow (see above). It is believed that in the early days some Lady Boughtons were used but any that survived are now only garden features.

Chapter 4
Maintaining the Park
The tree lined Avenue entrance

Land had been bought to provide access to the Park via a roadway linking onto Wealstone Lane. By the 1870 OS survey the Avenue was already tree-lined.

By the 1920s the Avenue was mature, with lopping and even some felling being undertaken. For many years the north side of the Avenue was lined with poplars. On the night of 1-2 December 1966 an 80 ft poplar fell on to the roof of 5 Gayton Close, Neston Drive and UPPA was charged the £24 cost of immediately removing the tree. As a result of this the UPPA committee had the trees inspected which resulted in the decision that the Council should take responsibility for all the poplars and they had them felled before establishing a new tree planting programme. UPPA did not accept responsibility for the felled tree. In 1970 the Council then planted a line of Cornish elm. The major tragedy of the Avenue came in the Autumn of 1979 when six of the Wych Elm trees were condemned with Dutch Elm disease and felled. Six new trees were planted the following spring.

Avenue trees numbered from the Park entrance onto Wealstone Lane

Trees/scrub along the boundary fence not listed

#	Tree	Status
1	Field Maple	Planted c1998 as a good mature tree
2	Sycamore	Established
3	Swedish Whitebeam	Planted 1980
	Elm	felled 1979
4	Norway Maple (red)	Planted 1980
5	Norway Maple (red)	Planted 1977
	Elm	felled 1979
6	Norway Maple	Planted 1977
	Elm	felled 1979
7	Large-leaved Lime	Planted 1980
	Elm	felled 1979
8	Whitebeam	Planted c1992
9	Sycamore	Established
	Elm	felled 1979, rings indicated tree was planted between 1860 & 1870.
10	Norway Maple (red)	Planted c1992
	Elm	Storm felled 1966
11	Norway Maple	Planted 1977
12	Sycamore	Established
	Elm	felled 1979, rings indicated tree was planted between 1860 & 1870
13	Large-leaved Lime	Planted 1980
14	Sycamore	Established
	Elm	felled 1979
15	Norway Maple (red)	Planted 1980

The 1940 accounts record Mr B Roberts being reimbursed £1 for laying the hedge in the Avenue. The minutes frequently record thanks to residents for tending to the Avenue, such as to keen gardener Tommy Trelfa of Treehaven for tending the verge. For many years now the verge grass has been cut by a contractor as a regular UPPA maintenance contract. A few years ago the then chairman Pauline Rourke organised bulb planting working parties and the Avenue now bursts into colour each spring.

The post-WW2 housing development alongside the Avenue was

seen to pose a threat to the whole of its environment. True Bond of London were the developers and at one time it looked as if 'unsuitable' housing was to be built. The personal intervention of UPPA Vice-Chairman Brigadier Stewart, meeting with True Bond, resulted in a change of plan and the properties alongside the Avenue are detached dormer bungalows.

Concerns related to the encroaching housing development are well recorded in the minutes. The 1956 AGM records the first formal consideration of installing an entrance gate, primarily to restrict the use of building contractors' lorries. Discussions continued until a formal proposal by Mr C W Wilson was supported at the 1960 AGM " *for a gate to be fastened in an open position, opening inwards and sited near the Wealstone Lane entrance to be easily seen*".

This was erected in 1961 much in the form as of today. For the next decade the minutes record frequent discussion on locking the gate and issuing keys. Locking the gate, with residents holding keys, was a measure very much religiously supported by some of the elder ladies of the Park, however on one occasion it is rumoured that a young lady, daughter of a past Park Chairman, finding the gate locked, let herself through and then hurled the lock over the hedge.

Replacing the lock and issuing new keys was an on-going saga amid pleas from some quarters for regular closed and opened periods. By the early 1970s even automatic locking was being considered but in 1971 a call for increased periods of locking was defeated. The locking gradually faded away – the gate has remained locked open now for some 30 years.

The Upton Park roadway

The practice for many decades has been for housing estate developers to establish an estate roadway acceptable to the Council for adoption. Back in the 1850s with Upton Park this was not the case. The covenant obliged each property builder to establish the roadway along their road frontage to the midpoint of the road. The cost of maintaining the whole estate roadway including the link roads was then covenanted to be shared between all plot owners. The standard to which the roadway should be maintained has been a point of Association debate through its history but has improved through the years even though rather erratically.

The roadway is much as intended in the early mid-1850s plan, but the cul-de-sac for plots 2-7 was never instigated. Before the Dickson Drive estate was built in the 1950s there was a track through to Dicksons nurseries. At times this access caused concern to Park proprietors and in 1939 posts were proposed to stop through traffic. Since the absorption of plots 2-7 into the Dickson estate all that remains is a small triangle of land made up as a simple border of shrubbery.

The post-WW2 housing boom produced development proposals around the Park boundary which incorporated additional access roads into the Park. However, the Park stayed intact as housing developments and playing fields surrounded it.

Another past gateway off the Park was owned by the Army between the late 1920s and early 1960s and gave access to their property in the Dorin Court area. Park accounts record an Army annual contribution of £1 – some 60% of the smallest property contribution – in 1960. As houses in the Park were built it has always been their duty to reinstate the roadway to at least the state before development commenced.

The roadway has remained private and maintained by the Park proprietors throughout its history despite consideration on several past occasions to pursue adoption by the Council. In 1947 the Council estimated a cost of £12,000 to instate a roadway to a standard that could be adopted. This ended once and for all any idea of seeking council adoption.

The roadway – the early days

No records have been identified to give any indication of how the roadway was established and the state of it for the first three or four decades. It is likely however that a surface was gradually established with chippings and potholes kept under reasonable control using fire ash from proprietors' properties.

The Minute book from 1899 and Accounts book from 1921 record periods with the services of a roadman and the delivery of

various materials and tools needed by him to maintain the road and boundaries. Until 1928, the earliest accounts ledger balance sheet showing road maintence costs, it is not clear from the minutes as to whether agreed proposals were actually carried out. For example significant work was proposed in 1904:
• 20 tons of 1-inch Macadam and 10 tons of half-inch chippings along with the services of a steam roller
• Kerbing using Lancashire kerbs (4" X 12") at an installed cost of 3s per linear yard.

For most of the years between 1928 and 1935 the balance sheet records roadman George Woodward's wages, tar chippings mainly from the Ceiriog Granite Company and tar spraying.

A shift in policy leading to roadway improvements 1935-37

The following is an account drawn from the committee established in 1935 which first seriously addressed the establishment and maintenance of the Park roadway. Council adoption was considered again, and again rejected in favour of independence and DIY. The newly proposed and formed committee comprised civil engineer Harold Sabine in the chair, with Mr Brocklebank as secretary, and Messrs Williams and Warner (and subsequently Mr Furley) as committee members. Minutes are well recorded in the old minutes book.

Initially tenders were invited from local contractors. There is no record of who drew up the enquiries but Harold Sabine was clearly the key player and had discussions with Mr W Starkie the Assistant County Surveyor – father to Ken Starkie who managed the roads during much of the latter half of the 1900s.

Mr Briercliffe of Chester tendered for £110, Mr Smith of Mold for £100 and Mr Thomas of Chester for £98.

From the scale of these costs (the Park balance stood at less than £10), the committee resolved "to do the work ourselves" by accepting Mr W Starkie's offer to hire two County Council men at 7s (35p) per day but to retain control of all labour and material purchase. The committee were to have full power to supervise the work and do as much of it as their financial resources would permit. Harold Sabine then interviewed a Mr Trew to ascertain the cost for certain sections of the roads (tarmac and spraying).

A special Park meeting was held at Mayfield (No. 31) on 28 June 1935 attended by 17 members – an unusually high turn-out – to sanction the committee proposals.

Two schemes were submitted for the meeting's consideration:
• Patching and tar spraying all roads for the sum of £58.
• Patching the Circle and Mill road and then tar spraying of the Mill road only, for the sum of £30.

The full scheme was adopted and a rate set at 1s 3d in the £ to meet the expenditure which turned out to be £73 18s 4d for the 12 months 1935-6. An objection to this was raised later by an absent landlord, Mrs F Ollerhead of Malpas.

The Park accounts for the year ending March 1936 record £45 paid to Cheshire CC for "patching/ spraying etc" and the committee meeting of 6 September 1935 records that the committee were satisfied with the work of Cheshire County Council. It was then agreed roads be kept clean and pot-holes attended to as soon as they developed. The roadman's wages for the 1935-6 years account were £10 19s 11d.

The next issue was subsidence opposite Roade Villa (No. 74). The brick main sewer had collapsed and had to be repaired in one place – 15ft removed and piped with 12in socket pipes. Also the road grid inlet piping was renewed and connected to this 12in piping. The cost of £17 6s 3d was just met from the year's higher rate.

By summer 1936, the Mill to Circle road needed attention again, and Harold Sabine dealt with Mr Trew of Cheshire County Council getting an estimate of £24 to patch and tar spray that piece of road. On Mr Trew's safety recommendation timber was replaced with Yorkshire flag alongside the grid opposite The Beeches (No. 23) the home of Harold Sabine. These costs were met by a lower rate for 1936-7 of 10d in the £ raising £52 18s 6d.

The roadway from 1938 until the late 1950s

The policy was now one of DIY, using the roadman for minor maintenance and engaging a contractor for more major tasks.

Some of the purchases for the DIY repair included:

1940 - 24cwt of tarmac from Foden Bros; 6 tons of gravel (3/8") from Moore & Brock - all for £3 18s 6d.

1941 - 40 gallon drum of bitumen at £2 15s.

1942 - 40 gallon drum of bitumen at £3.

The roadman, Mr Woodward, carried out some of this work but Mr Elson was also used. Scientific Road were frequently engaged as main contractors.

Immediately post WW2, the question of road adoption by Cheshire County Council was again unanimously pursued but following the £12,000 essential upgrade estimate, the committee ruled out any possibility of adoption and road repairs according to the previous policy were stepped up.

Ken Starkie's account of the road maintenance late 1950s to early 1990s

In June 2000, Ken Starkie wrote:

"When I moved into the Park in 1956-7 the Avenue (with a line of poplars on the north side and many trees, mostly elms on the south side) had been very lightly surfaced in places – but there was no footpath surfacing at all. About every 12 months it became so potholed that it was really dangerous and cars could only crawl up and down the Avenue, dodging the potholes. I organised a small gang of two or three men (all Cheshire County Council workers) to come on a Saturday morning and patch up the potholes – I'd ordered the necessary bituminous materials

Looking north from outside Hollybank (No. 17) and mainly featuring Nos. 48 and 44. Photo taken in the late 1960s.

from a local quarry for Saturday delivery. This worked well but it was after all only a temporary stop-gap.

"*The wide footpath alongside No. 60 in the Avenue was unsurfaced. I arranged to have this surfaced and then got a good quotation for surfacing all the road of the Avenue (using a Barber-Greene paving machine) with a layer of dense bitumen-macadam 2½ - 3 inches thick. We had previously tried (but not with my approval) a ½ inch thick cold asphalt surfacing around the circle and down to Mill Lane. However this started to break up so I arranged for the whole Park carriageway, including the Avenue, to be surface dressed with bitumen and chippings. This very effective method consists of chippings laid on hot bitumen – it is a very cheap process and served the purpose. I remember getting permission from the owner of the Mill and temporarily storing the chippings on the site there - no development had taken place then. This surface dressing, which was repeated 2/3 times, and was successful in waterproofing and sealing the Park roads and maintaining them.*

"*When the development was proposed at the Mill, the developers wanted to take access to the site from the Park and David Docherty (No. 68), Mrs Jones (No. 21) and myself were members of a sub-committee to*

Ken Starkie in 1976. As well as his road maintenance co-ordinator role, Ken also served as UPPA Treasurer and Vice Chairman.

negotiate with the developer. They agreed to pay a lump sum, I think it was £2000-£3000, and to include a requirement for all the new owners/occupiers in the Mill scheme to be liable for whatever individual Park rate was levied in Upton Park itself – this would have increased our income. The idea was to use the lump sum to completely re-construct the Park road from Mill Lane to nos. 18 &84 (the bend in the road), including drainage and one footway. I surveyed this length of road and prepared specification and contract documents and invited tenders. The lowest was Flathers.

"At the AGM the proposed access of the Mill development was turned down and this meant we hadn't the money to reconstruct that part of the Park road – that has always been a problem – still, 'c'est la vie'. The developers incidentally blamed the Park for back tracking for they had to re-organise their access as it now exists directly from Mill Lane.

"I found a copy letter in the files at Backford Hall (Cheshire County Council Highways maintenance department) dated c.1933 from my father W. Starkie (Asst. County Surveyor from 1930-35) advising the then Park chairman Mr. Sabine on how to treat the road. His advice, similar to mine, had been to 'tar spray' it after sweeping (surface dressing with tar – or bitumen – and aggregate). In those days the cost was 2d or 3d per sq.yd. In the early '90s we surfaced the footpath round the Circle. The footpath of the Avenue, formerly just compacted earth, had been properly surfaced some years earlier. We used a company, Road Maintenance Services (RMS), of High Legh near Knutsford, who had also carried out the road surface dressing from Mill Lane to Wealstone Lane and around the circle."

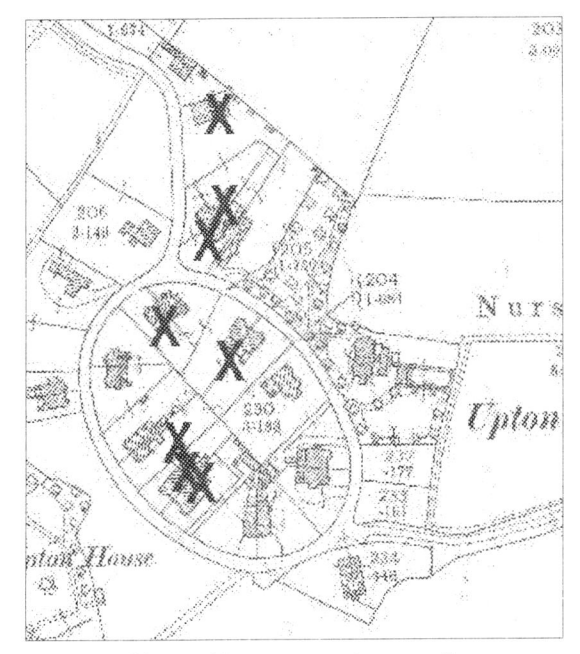

Sites of known previous wells

The utilities

Water

For the initial few decades the only source of water would have been streams and wells. Within the Park today the sites of only eight wells have been identified, as shown on the map above as X's overlayed on the 1898 OS map. It is thought possible that they are all on the course of an underground stream. The fall of the land is north to south suggesting that the stream may also be north to south.

Most of these have been filled in and covered over, often with a patio, but one that is 6ft in diameter has been restored recently to a depth of 12ft and with a working traditional handpump. The only other one still visible is on a garden boundary – one half covered over but the other half still allowing limited access.

The Park's water main was first laid, apparently, in 1890. According to Dee Valley Water by 1897 a fair part of Upton (pop. 1313, houses 124) was on mains supply from Chester waterworks.

In 1966 the Chester Water Company sought to improve their supply in Upton Park with the laying of a short length of main across the road opposite No. 56. In spring 1999 Dee Valley Water replaced the length of main on the west side of the Circle (between Nos. 1 and 23) due to unacceptable leaks.

Sewerage

In 1897 the 26 houses in the Park delivered sewage into a brook running through Dicksons nurseries. At this time new works were going on at the Asylum to treat their sewage as Upton was polluting the Bache brook and the River Dee. At least part of the main sewer through the Park was replaced in 1951.

Gas

When gas arrived has not yet been identified but UPPA minutes from the early 1900s urge proprietors to keep tree branches away from the street lamps. The 1926 Park accounts show a payment of 16s to the United Gas Company presumably for street lighting.

Electricity

The UPPA minute book records in February 1924, a letter from the City of Chester Electrical Engineer asking permission to lay cables in Upton Park. This was accepted by UPPA in accordance with terms and conditions stated. The account of the building of Rhossili (No. 4) records both gas and electricity with 'the electricity being very new'.

In 1963 MANWEB installed a high voltage underground cable from their substation, situated alongside No. 84, running under the Park's roadway into Mill Lane. This was part of a scheme to reinforce electricity supplies in Upton.

Chapter 5
The Proprietors Association (UPPA)

The work of the Association and its Committee

As put in an article by Bill Wilson in the 1979 Newsletter:

"There is a clause in the deeds of most of the houses in the Park which obliges owners to contribute towards the upkeep of the Park roads which are not adopted and, therefore, are not maintained by the Highway Authority. This condition is not included in the deeds of some houses which are outside the original Park area, but the owners of these houses have joined the association and have always contributed their share to the maintenance of the roads, trees, borders, etc.

"The function of maintenance and repair of roads, some drainage, trees and grass verges, is carried out for the benefit of all residents by a committee which is elected each year at the Annual General Meeting, usually in the month of May. Maintenance costs are kept to a minimum consistent with the wishes of the members as resolved at the AGM, when the Park rate to cover these expenses is fixed by a majority vote."

There is no constitution but certain resolutions made at general meetings over the last 100+ years, and other established custom and practice, do control the process of UPPA management:

• Today the Covenant is between all covenanted land owners. This group is the Proprietors Association and other proprietors of property within what is now Upton Park are taken as equal members of that Association.

• Between 1952 and 1954, rules to define a constitution were considered by UPPA with the help of a solicitor proprietor who acted as the 'legal advisor' on the committee. The conclusion was to leave things as they were.

• The Annual General Meeting is open to all proprietors. Proposals must be received before the formal notice. The notice calling the AGM is circulated at least 2 weeks before the AGM.

- Various minutes from the early 1900s define the officials but not until Harold Sabine's chairmanship in the mid-1930s was a working committee established as it is known today. The 'founding father' of the committee as a managing group was Chairman for over 20 yrs. He set about organising and maintaining an adequate roadway.
- The fair means of allocating 'sharing' in raising Park funds has been reviewed at AGMs and changed over the years.
- A budget for the following 12 months is prepared by the treasurer, discussed in committee and then put to the AGM to fix the levy for the year.
- The 1988 AGM resolved by a majority of 18 to 1 that a majority of 75% of all households (not just 75% of AGM voting attendees) was needed for significant expenditures from funds other than for normal road maintenance.

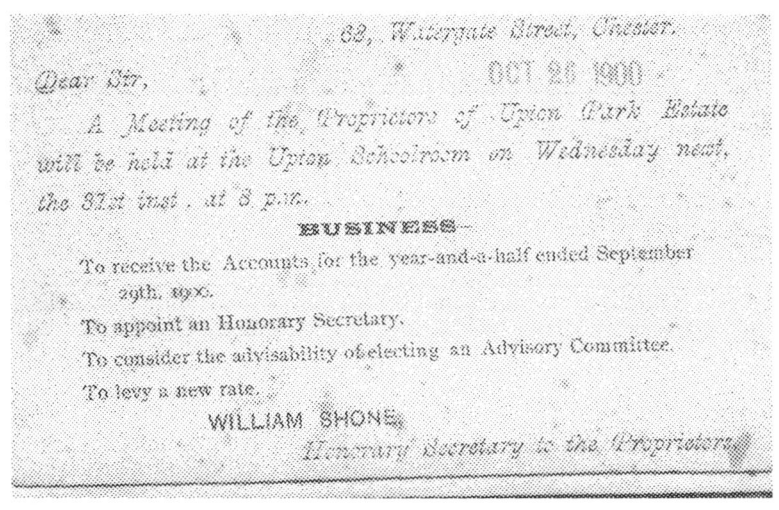

AGM notification for 1900 sent out by William Shone

- Established practice at the AGM has allowed only one vote per rate-paying household. The use of Proxy votes has been discussed and rejected by very high majority.
- The committee usually meets four or five times a year. Committee minutes are only circulated to committee members. Newsletters are produced and circulated throughout the Park

when deemed appropriate by the committee.
- Any issue for committee should be put in writing to the Chairman or secretary.

From the early days of setting out the Park until the end of the 19th century it appears that a rate was collected from proprietors by 'a collector' but no accounts are known to exist. On 25 July 1899 a meeting of Messrs J Smith (Chairman), Edward Dean, William Shone and the collector was called. A minute book incorporating limited accounts was started and a formality established for regular convening of proprietors.

A separate accounts book was started in 1921 initially naming proprietors and listing their Park rate contributions.

From 1899 until 1974 the minutes of both the committee and the AGM were recorded in a single bound minute book. These records have been summarised within the Reference section.

Today the rate is equal for each household.

Based on the Covenant, the rate was originally based on plot area but it appears that some owners with many undeveloped plots were often not paying and the system was seen as unfair. In 1928 the association changed the basis of the rate to be based on the Urban District Council set rateable value (RV) i.e. so much in the £. The Council would revise these periodically and as the decades passed, the newer properties which could command much higher rents, were having RVs several times more than old property on larger plots.

An equal rate was first formally proposed and discussed at the 1966 AGM but was rejected. Eventually though, the current equal rate was arrived at as the most acceptable when considering issues such as wear-and-tear on road caused by traffic and an acceptance that number of vehicles owned and number of motorised visitors was not related to the plot size or the previous RV (or today's tax band).

Pre 1970s the rate fluctuated widely according to maintenance costs. In recent decades the policy has been more towards a steady increase to build reserve and avoid sudden large increases.

Today's Park officials give their services voluntarily but in the past commission or honoraria were the order of the day..

The Park minutes for 1920 record L J Gowings as taking on the roles of Hon Secretary and Treasurer for UPPA on a commission basis of 10% of total Park rates collected plus reasonable out of pocket expenses and with authority to sign UPPA cheques on a newly established UPPA bank account at Lloyds Bank.

By 1929 the decision was taken to pay a fixed honorarium of £5 p.a. In 1940 the £5 honorarium was again stated.

At one point a single person held all the key roles with sole authority on signing cheques. Needless to say this situation was very short-lived.

And finally...

The Association is not a general interest club or a social club. While residents can raise concerns of a Park-wide nature, the Association's remit is managing the obligations of the covenant. The Association and the committee can choose to address some wider issues but not at the expense of meeting their covenant obligations.

Similarly, while many social events are arranged within the Park community, their organisation is independent of Association and committee affairs.

A quick tour of the UPPA Minute Book
(more details given in Reference section)
1899 - 1909

Annual meetings of 5-8 proprietors were held at the Mill, home of the UPPA Hon Secretary, and mainly addressed the Park rate based on RDC Rateable Value and road maintenance issues. There was strong consideration of seeking adoption of the road by the RDC but this seemed to evaporate. A managing committee was established to oversee the road maintenance needs. General meetings addressed other concerns such as the street lamps being obscured by trees.

1910 - 1919

Following pre-WW1 discussion, some land was acquired at the Mill entrance post-war for road widening to allow for turning of vehicles. Concern was expressed over hedges growing beyond five feet high and causing problems for cars – presumably driver visibility. No wartime meetings recorded.

1920 - 1929

Only owners or husbands of owners were allowed to attend meetings, this despite women having just got the vote nationally. The Avenue trees were now so established that lopping and even felling was carried out. The Accounts ledger that still exists today was started. The legal position of proprietors raised as an issue but no conclusions recorded.

1930 - 1939

The first few years saw little activity, just concerns over rate arrears from several residents and poor attention to their hedges. J Griffiths took on role of chairman, secretary and treasurer as sole signatory and all minor decision making. The Harold Sabine era then started in 1935. He established an active regular Park Management committee and the first attempts to establish and maintain a good Park roadway. Committee membership was now over-subscribed and elections held. The arrears problem was solved and maintenance offenders visited. Modern professionalism crept in with issues such as insurance. Towards the end of the decade the issue of road adoption was again raised but was inconclusive as WW2 beckoned.

1940 - 1949

There are no records of meetings and by mid-War no accounts records. Post-WW2 the issue of road adoption by the Council was finally ended when the Council estimated £12,000 for UPPA to put the road into a fit state for adoption. This post-WW2 period was dominated by the planning of the post-war housing development closing in on the Park. Dicksons Nurseries sold out but developments incorporating the Avenue remained on hold.

1950 - 1959

The decade was dominated by the post-WW2 housing development becoming a reality and covenant plots 2 - 7 were taken out of the covenant and out of the Park. All this building was leading to much increased building traffic and discussions started on closing the Avenue entrance with a gate. Legal status of UPPA again pursued with an in-house new legal advisor, Ken Davies, but all issues were dropped. The Avenue boundary did however get delineated.

Many changes happened with the working Mill closing and its sale leading to strong concerns about the implications for the Park. There was also friction with many other personally held views of proprietors regarding their personal building development plans.

Several new and younger proprietors, many ex-military, were now in the Park and active within the committee. These include builders and surveyors. The roadman eventually left complaining of 'too many bosses'.

By the mid-1950s the old guard could not cope with the changing times and the committee arguments. The Sabine era ended as younger members took over.

Contractors were now being used for the road maintenance and the Park rate escalated but the 10% prompt payment was introduced.

1960 - 1969

The new housing development got ever closer to home as the Mill grounds were sold and Nos. 86-104 were built. With this being an Upton Park development, issues and legal implications became very hot. Upton Park residents were also active in building with most of the potential in-filling taking place. In most cases plans were approved through the committee but there were cases of failed attempts to break the covenant. Notably this included the Orchard plot where the developer failed to break the covenant at the Land Tribunal.

Upton Park entered the City following boundary changes. The Avenue entrance became gated with residents having keys and being encouraged to lock it occasionally. The state of the road was causing concern again and the Park rate nearly doubled to start building adequate funds. With the Park rate still based on Council Rateable Values this meant that the new and often smaller properties were paying much more than the old houses since RV was based the rental income potential and tenants much preferred new property. Moves towards a fairer system for the Park Rate was at first resisted but the equal rate eventually came in. The

Avenue poplars were felled and some along the south side but replanting also took place.

This period saw Bill Wilson and Ken Starkie playing major roles – the former as guardian of the covenant the latter for road maintenance. The decade ended with an established pattern of turnover of Park officials and committee with typical service of two years in a post.

1970 - 1974

The decade started on positive notes of improving the Park. Trees planted along the school boundary with the Avenue, plans for a new water main and general appearance improvements through increased self-help with residents voluntarily tackling various jobs. There was concern over dogs and speeding traffic but the police resisted speed limits where they considered excessive speed could not readily be obtained. Beginning of the on-going debates about speed calming including speed bumps. Continual loss and replacement of the Avenue gate lock was an on-going saga. There was debate over whether or not the road was perhaps in too good a state, encouraging the through traffic speeding. The concrete lamp-posts appeared without warning from the Council. Development plans for the Mill site. Chairman's AGM report noted the trend towards young families moving into the Park and the noise this would add, but felt it was not for UPPA to intervene in any disputes between individuals.

Chapter 6
The Social Scene
Upton Park Safari Supper

Nicola Quartermaine (No. 19) writes:

"Every year in the summer and at New Year we celebrate Upton Park style with a Safari Supper in the Park, which involves eating, drinking and finding your way to the next house for the next course! It starts off with everyone meeting at one house for drinks, where you are given a card with house number and host for your starter. After the starter you find out where you go for your main course and so on till you stagger or crawl to the final venue for coffee, etc, and dance or talk the night away. It's a great way to meet your neighbours and create a friendly community.

"It started in 1987 with Hilary Williams (ex No. 9) and I knocking at every house in the Park to see if it was feasible. It took us three weeks but most people said yes, so we had the first one on April 1st with 40 people. It was a great success despite Brian Beard (ex No. 84) phoning me early on the great day to warn me he was cooking swan and was that OK? I was somewhat taken aback until I realised what day it was!

"From then on it has grown – our highest attendance was 76 and there is now a New Year's Eve version run by Megan Hinde (No. 3) and

Pre-drinks for safari party 1996

THE SOCIAL SCENE

A safari course in 1994

Margaret Measures (No. 50).

"We precede the Safari Supper event with a wine tasting evening to choose the appropriate wines. A very difficult task, but despite this, invitations to the wine tasting are very much sought after and newcomers to the Park are given priority. The organisers now include a Dutch contingent - Marianne Buck (No. 56) and Ineke Meijer (No. 13).

"It will hopefully continue as an Upton Park tradition for many years to come – I've even heard rumours that it has been included in estate agent's patter to prospective buyers!"

Right royal knees-ups

The earliest phographic record of any royal celebration is believed to have been for the **Coronation of George V** (right).

But the partying really started with the Queen's Silver Jubilee in 1977.

In the words of one of the organisers **Jennie Rogers (formerly of No. 52)**:

"It all began at the Mill end of the Park. Over a cup of coffee: 'Well, why not?', 'How about June 11th?', 'And let's have a children's tea party and an evening barbecue', 'Everybody bring a dish', 'Jubilee gifts for the children', 'Who will organise the wine and beer?' and 'What if it rains?'...

"Somehow it was borne in on the rest of us that Upton Park was going to celebrate the Queen's royal occasion along with the many thousands of jubilant citizens.

"Saturday dawned grey and wet. Nothing daunted, our organisers went ahead, putting up extra awnings, laying tables, preparing games for inside and out, rolling beer barrels into position and giving much time and attention to encouraging the enormous log fire to burn.

"Well, as you all know, rain didn't stop play and 50 children ranging in age from 5 to 15 years had a wonderful afternoon in Mike and Carol Ireson's garden, with three-legged races, bean-bag throwing, a darts competition, balloons, flags, pop and sandwiches. The sun shone brilliantly between showers.

"The agonies of the 'young at heart brigade', as they valiantly tried to outdo each other, considerably hampered by some white plastic sacks, was enjoyed by all! Loud cheers and several patriotic songs accompanied the ceremonial cutting of a gigantic cake made by Barbara Capstick.

"It was well planned, well run and, judging by the children's memories, well worthwhile. Our coffee drinkers Sue Matthew (No. 16), Doreen Judge (No. 20), Carol Ireson (No. 8) and Margaret Irvin (No. 32) could claim their first success.

"But more was to come. Back at Jim and Margaret Irvin's home (No. 32), the great bonfire was showing signs of life and the trestle tables set up in the decorated garage were beginning to groan under the weight of a magnificent supper. The party assembled at about 8.30pm, everyone suitably dressed in gaudy red white and blue, and although we walked there with umbrellas dripping, they were soon discarded as the sky cleared and it became a dry mild evening. Spirits were high, the barmen were most attentive and we ate and drank, chatted and danced on the patio until the small hours, when the glowing fire drew the hardy late-

THE SOCIAL SCENE

stayers to sit around it and enchant the night and themselves with the good old camp-fire songs.

"*It really was a splendid party and must stand in the annals of Upton Park as a most convivial occasion, long to be remembered.*"

So say all of us!

The children's party 3-legged race (above). Some of those present from left to right: Victoria Matthew (No. No. 16), Emma Lewis (No. 14), Alison Judge (No. 20), Nick Beard (No. 84), Ben Jones (No. 25), Chris Ireson (No. 8), Caroline Beard (No. 84), David Bennett (No. 24), Joanne Judge (No. 20), David Pye (No. 18), Emma Judge (No. 20), Emma Leadbetter (No. 12), John Jones (No. 25), Edward Irvine (No. 32), Veronique (No. Fr au pair), Matthew Ireson (No. 8), Annabel Jones (No. 25), Helen Feakins (No. 48).

In party mood for the Royal Wedding (see overleaf).

After the success of 1977 everyone was in party mood for the Royal Wedding on 29 July 1981.

The weather was much kinder and the garden of No. 80 was decorated with bunting and trestle tables laid for the children's afternoon fun and games and plenty of traditional party food (see photo on page 155).

After a slight pause to recover, parents and organisers then reconvened next door at Millside (No. 84), joined by others from the Park. The barrels had been set up and the next party soon got under way with everyone saying we needed an annual royal event – would there be the birth of a new prince or princess for next summer?

Fireworks and bonfires

From the immediate post-WW2 period through into the late 1950s, a major occasion of the Park's social calendar was November 5th Guy Fawkes night. It was held on Miss Crosby's field (now the site of Skellig, No. 36), and the local children would start building the bonfire well back into the summer holidays.

While Mark Rogers, Jim Feakins, Robin Parker and Peter Measures scythed the unkempt field in late October, sons Michael Feakins and Justin Rogers are seen here active with the hedge clippers.

THE SOCIAL SCENE

Come the event, contributions were raised around the Park and fireworks bought, as well as residents gladly getting rid of burnable items. Leo Jackson of The Nook (No. 42), chef at the Deva Hospital, produced the soup, and various mothers baked potatoes and later on toffee apples.

As there were plenty of military people about in this post-war period, the fireworks were impressive – many being ex-WD.

After a lapse of several years, the tradition was revived during the late 1960s and early '70s by the Rogers (No. 52), Feakins (No. 48) Measures (no. 50) and Parkers (No. 15). The loss of the land to build Skellig ended the tradition, as there was now nowhere on the Park suitable for a grand scale of bonfire.

Fireworks, of course, had to return on Millennium night. Park residents and friends gathered at No. 80 at 0030hrs on 1 January 2000 for a semi-professional display that kept the Park and its neighbours awake for a fair bit longer into the night.

A fireworks display at the 2001 annual Safari Supper was well received and so although the opportunity for a mass bonfire within the Park is now just a historic memory at least we are retaining the fireworks tradition.

Upton Park Christmas Eve carol singing

An important part of our heritage is the singing of traditional carols and what better than on Christmas Eve with a brass band, a big group of friends and plenty of hospitality with hot toddies and mince pies.

Upton Park is lucky to have brass bandsman Phil Mason (No. 26) as well as other musical (and not so musical) talent. Over a dinner party in early winter 1998 the idea was born to roam the Park on Christmas Eve collecting singers and entertaining those who just wanted to listen. Phil Mason did the honours by bringing along some friends from his band and that Christmas the starter group met at the Healds' house (No. 8) for a first hot drink and practice with the Bethlehem hymn sheets. Those less musically gifted rattled the tin and collected for the Honduras disaster fund. Staying within the Park, doors were opened and families and their visiting friends and relatives would join in for a few carols before returning to their own family Christmas.

Now established as an annual event, Christmas Eve 2000 saw the best turnout yet – more than 20 singers accompanied by our brass band. Each year the collection goes up – that's nearly £500 collected over three years – and each year a different charity is supported.

And yet again we find nothing is really new and in years gone by we had a carolling brass band.

For two years around 1980 Helen Feakins of No. 48 was in a brass band at Upton High School and along with some friends provided the band accompaniment during the round the park carol singing (see right).

Moving in the right circles

Recollections from the 1970s and possibly back into the 1960s:

The winter cocktail party scene got underway with invitations going out in October. There was a pecking order... No-one dare send out theirs until Dalzie Comyn had sent hers. Next in line were the Sherwins and then the Wilson, Lloyd and French families could follow. It was a great honour to receive an invitation. The Sherwins belonging to the City Club meant you were greeted with champagne served by waiters.

The format was strictly 'noon til two' though stories have emerged of unplanned events such as a resident happily playing away on the piano, enjoying their drinks, until suddenly with a crash they'd fallen off the piano stool.

Chapter 7

Park People

Surnames rooted in Wales have been in abundance throughout Upton Park's 150 years. Griffiths, Evans, Jones, Davies, Roberts seem to be featured during every era in its history. Often several families of the same surname, but apparently unrelated, have lived in the Park.

Occupations or means of dependence during the first 30 years can be seen in the census records. Those early days saw the influence of the railway with railway agents, clerks, guards, plate layers and similar frequently recorded as well as the influence from Chester's booming retail trade and new small businesses. The established professions of law, medicine, accountancy, science and engineering have always been represented throughout the 150 years. The post-WW2 period saw a large number of builders and surveyors. Of recent years medical and healthcare seem to have gone into dominance with science and engineering having declined, reflecting the reductions in the local process industries.

An age-spread of babies through to the very elderly has generally been the case, although there have been periods of very low household turnover and very few young families moving in.

The founding fathers of Upton Park

• **Founding Father William Pitt,** who was 30 years old in 1857, was born in Prees, Salop, the son of a farmer. He moved to Chester, becoming a railway clerk then a railway agent and cashier. In 1870 he was a trustee with two others of the Chester Benefit Building Society. He was married to Margaret Evans (daughter of another Margaret Evans) who died between the 1861 census and the 1871 census. Indications are that he built and moved into one of the first Park properties (No. 84) while owning other plots and building Hawthorne Villas (Nos. 19/21) and possibly Chatham Villas (Nos. 23/25). He relocated to Hawthorne Villa (No. 19), and rented out Chatham Villas, selling No. 84 and then his other vacant plots. Widowed with a young family, he then moved out of the Park before 1881. Records suggest that although he initially had a servant, his sister became his housekeeper after his wife died and no servants were employed. In 1881 his 17-year-old youngest daughter Caroline was a general domestic servant at Belmont (No. 33). All this suggests that he was not a wealthy man but dealt in land. He would seem to be the instigator of the Release of Covenant.

• **Founding Father William Shone** was the first of three generations of William Shones all associated with the Park, and was one of the founding fathers. His age is unknown in 1857 but he was described as a collector and agent.

William Shone (the 2nd) was born in 1848 and became an estate agent and accountant in partnership with Pritchard. In 1900 he was Hon Secretary of the Proprietors and his notice of the 1900 meeting gave his business address as 68 Watergate Street, Chester.

No records show William (the 1st) living in the Park but his son William (the 2nd) moved into the Park before the 1881 census, establishing the Shone estate of plots 18-21 with the double property Oaklea and Firdene (Nos. 66/68) unnamed during the Shone occupancy. The John Baichlin (or Bauchlin) Shone named in the 1870 Release of Covenant is a brother of William (the 1st or the 2nd). In the era of the 1870s and '80s Chester had an estate agency, Shone & Adams in St Werberg Street – the 'Adams' being Beresford Adams, grandfather of Philip Adams. William Shone (the 2nd) died on 17 April 1911. The Chester Archaeological Society journal of 1911 (Vol. 18) records an obituary of member William Shone noting his local archaeological history books. Whether this is the same William Shone of Upton Park is not proven but likely.

William Shone (the 3rd), born 1880, served in WW1 and during this time his colleague Horace Pritchard acted on his behalf through Power of Attorney. During the pre-WW1 and WW1 periods, the William Shones (2nd and 3rd) acquired and then sold several other Park properties (including Holly Bank and the Limes/Beeches), besides the family home of the Oaklea/Firdene estate. Documents from 1936 record a William Shone and Horace Pritchard accountancy firm in Chester, assumed to be the second generation of the Shone & Pritchard accountancy partnership

mentioned earlier.
- **Founding Father Thomas Wood** was born in Chester and was aged 32 years in 1857. He was known as a law stationer but also, maybe later, a Registrar of Births and Deaths. He moved into the Park with his wife Sarah (born in Ruabon) and son Thomas before the 1861 census. He died before 1881. His widow is recorded in census records for 1881 and 1891 as dwelling at Ivy Cottage and living on rents and dividends, with her son Thomas having left the Park.

The Rev Miles Hodgson Towers of Upton Church various tenancies from c1860-c1885

When Upton parish church (pictured below) was first consecrated in 1854 it was a chapel-of-ease, not becoming a parish with its own vicar until the mid-1880s. During this chapel-of-ease period the curate-in-charge from St Mary-on-the-Hill, Chester was the Rev Miles Towers.

His first stay in the Park is recorded in the 1871 census with the Horsfield family in No. 84. He was then aged 32. By the 1881 census he was in Westview (No. 80), the home of the Smith family. He is recorded as another family head and with his 17-year-old niece Mary Towers.

Indentures also record him as residing in No. 3 but without any indication as to dates.

The Smith / Pearson families of Westview/Roade Villa 1873-1953

William Smith was one of many early Park residents working on the railways. When he bought Westview (No. 80) in 1873 he was a railway plate-layer and by the 1891 census he was recorded as a retired railway contractor. By this time his first wife Margaret had died and his second wife was called Jane. His son William is not recorded as having lived at Westview for the 1881 census and may already have left home. His daughter Cecilia however was only a baby when the family bought the property in 1873.

William Smith Snr was born in Roade, Northamptonshire and when he had the property built next door on plot 17 he named one half Roade Villa. He died in 1895 leaving Westview to his two children but ensuring that his new wife had the rights to live out her life there.

William Pearson, a Chester chemist, is first recorded in the 1901 electoral roll as a lodger to Mrs Smith. A similar record in 1911 shows him still as a lodger to Mrs Smith but having more facilities provided. By 1904 Cecilia Smith had married William Pearson and had started formal arrangements with her brother William, then living in Leicester, to gradually buy out his interests in Westview. It appears that by the death of Jane Smith, Cecilia Pearson was the full owner of the property. William Pearson was chairman of UPPA from 1922-1925 and is named as settling the Park rates until his death c1930, and Cecilia until her death on 1 January 1936. They are still shown as owning Roade Villa (No. 74) during the 1920s and 1930s renting it out.

The Pearsons had two children, Marshall Smith Pearson and Constance Hilda Pearson, who were both reputedly very tall. Marshall, thought to be 6ft 6ins, was well-known in the Park as 'Tiny Pearson'. By 1939 Marshall is not named as living in the Park and Constance was in Westview as one of four women. In 1940 Constance sold Westview and left the Park while Marshall inherited Roade Villa (No. 74) and had moved in post-WW2 with his wife Leonora. Marshall was active in Park affairs and did not leave the Park until 1953. Reputedly he was a driving instructor but when he left in 1953 he went to Anglesey to run a pub.

Wannop/Trant families
of Laburnum Cottage 1873-c1970

Railway cashier William Wannop was 34 years old when he bought Laburnum Cottage (No. 9) in 1873 with his wife Emily. Still resident at No. 9 in 1881, with his widowed mother Fanny Wannop in No. 19, they then appear to have moved to Stockport, renting out Laburnum Cottage. They returned after his retirement in the pre-WW1 period and he died in 1915.

William Wannop

Their only recorded daughter, Ann Eliza, was born in 1874, presumably in the Park, and she married Captain Alfred William Vincent Trant, a sea captain who reputedly mainly sailed in the Far East. No relationship has been established between him and the Captain Edgar J Trant of the *Majestic* which replaced the *Mauretania*. By all accounts, though, Alfred fitted the image of the sea captain and Joan Compston (No. 4 in the 1920s) recalls his parrot pecking her as she passed it.

Captain Trant and Ann Eliza then took over Laburnum Cottage post WW1. He appears to have been a well-known character around the Park although he was frequently away at sea. He bought the vacant plot opposite from Dicksons and reputedly grew vegetables. Indications are that he died around 1934.

Trant had two sons, Vincent and Roger,, and two daughters – who both remained spinsters. The two sons were not really known as members of the Park but the two sisters were around for many decades. Margaret Patricia had the 'housewife' role and Mary Vincent was the organised 'military' breadwinner. Mary was Trant's daughter from a previous marriage, is believed to have been a Colonel in the ATS during WW2 and returned home after the war to look after her ailing step-mother. A formidable woman, she is remembered as having an 'Eton crop' and having had a senior post in the Red Cross. She had a car which at that time was quite unusual for a woman. In 1959 she caused quite a stir by erecting two garages without prior consultation with the committee. A proposal for a legal challenge over her breaching the covenant was defeated. It is rumoured that the younger elements in the Park sided with her but many of the old guard were not sympathetic.

There are many stories about them being exceedingly poor, having known better times. The rumours were that investments had been tied up in the Far East and these were lost at the outbreak of hostilities with Japan. (See 'Yarns').

Mary needed an income and set up a weaving loom in their coach-house. She sold the cloth and Margaret Millet recalls buying some for making a costume.

The sisters had two Pekinese dogs called Romulus and Remus.

Miss Mary Trant chaired UPPA for 1967 and 1968, stepping down in the belief that every resident should do their share in the running of the Park. She stayed active in Park affairs and is last recorded as attending the 1970 AGM. It is believed that she died shortly after that, ending nearly 100 years of the family's association with Laburnum Cottage.

The Prince / Gowings families of Millside 1876-1927

Leonard Gowings (pictured right), a Collector of Rates and Taxes, was appointed UPPA Secretary and Treasurer in 1920 and it is thanks to him that we have the Accounts Ledger. A very thorough record was established which has subsequently contributed substantially to the compiling of this history.

The following record of the family, who lived at Millside, is in the words of Leonard's daughter Margaret (Peggie), now Mrs Margaret Millett, who had a career as an actress.

"My grandparents, James and Elizabeth Prince, came to live at what was then known as 'Rose Cottage' after their marriage in 1876. Their first surviving child was Dora Louise, born in 1880. Next came Violet

Winifred, born in 1881, Raymond born in 1883, and finally Maggie Primrose born in 1887. Also living there at the time was James Prince's aunt, Elizabeth, aged 72, and a domestic servant, Margaret Jones, aged 33. My grandmother died at the comparatively early age of 44, leaving Maggie Primrose barely a year old. Margaret Jones took over the care of the house and children from the death of my grandmother in 1888. She was Welsh, quite untrained and did a valiant job. I think my grandfather became more or less a recluse from that time on. His aunt, Elizabeth, became senile and had to be sent to the local Asylum to live. My uncle Raymond emigrated to Canada when he was 17 or 18 and never came back. My youngest aunt, Maggie Primrose, was lucky enough to have been given an education at a well-known school in Edinburgh, by relatives who were sorry for this motherless family. She learnt to speak perfect French and German, had several excellent jobs in Europe and was not really living at Millside at all. My mother, Violet, first became a pupil-teacher and then went to a teacher training college in Oxford (nothing to do with the University). When she had qualified she found a job in Stepney, East London and boarded with the family of one of her fellow teachers.

"From about 1900, therefore, Millside was occupied only by my grandfather, my aunt Dora (always known as 'Daisy') and Margaret Jones. My grandfather had worked as a Collector of Rates and Taxes from the time he first came to Upton Park, and continued to do so.

"My father, Leonard Gowings, lived and worked in London, where he met my mother. I think they were married in about 1910 and continued to live in London. He had a varied and interesting life, but the only part of it that is relevant now is the fact that, quite as a coincidence, he had taken a training in Rates and Taxes. I was born in 1913, the same year that my grandfather died. My family then came to live in Millside and as he was a very fully qualified Collector of Rates and Taxes, my

James Prince (1838 - 1913) with son Philip Raymond (1884 - c1960s)

father was able to take over my grandfather's job in Chester. My aunt Daisy stayed on with us, and so did Margaret Jones. My sister, Isabel Mary (always known as 'Molly' and I was always 'Peggie') was born in 1920 and the family was then complete. We both went to a Dame School in Abbey Square, Chester, though at different dates of course, which was run by the youngest spinster daughter of the late Canon of the Cathedral. I am sure it was pure 'Jane Austen' – the eldest daughter was the housekeeper, the next was a music teacher and Miss Hilda ran the little school, partly in the Georgian home in which they lived. We got to know every corner of the cathedral, which is something I shall never forget. Later, for the next four years, I went to the Queens' School, Chester which I also much enjoyed.

Violet and Maggie Price

"My father was a talented tenor singer and was much in demand for concerts, many of them in Wales, but also in much of the North of England. He had sung in several of the London city church choirs and had also helped to start the Chester Operatic Society and sang in all their productions. In 1927, therefore it was decided that the only way to pursue his career as a professional would be for him to move to the centre of things – to London. So we all moved there in 1927 and of course, sold Millside."

Harold William Townend Churchill Sabine and family of The Beeches 1914-c1966

Harold Sabine lived in The Beeches (No. 23) from 1914 until c.1966. He was chairman of the Park for over 20 years, mainly from mid-1930s to mid-1950s.

Born on 8 November 1884 in Brondesbury Park, NW London, he was educated at Dover

Harold c1960

College and then The Central Technical College, becoming an Associate Member of the The Institution of Civil Engineers in 1910. His early engineering career was involved with electric batteries (accumulators) and by 1909 he was working for The Tudor Accumulator Company, in charge of the inspection and maintenance of some of the largest batteries in the UK.

He and his wife Rose had four children. The girls attended the Queens School and are remembered mainly for their horse riding. Their horses were frequently seen on the pasture-land which is now the site of houses 50 to 54. Pamela was a dancer with the Ballet Rambert. Roger followed his father into engineering after obtaining a Mechanical Engineering degree at Imperial College. Brenda was in hotel management in Bermuda and the UK.

Harold established the UPPA committee much as it is today, carrying out the role of managing the upkeep of the roadway. Being a civil engineer he provided the basic foundations of why today the Park roads are in a reasonable state compared to many unadopted roads. He was clearly a formidable character and guardian of the Park Covenant. When he and Miss Longworth-Dames finally resigned, unable to accept the

All pictured in 1941 at Roger's wedding: top, Brenda and Pamela; middle, Harold and Rose; bottom, Roger's wife Eileen, Roger and Barbara

changing post-WW2 world, it was the passing of an era. He remains a key name on any Upton Park Roll of Honour.

He left the Park a few years after the death of his wife in 1962.

Arthur Walter Snead Furley and son R Furley of various properties - c1920-1954

Mr A W S Furley was an electrical engineer running his own business based at Long Lane, Upton (the shop later became McFarlane's). He owned three Park properties and was an active Park committee member, as was his son R Furley.

A W S Furley and his wife Daisy Rebecca are recorded in electoral rolls as residing at three different Park addresses over the years - in 1921 at Laburnum Bank (No. 13), in 1929 at Firdene (No. 66) and in 1939 at Wyeby (No. 64).

According to the Park accounts he acquired Oakley and Firdene (Nos. 66 and 68) in 1925 from Brookhirst & Co. At that time they still had extensive grounds – some 6472 sq yards – but about 2000 sq yds less than when held by Brook Hirst & Co: This property and ground had once belonged to William Shone, the son of one of the Park's founding fathers.

A W S Furley is shown in the Park accounts as paying the rate for both Oaklea and Firdene from 1925 until 1946, and also for Wyeby (number unknown – possibly built in his grounds) from 1935 until 1946. The 'Furley' of Oaklea until 1954 is his son, R Furley, who played an active committee role regarding the road maintenance.

In spite of owning two (for a while three) substantial properties in Upton Park in the pre-WW2 period, A W S Furley nevertheless apparently lived above the shop in Long Lane. He was considered a astute businessman and after he had built up a substantial business in the area, engineering the utility transfer from gas to electricity, he secured a significant job advising on the electrical infrastructure of a new post-WW2 town being built in Scotland. It is believed that Mrs Furley had health problems and may have initially remained in the Park after her husband moved to Scotland.

One of the provisions of Furley's business was recharging accumulators for radios and many local people used this service.

The Parker family of Nos 7, 11 & 15 Residents for 60 years

The Parker family of the Chester building firm J C Parker lived in the Park for around 60 years with members of the family residing in Nos. 7, 11 and 15 at various times.

James Cecil (known as 'Cec'), his wife Elsie and their family Wendy, Paddy, Robin and David moved into White Cottage (No. 7) in 1938.

Cecil had joined the family building firm in amusing circumstances recounted by his son Robin:

"Cec had a strong love for motorbikes and during his adventurous youth had a burning need for a magneto. The family lived at Eccleston and his father James carried out many regular contracts for the Westminster estate. Cecil hearing that an estate lawnmower had a magneto that fitted the bill managed to acquire it. The deed went unnoticed until a cricket pitch required a mowing. The culprit was found and with the honour of J C Parker in the balance the only solution was to make him possibly the last convict sent to Australia. The cheapest route was chosen – by trans-Siberian during the winter when tracks cross frozen lakes. Three years' hard saving in Australia and the convict returned, not too pleased with father but eventually invited into the family business which he accepted."

Cec remained a builder all his

Cec (above) and Elsie (right) with Robin and David, who attended Mrs Brocklebank's nursery school at Mayfield (No. 31) during 1939

working life and retained his love of motorcars and motorcycles. He had numerous motorcycles and was also into aspects of country life – fishing and shooting. Robin tells that his father was a big friend of Bill Wilson, Arthur French and Marshall (Tiny) Pearson as well as sharing a common interest in cars with Harold Sabine.

J C Parker built The Hawthorns (No. 62) and carried out various extensions and modifications on Upton Park houses including Nos. 7 and 11 and the original Hawthorns (No. 19). Other significant work in Chester included the rebuild of St. John's church tower.

Elsie's daughter Wendy joined the ATS towards the end of WW2 and served as a forces telephone operator in Belgium. She married in 1948 and left the area to return in 1970.

Cecil died in 1970 leaving the garden of No. 7 full of old cars. His sons then converted No. 7 into two flats and rented the top floor to Shell. Daughter Wendy and Elsie moved into Loft Cottage (No. 11) and later into one of the flats when Loft Cottage was sold. Wendy left the Park in 1989.

Wendy is pictured (below) outside White Cottage after its conversion to flats. Her early memories include:

- Hiding with Robin in the basement of No. 7 and of the air raids with the sirens going about once a week as the German bombers returned from raids over Liverpool.
- Snowdrops in Garden House, the home of Miss Longworth Dames.
- Her father's car, ELG 122, towing a sledge during snowy times taking the children around the Circle.

Wendy's daughter Sally stayed briefly with her mother and grandparents during the 1960s and recalls:

- Being bitten by the Trant's dog.

- Gibbons in the copper beech outside her bedroom window!
- Nettie Crosby's field opposite and her donkeys.

Robin also recalls
- Mr Godwin's horse and cart delivering the milk and Robin setting up a booby trap in the tree outside White Cottage, unsuccessfully attempting to soak Mr Godwin as he went past.
- The field now developed with houses 50-55, being used for horses by Sabine's daughters and by himself for playing cricket.

William David Capstick of Redlands (1953-1973)

Bill trained as a house builder and started the building and contracting company Capstick & Owen Ltd. in about 1928 in Liverpool, with his two elder brothers, Thomas and Joseph, and with William Owen. In the 1930s the company bought land in Upton-by-Chester and started to build in 1936, starting with the four shops at the Bache. By the outbreak of war in 1939 most of Upton Drive and two houses in the Croft had been built. An area of land was reserved at the north end of Upton Drive for a railway station for the Great Western Railway Company.

Bill at a wedding in the mid-1950s

In 1938 he married Kathleen Joan Lanham of Redland, Bristol and they had two sons. David was born in 1940 and Richard in 1945.

During the war the company was employed on bomb damage repair or demolition in Liverpool.

He built Redlands (No. 54) in Upton Park and the family moved in on the 5 November 1953. The house is very similar to the family house which he had built in 1938 in Liverpool and has not been changed significantly since then.

By 1953 the company was able to start to build again in Chester, and Upton Drive and Pine Gardens were completed, then the Croft and Orchard Close, together with two houses in Bache Drive. The land at the end of Upton Drive was no longer needed for a station so it was given to the 1st Upton Scout Group to build their new Scout Hut in 1957, however about half the land was acquired a few years later for the widening of Liverpool Road. The company had acquired a large piece of land in Hoole containing a derelict house which was demolished and about 50 houses were built on Hoole Road and Woodfield Grove by 1961. The company continued to build houses at Whitby, Lymm, Duddon and Great Sutton until the late sixties when it closed down and the two remaining partners retired. The company also owned the land of Nos. 50 and 52 but sold it to Peter Dentith who built these two houses in 1965.

Bill was a keen golfer and a member of Upton Golf Club, he was also stage manager of Upton Dramatic Society for many years and acted a not very convincing detective and furniture removal man with Bill Wilson.

Very soon after moving to Upton Park, Bill was on the UPPA committee – his knowledge of the building trade being very useful. He continued to serve on the committee through the 1960s. Bill and Joan left Redlands in October 1973 when the house was taken over by David and Barbara Capstick with their two children, Joanna and Anthony.

Thomas Gerald Scally of Fairfield (1954-1969)

The following account is from his eldest son Thomas Clive Harold Scally:

Thomas Scally was born in 1912 and sent out to Australia by his father at the age of 16. There he married Australian Suzanne Ellison Scally and started a family before returning to England in 1946. After working in Australia House in London and as a clerk for Cammel Laird in Birkenhead he decided on nursing and the move to Fairfield (No. 16) was the result of eventually working at Chester Deva Mental Hospital.

Tom stood as a local Labour candidate for Upton prior to the

Wilson Labour Government years. Those who voted for Thomas G Scally would have seen his motto as *'a sick world needs nursing not cursing'*.

He often appeared in the Chester Chronicle, sometimes under unusual headlines. One such incident was his plan for putting an ex-RAF rescue launch on the River Dee in Chester. He was very patriotic and named the family's English bulldog 'Victor'. Amongst his old car collection were three Jaguars, a Riley and a hooded Packard, although he often cycled to work at the Deva hospital.

Thomas Scally in the 1970s after his retirement to the Isle of Man

Before the move to Chester the family had five boys – Thomas Clive Harold, Maxwell Ellis, Lancelot Derek, Stafford William and Carl Gerald. Mrs Sue Scally always wanted a daughter and four more children were born in Upton Park – Rex Parker, Victoria Suzanne, Diana Elizabeth and Pamela Anabel. All the children attended the local Upton schools over the period. The front room of Fairfield became the 'best' room and was 'out of bounds' to all the children. It was used to impress invited visitors and show off the family trophies.

Tom retired in 1969 and the family moved to the Isle of Man where he had plans to start a golf course. The photograph shows him in the IoM with a boat in the background. He had a dream to cruise around the world but that never came off. He died in 1976 at the age of 64. Mrs Sue Scally, ten years his junior, returned to the Chester area and died in 1989.

Carl is now in Australia but the other children are still in the UK, some local in the Northwest. Clive and Max both worked at Browns of Chester, Clive then joining the RAF in 1965. Stafford was apprenticed to British Aerospace.

Bill Wilson of Hawthorns

Born in 1914 and educated at the Kings School in Chester, Bill was a Provost Sergeant in the TA and commissioned for WW2, reaching the rank of Captain when he was demobbed at the end of the war. He became a Fellow of the Royal Institute of Chartered Surveyors and worked as a valuation office for the Government. In later years he was a consultant with Beresford Adams in Chester.

Bill and Joan came to the Park in 1951/2 initially to live at Hawthorn Villa (No. 21). By 1954 Bill had joined the committee and along with others, joining post-WW2, provided the younger views on a committee that had been dominated for a good while by an older guard. Over many years, Bill was an active committee member raising many issues specifically regarding the tidy and well-behaved manner of the Park. Passionate about the Covenant, he put considerable energy into fighting any proposed breach and in leading campaigns where cases were referred to the Land Tribunal. He became Chairman in 1962 staying until 1967 when he stepped down on the grounds that the chair should be with someone more available. When time allowed, Bill returned as chairman serving for several more years before retiring to remain an active member of the Association, keeping members on their toes and expecting them to retain the whole Park to a high standard.

Bill in 1977

A keen rower from his youth, Bill became Captain of Grosvenor Rowing Club and as an active member of the Upton Dramatic Society helped Bill Capstick in building scenery, while never really seeing himself as an actor.

Andy Lees
of The Garth

Andy Lees has lived in the Park since 1950 after marrying Mrs. Loadman's daughter Mary from No. 6, so his first-hand knowledge of the Park goes back well over 50 years.

Andy was born in Aberdeen, Scotland and began an electrical apprenticeship there. He then joined the RAF for six years, during which time he was stationed at Hawarden near Chester and met his wife. Demob saw him getting into the teaching profession via the post-war emergency teaching scheme. He progressed through primary and secondary levels, and then into college lecturing. For 32 years he commuted by rail to Crewe where he was Senior Lecturer in Electrical and Electronic Engineering at Crewe Technical College. He retired in 1981 and is now regularly seen cycling through the Park.

He has audited the UPPA accounts since 1959, having worked with at least eight treasurers including Gilmore, Starkie, Morris, Fieldhouse, Mounsey, James and Hedley.

Chapter 8
Reminiscences
Margaret Millett (née Gowings) of Millside (No. 84) c1915-1927
Personal memories of the Park

"The room I slept in, at the front of the house, was opposite the place where the Johnsons (No. 28) kept their hens and I can remember most mornings waking up to the sound of contented clucking and scratching and the occasional crowing. Sometimes Mr Johnson would stop for a chat on his way home and he used to say, "When I get to about here, I would ring the bell 'ting-aling-ting-tay, ting-a-ling-ting-tay' and mother knows it's me and puts the kettle on!"

"I remember something rather special about Grace. I was said to be a delicate child and my parents decided to send me to the Convalescent Department of Rhyl Children's Hospital, but I found myself in the Surgical Department because Grace was in charge of the ward there and would look after me! It was an unusual experience for me and I enjoyed it.

"My first friend in the Park was Gwynneth Twist Jones, who lived in Ranmere (No. 18), almost opposite Millside. Her parents were Welsh (almost everyone in the area seemed to be named 'Jones' but this was the only family named 'Twist Jones') and we played together in each other's homes before we were old enough for school. We were both only children, so it was good for both of us.

"Just before I went to the Queen's School, when I was about ten, I got to know a completely new family – so new that we all watched their house being built, from the foundations up, and wondered what sort of family was coming there. The family was named Compston and the house they were having built was called 'Rhossili' (No. 4). They used to live in South Wales and so named the house after one of the places on Gower that they particularly loved. Charles Compston was an engineer and I think he used to design boilers, and he worked from home. His wife was Margaret, his son Geoffrey and his daughters Kathleen and Joan. Joan and I hit it off immediately and we have never lost touch throughout our lives. She is nearly a year older than I am and now lives in Wiltshire. We talk on the phone about once a month.

"Betty Carbutt who lived in The Limes (No. 25) was another good friend of ours and also went to the Queen's School.

"I got to know Margaret Trant and her family at Laburnum Cottage (No. 9). I think we started at the Queen's School at the same time. Her father was very often away at sea and her two brothers, Vincent and Roger, also seemed to be away from home. She also had a half-sister named 'Mary' who was the child of Captain Trant's first marriage. She was a very interesting young woman who drove all sorts of vehicles, which was rare for a woman at that time. Margaret, who became 'Meg' to me, used to call for me every morning on our way to school. We would both run like mad to catch the bus at the Mill. She was always punctual but I tended to be rather 'last-minute'.

"There was a family named 'Catchpole' and I believe they lived in the house called 'Ravensworth' (No. 5) but that was not its name at the time. They had two sons, named I believe, Donald and Alec, and a younger sister named Silvia, who was a friend for some time, but then the family seemed to disappear.

"Ted Dean's two elder sons, Geoffrey and Frank(?), seemed to call at our house fairly often, possibly on behalf of their father.

"Margaret Jones, our maid, was always known as 'Margie' (hard g) and Margie was always talking about 'Mary from Shones' who seemed to be a great buddy of hers.

"E Hylton-Stewart was from a well-known Chester family, I believe, and I can often remember hearing him mentioned. I think he was an owner rather than a resident.

"The name 'Haswell' listed as The Nook (No. 42), certainly rings a bell. I never knew him of course, but my best and oldest friend, still very much alive and living on the Wirral, was a Miss Haswell and I understood that her father's family had old Chester roots. Possibly the man at the Nook, was some connection.

"George Woodward, who was certainly 'tuppence short of a shilling', as the saying went, was the roadman in the Park. He did a few odd jobs for us and possibly came to the house because it was my father's job, as Treasurer of the Proprietors Association, to pay him.

"Two names of people not living in the Park, but who seemed to be involved with local events very much, were B C Roberts and A

Crompton. They both lived in a very grand houses in Upton Village and I can remember my mother talking of the garden parties that B C Roberts held for the entire community. When I was about ten or eleven I was taken to what was known as 'Elocution', and I have a small handbill advertising a concert in aid of the Upton WI at which I was performing and A Crompton was chairman.

"I have said that my father was a Collector of Rates and Taxes and, because of an operation he had at the London Hospital, he was not allowed to join the armed forces in the 1914 War, so he carried on doing his job. The Government of the time introduced quarterly payment of Income Tax for manual workers, so many of whom were engaged in making munitions in the area, and of course my father had to collect them. He had to travel over dark lonely roads on his motor-bike, all of which became more difficult, particularly in winter, so he managed to buy an 8 hp Rover car for £50. It would take me ages to describe the whole of the 'primitiveness' of this car, but I'll tell you that it had one single cylinder, oil lamps, plus one acetylene headlamp, two seats with a hood and a 'dicky-seat'. But it could go anywhere, including the Derbyshire Peaks, and took him safely over the Cheshire countryside and the Welsh Marches during the whole of the War, in very low gear. That was my first experience of a car and the next was different. At the Abbey Square school one of the pupils was the daughter of Mr A Crompton and on most days, I was taken home in the chauffeur-driven Rolls-Royce belonging to him. I always went to school by bus and, if the Rolls was not available, returned the same way.

"Train travel was enormously important of course, and I note that several of the residents of the Park had jobs relevant to trains. My aunt (Daisy) owned a bungalow in Prestatyn, North Wales, and my whole family always went there for our holidays. I believe I can still remember the names of all the stations between Chester and Prestatyn – each one getting nearer to the Promised Land! I can still visualise the rear end of the pony attached to the trap, the local version of a taxi, taking us to the bungalow."

Margaret's memories of Millside (No. 84)

"The house-name must have changed from 'Rose Cottage' to 'Millside' while in the ownership of my family but I'm not sure exactly when. It doesn't look very different externally from our time to the pres-

UPTON PARK, CHESTER

Violet and her daughter Margaret (Peggie) Gowings outside Rose Cottage.

ent time except for the modern double garage replacing the stable and coach-house (and now the conservatory). I do not recall any stories of it originally having been a pair of semi-detached cottages – the internal arrangements during our era did not suggest that.

"*There must always have been a front door because it would have been extremely difficult to gain access through the little back door, as the field was so close. Above the porch, with its partly stained glass inner door, was a space, always known by the Prince girls as 'the landing', and when my sister was born my father made it into a little bedroom for her.*

"*As a family, we used the dining room for most activities. This was partly because my father used the 'drawing room' a good deal for his singing practice, and in the winter particularly, it was somehow a much cosier room. There was an oak bookcase, made by my father, beside the fireplace and I had a little stool on which I sat to read everything (more or less) in the bookcase. This was undoubtedly my favourite occupation.*

I think I used to badger the grown-ups to read to me and made myself such a nuisance that they taught me to read as soon as possible. This room overlooked our front gate which was very convenient. The sitting room was very pleasant in the summer and I remember it had a lovely window-seat, with cupboards underneath, and there was a delightful view of the garden.

"*Just beside the staircase there was a narrow passage leading to a sort of lobby. This back lobby had three doors, the left-hand one was to the working kitchen, in middle one was the back door to the outside and the right hand one was to a dark little room, down three steps, known as the back kitchen. I believe all this back extension to the original house was built during my grandfather's time. The kitchen was a reasonable size and had a coal or coke fired kitchen-range, which was used for cooking and also to heat the water for use in the bathroom. All the cooking was done here, and much sitting and chatting over cups of tea. The back kitchen was so dark because the only window, which was over the sink, faced into the wash house. This was typical of the period, with a boiler which had to be filled with cold water and a fire lit under it. There was a small gas cooker in the back kitchen and beyond that was the larder, called the 'pantry' for some reason.*

"*The back door opened on to a passageway, partly walled in and roofed, but with part of the outside wall open. Turning right by the door, you entered the wash house, which had a door the other end which led into the garden and the clothes line. If you turned left as you came out of the back door into the passage, you came to the yard which contained a kennel for our dog, Bob, a boarded-off part for the coal, an earth closet (originally the only sanitation) and a ladder up to the loft.*

"*My grandfather had had a pony and trap, used basically I think for him to visit the various place where he had to collect taxes or rates, so there was a stable and coach house. The loft was for the pony's hay, and I found it tremendously interesting. Once I discovered in it three full sized bows with arrows and a target. I was told that archery was a very popular sport for 'young ladies' when the Prince girls were young.*

"*Now we return to the first floor of the house, up those very steep stairs. There were originally four bedrooms, two the same size as the living rooms down below, and two tiny ones squeezed in behind them. I had shared my Aunt Daisy's bedroom when I was very small but later I had the smallest room of all, with a window so high up that you couldn't see* out. When my sister was born, my father made a little bedroom for her in space above the porch. He did this by making a sort of wooden frame with opaque glass walls. There was already a good window above the front door. To get from this oldest part of the house to the extension, you went down two steps from the top of the stairs. On the right (over the back kitchen and wash house) was a room that my father used as an office. He was employed by two local Councils as well as the work he did as Secretary and Treasurer of Upton Park Proprietors Association, so he needed an office. I can well remember the enormous safe that was there and also one of those original telephones, which were black and you hung up the receiver on a sort of stand. The other room was a bathroom. It was over the kitchen, so the kitchen range provided the heat for the water, and the tank was surrounded by an airing cupboard. It was fairly large and also contained, beside the bath and wash basin, a chest of drawers, a small wardrobe and a medicine cupboard. Between these two rooms was a WC, a genuine water closet. I think that my parents had the bathroom and WC installed when they took over the house, because my mother and aunts told me about the baths they'd had in a tin bath in front of the kitchen fire when they were children.

"Gas was installed and most of our lights were gas, with gas mantles, though a few of the bedroom ones seemed to be just blue flames. Our bedside lights were just candles and often I read far into the night by candlelight. Of course there was no electricity and I think the Prince family must have managed with oil lamps. Heating was by coal fires and every bedroom had a small fireplace, though I never remember them being used.

"Most of the garden was in a sort of triangle to the right of the house. We had a 'Cabbage Rose' in front of the stable block – this was dark red and had an exquisite perfume. There was a Monkey-Puzzle tree almost opposite our front door and the front boundary hedge was very close to the house. There were several large fruit trees, many gooseberries, raspberries and currant bushes, and I particularly remember two Victoria plum trees on the small lawn right next to Westview. They fruited every other year and on each occasion the yield of plums was so great that small branches were broken off. One of these trees was still there when I visited the house a few years ago.

"To explain about the garden extension I have to digress outside the boundary of the Park. Upton Mill, a windmill, was used mainly to grind wheat, etc, for the making of bread. Edward (Ted) Dean lived in the house

REMINISCENCES

Molly Gowings in the garden of Millside c1923 - showing the tennis court.

there and was a very successful miller and baker. 'Dean's Wrapped Bread' was the first that anyone had heard of and of course it was sold in the shop next to the Mill, a very popular place. It was very much the era of the horse and they had several huge cart-horses to dray their huge wagons. They owned two fields behind our house, one of which came right up to our house boundary wall. One of my great delights, as a small child, was to wait by our back door in the evening until two of the horses came galloping towards a large farm gate through which, when the carter had opened it, they charged into the field and rolled on their backs, so glad to get out of the harness that they had worn all day. Then they would quietly graze and during many summer days when the horses were not there, I loved nothing better than to wander in that field sometimes trailing a huge bow and arrow. At the end of the First World War, my parents bought a piece of that field from Ted Dean, enough to make a tennis court, build a summer house, create a good vegetable garden and grow more flowers. At least we had a garden that we could get into from the back door, which was wonderfully convenient. Poplar trees were planted round the boundary, which I am sure would be there still, probably also the passage way that was left for the horses when the garden was extended."

Miss Grace Johnson of Nos. 3 & 28, c1900-c1920

The following extract is from a letter sent around 1980 to Mr and Mrs Wilson. It is from Miss Grace Johnson who lived for much of her childhood in Upton Park (No. 3 and then No. 28) before moving to South Africa in 1920:

"We first came to Upton Park when I was about nine. It was a freezing day and I slid along in front of my parents, my hands snug in a muff. The house was on the left, called Vron Deg (No. 3), opposite to the Martyns (No. 32). I hear it now has a new frontage but we were quite happy with it as it was. The rent, if I remember rightly, was £25 per annum. There were four bedrooms, two loos, one upstairs and one down in the garden.

"The garden was full of fruit trees of which I remember most, with a watering mouth, the Jargonelle pear and the Cox's Orange Pippin apple as well as tall beurre d'oeil pear trees and Victoria plums and many gooseberry bushes.

"In those days the only transport to Chester was the "Shanks' pony", which we reckoned took about 40 minutes, or a bus drawn by two horses which left Bache Hall on the hour, parked in the Market Square and left for the return journey in time for the next hour. Father always had his bicycle – I remember his early bike when we lived in Walpole Street was a penny farthing, on which we children were often given a ride with father holding the saddle.

"The Mill was in working order then, with sails revolving with a clanking noise. Dean's shop was a very useful asset, famed for its delicious bun-loafs. Once as I walked home from school, I heard squealing

Grace Johnson with Joan Wilson

and climbed on a wall to see what was happening in Dean's yard. To my horror they were killing a pig in the most barbarous way. I fled home in tears, shut myself in my room and howled for hours.

"When I was seventeen we bought a dear little house called Sycamore Cottage, on the opposite side of the road. We paid £1000 for it and then had it extended on both sides. Stairs were put up to the attic. The garden became a showpiece under my mother's skilled care and father's patient digging. They planted sweet briars on poles all along the front of the house and people passing used to exclaim at the sweet scent, especially in the damp weather. We called the house 'The Briars'.

"The church was 10 minutes away and there were only fields up to the crossroads – half way up on the left was a large granite stone, square and smooth, placed there for old Mrs Longueville to rest as she walked back from shopping at Deans (the Mill bakery). She owned a snuffly pug which was also probably glad of the respite. There was no zoo in those days and only a lovely park-like estate owned by Mr B C Roberts. The most usual form of transport then was a bicycle, unless one was lucky enough to run to a pony and trap or, to the envy of the Johnson children, a governess cart.

"These are some of my early memories of Upton, before I left in 1920 to take up a teaching post – Senior Latin – in Johannesburg.

"With warm greetings to all Park dwellers."

Footnote: The Wilsons of No. 62 met Grace in South Africa prior to 1981. At the time she was 91 years old. They understand that hers is the first name on the Honours Board of the former City and County School in 1902, now called the City High School.

Joan Robinson (née Compston) of Rhossili (No. 4) 1920-30s

Joan's parents had Rhossili (No. 4) built in 1923 and she lived there until she left for University and went on to teach in Birmingham. She made frequent visits home until her parents moved in 1934.

She has remained a close friend of Margaret Millett and recalls her adolescent days in Chester during the 1920s:

"We spent our free time as rather frivolous young people on the

river. Many of our friends had their own boats – the young ones had canoes – and the weather was going through a warm sunny period about then. There was a dance arranged by the Council in the Town Hall on Saturday nights in the winter where we met up. Most respectable."

Michael Brown of Westview (No. 80) in the 1950s

Michael Brown lived at Westview (No. 80) as a young boy in the 1950s. He revisited his old home in the late 1990s and reflected:

• Horsedrawn milkcart and sledge in winter. Browns had an old army sledge and Michael would help the Bache shop milkman deliver to the Park.

• Putting out fire ash to fill the potholes in the road.

• Cattle in the field (now the council playing field), the pond and a big deep hole in vicinity of where putting green is now. At least 20ft deep and good for winter sledging.

• The 'elite' Park ended at the covenanted boundary. It wasn't done to mix with those 'in the lane'.

• Garden House still had the large orchard. An old lady lived there – very strict and old-fashioned with a maid wearing a blue chequered skirt.

• The Mill orchard still existed.

Rhoderick Davies of Holly Bank (No. 17) 1950-60s

The Davies children, Howard, Rhoderick, John and Elizabeth, all spent the formative years of their childhood at Holly Bank (No. 17), and all have many happy recollections of it. Their memories of Holly Bank are recorded elsewhere under the entry for the house. Here, Rhoderick recounts some of his many recollections of life in the Park:

"For much of the 1950s, we would buy our fresh Country Maid bread from the Mill office, situated just inside the main entrance on the right. The aroma from the bakery used to greet us while waiting for the No. 13 bus to and from Chester.

"During our time in the Park very few new houses were built, the

REMINISCENCES

Ken Davies – the Park's legal advisor – enjoying a pint of cider from a keg stored in the garage.

Possibly playing in the field opposite home (now site of Nos. 50 & 52)

Back garden snaps

first being Redlands (No. 54), which was built opposite our next-door neighbour Mrs Dobie. Prior to Redlands being built we had a direct view from Holly Bank over the meadows into Chester (Dicksons Drive and the railway were a distant vision). The grass in the meadows was high enough to play hide and seek in and not to be found. The field opposite the site of Redlands and the neighbouring house was used by Mr Godwin (of Godwin Dairies at the Bache) to graze his horse Polly. All three of us boys were co-opted to help Mr Godwin – a weathered old man, in a milk stained brown homburg and a khaki overall reeking of stale milk – on his rounds. These took place with an open cart and horse drawn by Polly. The milk was ladled out of churns in the early days and later delivered in bottles, but still by horse and cart, both of which were stabled next to the old post office at the Bache (opposite the Egerton Arms car park). Mr Godwin's niece Miss Nixon was postmistress. We seem to remember being paid for our labours the sum of 1s 3d (the price of a ¼lb of Black Magic chocolates).

"The land to the west was undeveloped, a tangle of bush and neglected woodland, which formed the grounds we think of the old Upton House. I remember playing among the levelled foundations.

"Between the Mill and Millside (No. 84) was a dense copse with a sinister aspect, which we used to hurry past at night prior to the development of the new houses.

"'Bob a Job' week was another time when we boys used to exploit the generosity of Park residents to raise money for the Boy Scouts (1st Upton by Chester Troop).

"There are so many recollections that it was a privilege for all the Davies children growing up in Upton Park. We were able to play with complete safety, and the families that lived in the Park with or without children were some of the nicest people around."

Judith and Jonathan Pender of The Cedars (No. 70) in the 1960s

Judith recalls:
"The Cedars was our family home for many years even though we only lived there properly from 1962-1968. My brother Jonathan was pre-school age when we first arrived.

"After 1968 my father who, as a chemical engineer, had been Head Technologist at Stanlow, was posted abroad with Shell and spent the next 14 years travelling to Venezuela, the Sudan, and The Dominican Republic. My brother and I went to boarding school. However, we used to come home on leave every year and The Cedars always felt like home. To me it is synonymous with a very happy childhood.

"There were two sheds in the garden and a little Wendy house attached to one of them .

"It had 'Garden House' painted on the door and was my little domain. I had small wicker furniture brought back from postings in India and a little toy kitchen. There were curtains at the side and back window. The piece of garden beside it were considered its lawn and flower bed. I spent many happy hours in there. We had a brown standard poodle that we had rescued in India called Spicy.

"My father used to work in the garden every Sunday producing an array of vegetables for Sunday lunch which we then ate while listening to Gardeners' Question Time. Only years later did we learn that he hated gardening as a chore that had to be done.

"There was a gate into the field at the back and we would go through it to walk to school in fine weather. We would also go through to play in the field and Jonathan recalls being attacked by the horse and collecting rocket

The back garden

sticks on November 6th. On Sundays fathers and sons would fly remote control planes which we could always hear in our garden.

"Upton Park was a very safe place for children to play in. I used to roller skate right around the ring although I was asked not to skate past our neighbours

Side border to the field

house (Mrs Mason) as it used to upset her dog. Jonathan would cycle round and round pretending to be one of the Q Bike Kids. He also happily recalls other places to play such as the strictly 'out of bounds' ruin of the mill to explore and the orchard plot before the new houses were built. Getting there meant passing Mrs Lloyd's house and being given sweets.

"Jonathan remembers being told that the gate at the end of the avenue was only locked 'once in a blue moon' and ever after looking for when the moon was blue. Once he was rushed in Mummy's arms to the dentist's house in the Park after knocking a tooth out."

John Gilmour of Grange House

- The Christmas round of parties
- The nice gates put up by his father for their house – Grange House.
- The goat kept by next door – Roade Villa – to keep the grass down.
- Godwin the milkman, who delivered 365 days of the year. Everyone tried to get him drunk on Christmas Day so he often didn't come till mid afternoon. He was bent double when he retired but the physiotherapists straightened him and made a new man of him.

REMINISCENCES

and finally, some snapshots from the photograph album of Marjorie Adams of Belmont

Above: Marjorie in the garden
Right: David and John in the drive
Below: The Adams children and friends in the garden

Chapter 9
Military connections and wartime experiences

Currently no Upton Park residents are military or ex-military people who still use their ranks as titles. However in the past a fair number of former military officers have been residents. This is largely influenced by the fact that Chester has been a garrison town until recent times. Around WW2 it was the HQ of Western Command and had many Army and RAF bases. Upton Park's former neighbour Government House (formerly Dorrin Court), which was demolished in 1973, was purchased by Western Command in 1920 and used for a succession of G O C's. Stories suggest that Government House accommodated Haile Selassie during WW2 and was visited by Field Marshall Montgomery.

The following list records some of the ex-military people who have lived in the Park:

• Brigadier Stewart of Carden Bank (No. 15), a former UPPA Vice Chairman. He is believed to have served with REME and/or the Royal Ulster Rifles. He apparently got married while in Constantinople.

• Brigadier B L Rigby CBE, who lived in Holly Bank (No. 17) from the mid 1960s to mid 1970s. He served with the Cheshire Regiment and subsequently was the author of the regiment's history 'Ever Glorious' and other histories including one on the Malta Railway.

• Colonel Taylor of The Limes (No. 25), who was UPPA Chairman in 1962.

• A Colonel was reputedly billeted in (No. 7) with Parkers during WW2.

• Group Captain Evans of Belmont (No. 33).

• Wing Commander Ron Lloyd DFC AFC, of Garden House (No. 28). Ron trained at Cranwell and was a bomber pilot with 50 Squadron. He also served as CO of 110 Squadron in Ceylon.

• Lt Col Flavelle, Royal Army Dental Corp, of Millside (No. 84).

- Lt Col E A French of Roade Villa (No. 74) was with the Royal Army Dental Corp. He served in India during WW2 and also in Japan during the Korean War.
- Major J S Smith of Millside (No. 84).
- Major W T Whitley of Belmont (No. 33).
- Major Hyde of Holly Bank (No. 17) after WW2.
- Major (later Lt Col) Frederick Matthews (No.14).
- Major Brown of Westview (No. 80).
- Major Brunton of Norland House (No. 21), who was Park Secretary in 1965.
- Squadron Leader Davies of Holly Bank (No. 17) served in the RAF as an Intelligence Officer during WW2.
- Captain Arthur Garrod of Elm House (No. 64) was a Royal Engineer in Queen Victoria's Own Madras Sappers & Miners; also Jean Garrod, who was a Junior Commander in the ATS.
- Captain Wilson of Hawthornes (No. 21 and No. 62), served as UPPA Chairman. He trained at 170 (MG) OCTU, was commissioned in the Cheshire Regiment during WW2 and posted to 24 MGTU at the Dale.
- Lt. Tom Griffiths (No.104), who served during WW2 in the Fleet Air Arm having been in the Navy as a rating before the war. He flew Swordfish protecting the Atlantic crossings.
- Mr and Mrs Lees (No. 10) both served in the RAF during WW2.
- Jim Irvin is believed to have been in the RAF.
- Mary Trant (No.11) is believed to have been an officer during WW2.
- Harold Sumption (No. 4) had WW2 service in the RAF or Army.

Meanwhile on the Home Front:
- Cecil Parker was a motorcyclist in the Home Guard (see letter and photo overleaf) as was Ron Ross who later lived at Oaklea (No. 68) during the 1960s. Albert Warner of Heatherlea (No. 8) became the local chief of the ARP Warden service.

There is no record of the Park suffering any bomb damage although the following incident occurred at the Mill:

UPTON PARK, CHESTER

On 1 July 1941 a 2-seater Miles Master N7833 crashed into the outbuildings of The Mill killing the trainer and student. Both were French Canadians, Pilot Officer J M Milmine and Sgt H A Womack, both from 57 OTU at Harwarden.

There are no Proprietors Association records between February 1915 and October 1918. When they restart the issue of widening

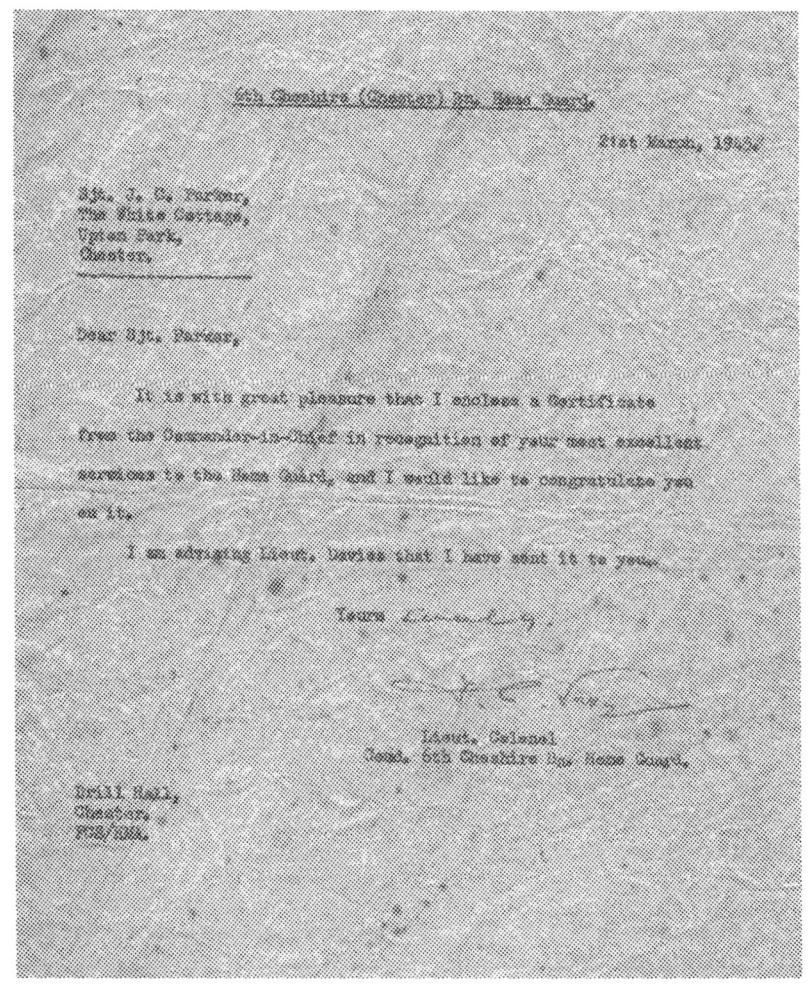

Letter of thanks to Cec Parker, 21 March 1945

MILITARY CONNECTIONS AND WARTIME EXPERIENCES

Cec with his sergeant's stripes is 6th from the left in this 1940 photograph

the mill entrance, as raised in 1915, is taken up again and seems to be quickly actioned. Also the road workman's wages were increased to five shillings, presumably reflecting the shortage of post-war labour.

There are no Proprietors Association records between the committee meeting of December 1940 and the AGM of July 1945. At the committee meeting Mr Furley brought to the notice of Proprietors that stirrup pumps could be bought from the Rural District Council at £1 each. The 1945 electoral roll records many Park residents as serving away on military service.

Post WW2 communal air raid shelters remained on the mill orchard plot opposite Nos. 8 and 10.

Chapter 10
Yarns

The Park has not been short of colourful characters over the years, leading to several stories. Have you heard the one about...

Miss Longworth Dames and her maid Eva

Miss Longworth Dames of Garden House (No. 28) had a reputation as being very aristocratic and very strict, though she was known to be a big horse racing gambler. She would walk around the Park as if she owned it, waving her stick and ordering residents to trim their hedges, tidy up, and so on.

She had a live-in maid known as Eva who was always dressed in black and white. A tale about Eva is that when she was ill, Helen from No. 76 was sent to the chemist to collect her prescription. When asked the name for whom she was collecting the medicine, she used the only surname she knew for Eva – 'Miss Brick'. The Gilmore boys at No. 76 had always referred to her as 'Eva Brick' .

Graham Hinde (No. 3) remembers her from when they first came to the Park in 1958: *"Miss Dames, who lived just across the road from us, was a lady of extremely imperious demeanour. It was an ordinary occurrence to receive notes informing me that the hedge needed cutting, or the house painting. I cannot recall that she ever demeaned herself sufficiently to actually speak to me."*

When the Rev. Wheldon Williams joined the parish, he had the temerity to pay a pastoral call on Miss Dames. She listened whilst he introduced himself, and said: 'Well you can bugger orf, I'm an atheist'.

Betty Lloyd recalls Wheldon Williams recounting this to her and adding that he was subsequently asked by Miss Dames' niece to bury her – and he was glad when the deed was over. Letters from bookies continued to arrive, well after the Lloyds moved in!

Betty Lloyd's dream of Garden House before even seeing it

Before Betty Lloyd moved into the Park she had had a recurring dream of being in a house of Victorian 'doll's house' style with Minton hall flooring and very specifically a black traditional telephone upstairs. Not being given to such psychic behaviour normally she was teased by the family, but they were later to be shown up...

Thinking of moving to a larger house, Betty saw an advert saying that Garden House was up for auction. With her husband Ron and her cousin she came around one day and finding the house all locked up, peered through the letterbox only to see the Minton floor.

Clearly an appointment to view inside was needed and at a time that their son Jeremy could attend. While Betty stood 'blood running cold' and looking at the hall and ground floor, Jeremy rushed upstairs only to run down again declaring that there was the black telephone in the upstairs room.

The Misses Trant who lived at No. 9

Graham Hinde recounts that the Misses Trant might accurately be described as gentlewomen of reduced circumstances. *"They were, in fact, as poor as church mice. Margaret was not in the same dimension as everyone else. Mary, however, had been a fairly high ranking officer in the A.T.S. and exercised a sort of* droit de seigneur *(or whatever the female equivalent is), over the Park. In those days most of us had solid fuel boilers. Miss Trant was out of fuel, as she hadn't paid her bill (one didn't pay tradesmen in her world). I felt sorry for her and foolishly invited her to take some fuel from my bunker to tide her over. She took me at my word, came with her wheelbarrow, and removed close to a ton of anthracite whilst I was at work. She never alluded to the incident again, even to say 'thanks'".*

Netta Crosby from No. 42

Graham Hinde recalls Netta who used to have the Meals on Wheels service. *"However, she believed that in order to qualify, one needed to be bedridden, so when they arrived she would dash upstairs*

and leap into bed, fully clothed and not infrequently straight from the garden in her wellies. All the children adored her. I think they recognised a kindred spirit.

"She used to sit by the window in the front bedroom, the light from her television bathing her in an eerie glow. They say that, when the moon is full, and Coronation Street is on, you can still see her sitting there..." (Ed: Graham's imagination is running riot!)

The chairman who paid his rates ... ... a little late

In the early 1950s with the AGM taking place in the rather grand setting of the garage at Belmont (No. 33), the Treasurer hastened to add that the Chairman had not yet paid last year's rate. At that the residing Chairman withdrew the money from his wallet and, throwing it on the table, then proceeded with the meeting.

Shift that piano!

Friends and neighbours of Ian Pillow (No. 13) recall the occasion when he was visited by family friend, the astronomer Patrick Moore. Patrick was giving a recital at the Town Hall and Ian's piano was required. Ian – a violinist with the Liverpool Philharmonic – needed some muscular help and so it was a case of "volunteers who like music ... shift this piano!"

Sell through the committee – to get the right type of person moving into the Park

One long-established resident recalls an early visit from a Park official. Yes – it was nice to be welcomed into your new home – but then came the statement: "If you come to sell, the right procedure is to let the committee know and they might know of someone suitable. Mr X who has just sold to you didn't do that, and we don't want the wrong sort moving in!"

"Have I passed the suitability test?"

... but putting it another way, as in the 1976 Newsletter:

"Selling your House?

"While Upton Park remains one of the most attractive residential areas in the City, homes in the Park will be eagerly sought after.

"It has been suggested that anyone with a house for sale should first notify fellow residents – who may wish to buy or know of a buyer – before approaching an estate agent. This action could result in a considerable saving of estate agent's fees."

The elephant paraded thro' the Park

John Gilmour of Grange House (No. 76) recalls the occasion in the early 1950s when their dog Raq was suddenly startled, with hairs bristling on his back. Passing down the road past their house was a Mahout leading his elephant. Apparently the elephant had come up by train and was on route to the zoo. The route through Upton Park was obviously seen as the best way...

... events even led to residents bursting into poetry ...

Poem by Peter Holmes after the beech felling

Peter Holmes of The Beeches felled the large beech tree in front of his house in the early 1980s. Not surprisingly, since this was one of the Park's finest trees, the action caused a great stir – prompting the following poem from Peter:

If you can make a mountain from a molehill
and use it thus to fly your little kite;

If you can spurn the view of council experts
because you claim that you are in the right;

If you can hint your case has legal substance
when all the time you know that is not true;

If you can write a load of childish rubbish
and get committee backing for it too;

Then you are round the twist my son
and what is more, you've nothing else to do.

(usual apologies to Mr. Rudyard Kipling)

UPTON PARK, CHESTER

Reference Section

Abstracts from the Upton Park Minute Book

1899-1909

- The first few meetings were held 'off-Park' then they settled at Upton Mill, the home of the Hon Secretary, Edward Dean Jnr.
- There was no appointment of an Association chairman but rather each of the early minutes seems to have been signed by a different name as meeting chairman.
- Typically there were only between five and eight attendees but when only three turned up, the meeting was abandoned.
- The rate was based on acreage, fixed annually based on need, typically about 4d per 20sq yds (totalling about £50) but 6d when flooding problems in one garden needed attention. Kerbing of the pathway was proposed and a committee was formed to prevent the flooding!
- There are references to Park lamps and the need to stop trees obstructing them. These were gas – the 1926 accounts still showed payment of a gas bill.
- Meetings were very much about the condition of the road – either decisions for more chippings or complaints about the state of the road and inadequate tree pruning.
- A worker William Dodds was employed at 3s 4d per week for road maintenance but was then dismissed following complaints that the cost was excessive for the amount of work that had been done.
- There was unanimous support for a meeting to consider the advisability of seeking road adoption by the Rural District Council. That meeting was then silenced on a point of order and another was convened. Only three people attended and the decision was taken that no business be transacted. The adoption issue does not appear to have been raised again in this era.
- The Avenue and other footpaths were put in order.
- An Advisory Committee of Management was formed to meet at least twice in a year – inaugural members were Dean, Robinson, Fitch, Mason and Shone.
- References to 'proprietors and tenants'. (At the time a lot of residents were tenants whereas UPPA was intended for the proprietors).
- Notice was given to householders that no rubbish was to be deposited on the Park estate.
- Mr Walls, the builder of Nos. 12, 14, 16 and 18, was instructed that he should not spread cinders on the roadway without the express permission of Mr Shone.

No record of 1909 meetings.
No record for 1910

1911-1919

- Decision for annual meeting in January to fix rate levied on estimate for the current year.

- Letter of complaint re need for tree pruning, hedge trimming and rubbish removal. The committee sent a letter to one resident stating their hedge to be kept under 5ft.
- Mr W Shone was appointed Treasurer and rate collector in succession to his late father.
- References to the Park gates – easing them so as to open/shut if required and decision to set them back 5 yards.

No record between October 1912 and February 1914.
- Rate typically 2.5d per 20sqyds throughout period.
- Again concern over hedges being kept under 5ft high due to danger with motor car proprietors residing in the Park.
- References to widening the Mill end entrance 'for the turning of vehicles' even acquiring of some land opposite the Mill for setting back the gate pillars.

No record between February 1915 and October 1918 (WW1)

- First post-war meeting approved expenditure of £24 to improve Park entrance (assumed to be Mill-end) with requests to District Council for gas lamp on path opposite entrance and to the Postmaster for removal of postbox and resiting in the wall (presumably where it still is today).
- Mr White was still retained as maintenance man with his wages increased to 5s (no period stated).
- In March 1919, thanks were expressed to Messrs Dean (the Mill) and Dickson Barnes & Dickson (the Nurseries?) for giving a portion of land to improve the Mill end entrance.

1920-1929

- Following an interview Mr L Gowings was appointed Secretary and Treasurer on the basis of being paid a commission of 10% of gross rates collected plus reasonable out-of-pocket expenses. Account with Lloyds in the name of 'Upton Park Proprietors', signatory L Gowings. (It is possible that L Gowings was not a resident but Edward Gowing was an attendee of meetings).
- References to Mr Sabine's garden fence 'along the Avenue'.
- Nuisance of Guy Dickson's cockerels crowing and letter asking him to abate the nuisance.
- Letter from Dicksons Ltd regarding the need to lop trees in the Avenue. This resulted in the lopping and even felling of trees, carried out by Dicksons at cost of 16s 6d per man day with total cost not exceeding £36.
- Resolved who should attend meetings – only the owner, or the husband

of an owner, of property on Upton Park Estate be allowed to attend and vote at Proprietors' meetings. Messrs Brook Hirst & Co were allowed to send a representative.

• Gerald Martyn, Solicitor, was instructed to investigate the deeds (held by Messrs Shone & Pritchard) to Upton Park with a view to ascertaining the legal position of the proprietors and if necessary to obtain counsel's opinion on the matter.

• The Post Office was requested to lay telephone cables underground rather than use poles.

• In 1929 the Park rate was stated as 1 shilling in the £.

• A special meeting was called in 1929 – the paid Secretary resigned and a new resolution was passed to pay the Secretary £5 p.a. rather than a percentage. All cheques were to be signed by the Chairman and Secretary

• In 1929 an Executive committee replaced the sub-committee to oversee road maintenance. It comprised the Chairman, Secretary and three members.

• In 1929 the idea was re-instated of employing a roadman as previously – now offering 1s per hour.

1930–1933

• Records of AGMs only and then with little (recorded) activity, only about 10 attending and a rate sustained at 1 shilling in the £ until 1933 when it was reduced to 9d. A Park roadman was still employed.

• Started the 1930s with a credit balance of £5 17s 1d and the AGM decided that in future a set of accounts should accompany the AGM notice.

• Running costs were met such that the balance mid-1931 was £6 5s 11d. With such funds in austere times the AGM agreed to investigate the purchase of a reasonably priced lockable shed to store Park property.

• Concern was expressed over the bad state of some hedges, particularly at the foot, and householders were reminded of their responsibility. The 1933 AGM proposed approaching Mr Grimes regarding the use of the Park roadman to trim Mr Grimes' hedge at Mr Grimes' expense.

• Overdue rates from several householders led to personal visits from the Chairman and communication with Mr Jeffs, c/o Brown & Co of Chester – presumably solicitors.

• At the 1932 AGM, Mr J Griffiths became Secretary and Hon Treasurer as well as his current role as Chairman. He accepted the joint posts conditional on being sole signatory and given a free hand to deal with the minor business of the Park.

1934–1937

• At the May 1934 AGM Harold Sabine proposed a road committee to discuss the road question thoroughly and decide upon the best method of treating the roads.

• At the May 1935 AGM this committee formally took on the management of the Park and agreed to meet periodically.

- J Griffiths resigned all three posts at the 1935 AGM and Harold Sabine as road committee Chairman took over as Park Chairman at the July 1936 AGM after a brief chairmanship by Mr Martyn.
- Committee membership was over subscribed – only three (Sabine, Williams & Warner) of the five balloted (but Furley who owned more than one house was later admitted) – to work with the Chairman (Martyn) and Secretary (Mr Brocklebank). Quorum set at two plus the Secretary. By September 1935 this committee resolved to meet monthly.
- Mr Pinnington, now the only Park rate defaulter, promised to pay future rates if arrears were ignored. The suggestion was rejected.
- A recommendation made by Mr T E Williams and heartily endorsed by the meeting was that during the fruit season, children should not be encouraged by gifts of windfalls, as this practice encouraged thieving.
- Complaints about certain people's hedges were still an issue. Lyndale was the culprit in 1935.
- The recently revised Urban District rateable values were adopted in 1935 as the basis for future Park rates. Although this resulted mainly in increases there was a mixed effect across the Park taking many of the 'grander' properties up (The Beeches from £36 to £45 and Mr Martyn's Rock Cottage from £38 to £56) while others went down a little (The Cedars down from £32 to £30)
- Another sign of the more business-like approach of this new committee was the fact that the need for insurance was raised when employing the roadman and other casual labour.

1938–1939

- Consideration of adoption by Chester CC of the Park roads was once again proposed but there is no record of any conclusions being reached with CCC.
- Several notes are recorded regarding arrears of the Park rate, including visits by Park officials to the guilty parties and in some cases to their tenants. It was agreed that future annual accounts would state arrears.
- Foden and Parker, both builders, joined the committee and assisted with road repair issues.
- There was an enquiry from Messrs Gair, Roberts & Co. regarding a purchaser wishing to build between Lindum and Dickson's gate.
- Mr B Roberts paid £1 towards the cost of laying the Avenue hedge.
- An honorarium of £5 was paid to the secretary for services to UPPA.

1940

- It was suggested that a stirrup pump be purchased for the use of the Park. No accounts record any purchase and there is no record as to whether this happened.
- Mr G S Martyn of No. 32 was requested by the AGM to interview Mr H Williams, Clerk of the Rural District Council, concerning conditions upon

ABSTRACTS FROM THE MINUTE BOOK

which Cheshire CC would take over maintenance of the Park roads.
- The AGM confirmed a letter of protest to the Chester Town Planning scheme (topic unknown).

1941 – July 1945. No meetings

1945
- The 1940 minutes were signed as correct, dated 13 July 1945.
- A circular was to be sent to those whose Park rates were in arrears.
- The committee agreed to spend up to £12 repairing pot holes.

1946
- At the Committee meeting held on 1 January 1946. Chester City Surveyor Mr Coleman presented a plan to build houses on Dickson's Nurseries. This suggested road(s) linking the new properties into the Park. It was agreed that the committee should establish what legal rights they had to close the Avenue road.

No further meetings were recorded.

1947
- Letters were tabled from London-based architects for a proposed new development, requesting UPPA's agreement to the closure of the Avenue. The committee agreed to let the issue remain on the table since any development was seen as some way off.
- There was unanimous committee agreement again for Mr G S Martyn (possibly with Council connections) to approach Cheshire CC regarding the conditions under which they would take over the Park roads. Cheshire CC representatives visited the Park to discuss the matters on 29 April 1947. They concluded that the cost of putting the roads in a fit state for the Council to then take over would be in the region of £12,000. The next committee meeting then agreed that this estimate ruled out the posssibility of dealing with the matter and that road repairs should be continued on the same basis as previous years.
- The Chairman interviewed Mr Roberts about removing the caravan from his field. Mr Roberts agreed to order the owner of the caravan to leave.
- At the May AGM, the rate was raised considerably to 1 shilling in the £, with the option of paying in two 6d stages. This was needed for urgent road repairs.
- Besides the housing development proposals for the Nurseries, already tabled, another planning proposal was in hand to the east side of the Avenue. This wished to incorporate the Avenue within its plan. Again this proposal was not taken up by UPPA since it was seen as several years ahead. (Clearly, post-war, extensive housing developments were under consideration and it was far from obvious at this time which ones would get the go-ahead).

1948
- Mr Martyn had now ascertained from CCC that plans for housing development along the east side of the Avenue had been shelved for the time

being.
- Upton Parish Council was approached to re-instate adequate street lighting.
- Cheshire CC requested permission to excavate in the Avenue for drainage and sewerage. This was agreed conditional on surface re-instatement.

1949

- There was a deterioration of the roads due to heavy vehicles and the transport of materials for building married quarters behind Government House. A letter to the War Dept requested an interview. Later in 1950, the accounts record the War Dept paying £175 for damage caused to the road.

1950

- An application was made to the War Dept regarding serious damage caused to the Park roads due to their use during the construction of the married quarters. Col Jones offered £125 without prejudice but the committee requested £300 to be considered. Accounts record £175 received.
- The War Dept was asked to increase its rate for the Army gateway from the current 5 shillings. The subsequent offer of £1 was accepted.
- It was agreed that the passage between No. 44 (recently built in 1947) and No. 48 be suitably blocked at the Park end.
- The Park rate was set at 1 shilling in the £ payable in two instalments. There are also references to a Special Road Fund (see 1952 AGM below).
- Chester RDC were chased regarding a decision on repairs to The Park's main drainage. By June they responded that sewer repairs were required and would be dealt with by them. Messrs Flather then began work on a new sewer under direction of the Chester RDC who recommended further work at UPPA expense on road surface water drainage into the sewers.
- Sabine and Furley were asked to to instruct Flathers on UPPA work, laying additional 4in pipe connecting surface drain water in the area of Millside (No. 84) into the main sewer and also provide a new drain water gully opposite the Garden House (No. 28).
- Road repairs were largely on hold pending the sewer work but it was decided to carry out some minor work and gather contractor estimates for the major work to be carried out after sewer repairs.
- Mr Furley was asked to pursue Cheshire CC via the Chester RDC with regard to them carrying out Park road repairs in association with repairs to their own adjacent roads.
- Chippings, bitumen and emulsion were ordered and Mr Parker was asked to technically assist with administration of the road repairs. Accounts show around £100 spent on road repairs (labour and materials).
- The lowest tender for repairs from Scientific Roads of Queen's Ferry was provisionally accepted but put on hold.

1951

- The main sewer was completed and the trench filled in but the proprietors were not satisfied that the road had been re-instated to its former condition. Mr Furley and Mr Parker subsequently met with eight members of the RDC and obtained an offer of an ex-gratia compensation payment of £72. The offer was held in abeyance pending a quotation from Scientific Roads for this work as well as for tar spraying the whole of the Park roads and for the Avenue. On receipt of the estimate, Mr K Davies was nominated to approach the Clerk of the Council to negotiate the best possible settlement.

1952

- The Hon Secretary was empowered to settle road maintenance accounts directly without recourse to the committee up to £10 at a time, £30 in a year. The cheques were still to be countersigned by one of the two members of the committee as authoriased by the 1950 AGM.
- Compensation payment from the Council was still under discussion, with the Council requesting submission of three estimates from contractors and then further meetings.
- 20 members attended the AGM which covered many issues.
- Relative newcomer Mr Oldham (No. 44) proposed that all ratepayers be entitled to attend meetings, vote and elect the committee. A decision was taken to give the Hon Secretary (Miss Longworth Dames) voting rights – which had been presumably not the case before, even though she was a proprietor. The new proposals were carried but the entitlement prior to this has not yet been identified in the research.
- Mr Davies of Holly Bank (No. 17) recorded as 'Legal adviser' and joining the committee proposed that a sub-committee be appointed and draft a set of rules to define a constitution for UPPA. This was carried.
- Proprietors who had contributed to the Special Road fund were named at the AGM.
- A proposal was agreed that a short statement of accounts should be prepared and circulated at the AGM.
- It was decided that the replacement of the wooden posts across the track leading to Dickson's nursery should be postponed but any steps needed should be taken to protect the rights of Park proprietors.
- Two committee meetings were held, in February and September.
- The Chester RDC offer to fund Scientific Roads' quotation of £94 10s for road re-instatement post the new sewer was accepted.
- The Scientific Roads' estimate of up to £232 13s for the repair of potholes, tarspraying and limestone chippings on the Park roads following the re-instatement work, was also accepted.
- A Constitution sub-committee was appointed (Mr K Davies, Harold Sabine and Mr Pearson). They were mandated to draw up a set of rules to define the constitution of UPPA and also to report on legal aspects of the path into Dickson's nursery.
- It was decided to close the pathway entrance to Dickson's nursery for one day per year commencing 1 January 1953, with Mr K Davies to arrange advertising in the local press if necessary. Any decision to close this entrance

permanently to be referred to a GM of UPPA. Present posts across the entranceway to stop vehicles were to be replaced or renewed as necessary.
- Work carried out by Scientific Roads was deemed satisfactory and it was agreed to settle the invoice in full. The 1952 accounts record £219 17s paid.

1953

- The AGM was held in the Village Hall on 16 March 1953 following an adjournment from January. Fourteen people attended.
- Mr Parker proposed restricting road maintenance expenditure in 1953 to £20 and to build up a reserve account. The rate was kept at 1 shilling in the £.
- Building plans for Mr Capstick's house (No. 54) were viewed and a letter agreed welcoming him to the Park, informing him of the Park rate and requesting that he make good any road damage.
- It was agreed that immediate attention should be given to the matter of closing or otherwise the pathway into Dickson's nurseries.
- The named sub-committee to consider rules for UPPA constitution was accepted, but the sub-committee had nothing to report as yet.

1954

- The AGM was held in the Village Hall on 29 March 1954. Sixteen attended. The balance sheet was now circulated to all members. A rate of 1 shilling in £ was retained.
- Tribute was paid to the late Mr Warner of Heatherlea, Vice Chairman.
- New members Capstick (No. 54), Wilson (No. 19) and Fletcher (No. 56) were welcomed. All three were then elected onto the committee with long-serving members retiring.
- A decision was made to discontinue any proposal for a set of Rules for UPPA and that things should remain as they were at present.
- Regarding the Dickson's nursery entrance, it was agreed to let present arrangements stand.
- The purchase of a wheelbarrow and other tools was considered. The Committee later decided to buy one wheelbarrow and top, one pair of shears, one brush and one rake – and a scythe at a later date.
- The parking of caravans in vicinity of the Park was discussed with the probabilty of a caravan coming to the field of Grafton Villa (site of house No. 36 now). It was agreed to send a letter to Miss Crosby of Grafton Villa expressing strong resentment of her proposed letting of a caravan and saying that if she went ahead representation would be made to Chester RDC.
- In committee, Mr Wilson raised concern about rubbish left by Council dustmen in the Park. This was substantiated by other committee members, and it was agreed that Brigadier Stewart (newly appointed Vice Chairman) should see Mr Morgan of Chester RDC personally. At the next committee meeting Brigadier Stewart reported back that improvements were evident since his meeting with Mr Morgan.
- Mr Capstick and Mr Parker both took up the issue of enquiring into price

ABSTRACTS FROM THE MINUTE BOOK

of road materials (gravel and tar barrels). Mr Wilson was asked to enquire of Cheshire CC about future road repairs.

- At the 2nd November committee meeting, Chairman Sabine revealed correspondence with Letts Bros appertaining to the new housing development on Dickson's nurseries and revealed his acceptance as Chairman of their invitation to a meeting. This was strongly opposed by Messrs Parker, Wilson and Capstick and the Chairman declined to take a vote on the issue.
- Mr Davies was instructed to write to Letts Bros stating that owing to the name given to the new estate, heavy traffic was coming through Upton Park and if they still continued to use this name they would be held responsible for the maintenance and repairs of the roads.
- Six weeks later at the committee meeting of 13th December, Sabine stated that the Davies letter had not been sent and that he, Sabine, had again been asked for a meeting. Opinion on the desirability of a meeting was again divided.
- There was discussion regarding the piece of land (plots 2-7) which Mr Parker claimed used to belong to Pritchard and Shone. Messrs Sabine, Wilson and Davies were asked to investigate the current ownership.
- Notice boards at both ends of the Park were to be repainted to state: *"UPTON PARK, Private Road, HEAVY Vehicles Prohibited..."* together with notices of the 1932 act.
- Complaints were received about speeding motor vehicles in the Park. It was agreed to send a letter to all residents in the Park, requesting more care and caution particularly in view of the fact that there were now nearly 40 children in the area.
- Chairman Harold Sabine, Vice Chairman Brigadier Stewart and Hon Secretary Miss Longworth Dames all resigned and the remaining two members, Capstick and Wilson, called for an EGM in January 1955. Brigadier Stewart suggested someone younger should take on his role.

1955

- After the resignation of Chairman Sabine, Vice Chairman Brigadier Stewart and Hon Secretary Miss Longworth Dames, Dr Sconce chaired the 1955 EGM. Stewart and Dames were absent but Sabine attended.
- Miss Dames agreed to continue as Treasurer.
- Sconce was appointed Chairman; Parker became Vice Chairman and French was Hon Secretary.
- The Committee consisted of Oldham, Wilson, Lloyd, Brown, Gilmore, Capstick andDavies.
- A decision was taken to close the entrance to Dickson's nursery, opposite No. 21, with a fence, notifying the appropriate authorities.
- The committee was to consider a letter to Letts Bros about use of Upton Park roads.
- The committee decided in May on some self-help for road repair. Bill Wilson was to acquire tools and materials. The July committee meeting aban-

doned the notion and considered using a contractor at a cost of £15.
- Repeat letters were sent to the Mill requesting that they repair their delapidated wall along the Park entrance.
- The committee was brought into a dispute between neighbours, Laverstock and Fairfield, regarding access and parking in the front garden. Regretting the non-co-operation of the neighbours, the committee resolved that it could do no more.

1956

- There was discussion around forming UPPA into a legally constituted body but the issue was shelved in view of anticipated difficulties.
- It was decided to delineate the boundary of the Avenue along its south side, now bordering onto the new Letts housing estate, and also adjacent to Dickson's gateway. Five-foot mesh fencing was proposed.
- Similarly the AGM considered ways of closing the Avenue entrance, but left the committee to make firm a proposal. The first committee thoughts were of a lockable tubular gate across the Avenue entrance, with the ratepayers having keys

Both above issues were still being discussed as the decade ended!

- There was continuing concern over Letts describing their estate as 'the Upton Park Estate' thereby causing general inconvenience and annoyance to UPPA members. Support was sought from Upton Parish Council.
- New Council rateable values resulted in the Park rate changing, as the Park rate related to the Council rate.
- Mr Walley was asked to see to the Park road potholes again as he had done in 1955.
- It was resolved to change Park notice boards from:
"*Heavy Vehicles Prohibited*" to "*No Thoroughfare*".
- At Brigadier Stewart's request, the Hon Secretary was instructed to write to Upton Parish Council requesting that they pursue the establishment of a local Upton library. By June 1957 a site had been agreed.
- Concern was raised over the Avenue trees which needed expert advice and insurance against consequential damage.
- Builder Mr D Jones of Upton Heath submitted plans to build a bungalow in grounds of Mona Villa (No. 58). The plans were viewed as being of a low standard as well as being contrary to the covenant.

1957

- The committee was retained except for the Hon Treasurer's role, with Mrs Gilmore taking over from Miss Longworth Dames.
- Bill Wilson was appointed accredited representative for UPPA at an inquiry into the change of use of the Mill to a shopfitting business. Approval was given but on the proviso of no overtime being worked – a condition likely to scupper the proposal.
- There was a good turnout for the AGM, with over 30 present.

ABSTRACTS FROM THE MINUTE BOOK

- Mr Walley was asked to continue with his road repairs when next working in the area.
- The Letts proposal to break the restrictive covenant for that part of their development plans that lay within the original covenanted area (plots 2-7) was considered. It was agreed that UPPA should instruct Messrs Walker Smith & Way to act on its behalf.
- The committee reviewed plans for No. 72 submitted by Dr Doran for his use. No objections were raised.
- The roadman suspended in view of his habit of sending an OAP to do his work.
- There was concern over the Scally children darting in front of cars passing their house.

1958

- The committee was retained with only the Auditor resigning but Brig Stewart proposed a lady householder be appointed. Mrs Evans was duly added to the committee.
- Mr Lees was elected as Auditor – a post he still held in 2001.
- The rate was increased by 50% but with the introduction of a 10% discount for payment within one month.
- After lengthy AGM discussion on funds and reserves, it was decided not to limit expenditure but leave it to the committee's discretion.

1959

- The committee was retained but there was a change of officials at the late 1959 AGM.
- With the Mill up for sale, concerns over the Mill entrance were raised but a 'wait and see' policy was adopted leading to the threatened resignation of Bill Wilson.
- By the next committee meeting, builder Mr Austin was proposing to erect flats and garages on land adjoining the road. "Feelings on the matter were strong..." Ken Davies, as Legal Adviser, proposed consistency in approach, not allowing Mr Austin "to ride roughshod over us". As a private road Mr Austin needed to establish by written consent from UPPA any ingress and egress with the private road. As the year progressed Mr Austin continued to use the Park road for his delivery lorries and committee hostility was raised.
- Miss Trant erected two garages without first informing the committee of her intent. A proposal to take legal advice on a possible breach of covenant was defeated, but clarification was sought that the use would be only for residents of Loft Cottage.
- Objections were made to Miss Nixon having established a gateway through the hedge boundary on the north side of the Avenue. Legal action was threatened if she did not cease and re-instate. Later that year she had satisfactorily re-instated the hedge.

- There was a proposal to convert Mayfield (No. 31) into flats. The committee objected on grounds of the restrictive covenant and the matter was amicably settled.
- The committee was still trying to appoint a new roadman.
- There was more heated discussion as the chairman, Dr Sconce, justified his new drive that would also be used to access a new house outside the covenanted area. A proposal by Messrs Wilson and Capstick that Sconce withdraw from the discussion was defeated and Mr Gilmore's proposal to proceed with the agenda was accepted.
- The 1959 AGM was held in late October. Lt Col Taylor was appointed Chairman with Major Flavelle as Vice-chairman. and Mr Myles as Hon Secretary. Otherwise the committee was largely retained.
- Mr Wilson reported that Mr Thelwell of Mona Villa would pay his Park rate arrears if the proposed Sconce development was dealt with in the same way as his earlier application even though the Sconce proposal was not to develop on covenanted ground.
- Other proprietors were named as in arrears.
- Chairman Sconce resigned on the grounds of constant committee argument.
- Committee expenditure on legal matters was restricted to £10 in any one year without AGM/EGM approval.
- Mr Austin was now intending to forward plans for his development of flats and was prepared to take part in a scheme for the upkeep and maintenance of the private road.
- It was reported that the roadman had now left, complaining that there were "too many bosses". No-one had been found to replace him.
- By the November committee meeting the Sconce development was accepted as a *fait accompli* and the new house owner was asked to contribute to the Park rate.
- Concern was raised over road subsidence outside Nos. 84 and 72 due to utility companies.
- Mr Capstick offered to repaint the Private Road signs.
- Mr Austin was now planning to acquire more land – buying from the War Dept land agent – and it was time for the committee to agree on what terms to offer him for road access. Two options were considered – a single lump sum of £500 with no further annual rate or £300 plus annual rates from the property owners. The opening bid was left to come from Mr Austin.

...and finally...

the committeee was still discussing the gate and fence, agreeing to proceed with Mr Capstick and the Secretary trying to get better prices.

1960

- Lt Col Taylor was in the chair for the AGM with Major Flavelle as vice-chairman. The chairman suggested the committee be reduced to seven by not replacing any retiring members.

ABSTRACTS FROM THE MINUTE BOOK

• Austin's proposal for flats fronting onto the Mill arm of the Park roadway was generally approved by the committee.

At the beginning of the 1960, Mr Austin was asked to pay UPPA £400 with a further deposit of £250 returnable with interest on the satisfactory reinstatement of the roadway and utility services. The flats would then be subject to the same Park rate as the rest of the Park – currently 1s 6d in the £. By the October AGM it was apparent that the issue had to be dropped since it could not be enforced, with Austin's solicitor requiring proof of ownership of the road.

• The Rural District Council was still being chased regarding the hedge planting along the Avenue entrance.

• Dr. Doran was to be politely reminded that proprietors were responsible for their own drains – problems with his were causing road subsidence. It was agreed that the dangerous gully outside Doran's house (No. 72) was however UPPA's responsibilty and should be repaired.

•· The committee finally acquired materials for the Avenue boundary fence so work could start "as soon as possible".

• Mr Wilson drew attention to the state of the front garden of Derrimore especially the old car left lying on its side. "This must especially be a great eyesore to neighbours," it was said. It was agreed that a very polite letter be sent to the occupier.

• Hedge cuttings were dumped along the Avenue by certain members of the Park.

• Proprietors were encouraged to keep an eye open for hooligans smashing the road lamp bulbs.

• and finally, at the AGM, Mr Wilson proposed a gate at Avenue end to be kept fastened in open position and only closed on special occasions. The proposal was passed unanimously.

1961

• Generally the same officials and committee.

• Austins the builders were now requiring further access into the Park with plans for four more flats. The committee decide to put the issue in hands of the Park solicitors.

• The bad state of the Park roads was causing concern and a decision was made to apply the usual tarred stones once the frosts were over.

• Furtive effort was needed to get the outstanding Park rates paid. Offenders were named at the AGM. Mr Kermode, who was new to the Park, pointed out that not all newcomers were aware of this rate.

• A working sub-committee was established to invest Park funds to produce a small income.

• There was concern over the Parish Council's failure to attend to the painting of the Park lamps. Brigadier Stewart encouraged Park residents to withhold their votes at the next Council election.

1962

- The first typewritten minutes, pasted into the Minute book.
- The committee agreed to settle an account of £52 10s with Potts & Balls (Solicitors) regarding the legal expenses incurred dealing with Austins the builders.
- A letter was received from Birch Cullimore & Co regarding property development on plot 15. The response was that there was no objection if it was within the covenant and a request to see the outline plans.
- Mr Wilson's plans for a new property (No. 62) were agreed. Mr Wilson agreeed to make good any disturbances to the road.
- Mrs Comyn requested to submit plans for her bungalow (No. 27) when Council outline planning permission granted.
- Upton Parish Council submitted plans to convert the existing street lights and to install seven new lights.
- Oldham & Starkie offered to make arrangements for road repairs. The offer was accepted.
- Two committee meetings were held, with no minutes being recorded in the book.
- Mr C W (Bill) Wilson took over as Chairman following the departure of Lt Col Taylor from the Park.
- Strong concern was expressed at the AGM by former chairman Dr Sconce that the committee had approved legal expenses of £10 plus £52 10s despite an AGM resolution limiting such expenditure to £10 p.a. without an AGM or EGM. Lt Col Taylor as chairman had personally carried out most of the negotiations with the Solicitors.
- The Hon Secretary and Hon Treasurer were both offered £5 honoraria at the AGM. Ken Starkie accepted the treasurer's role with Major Brunton later agreeing to be Secretary.
- The AGM agreed to spend up to £200 surfacing the pavement with tarmac and tar-spraying the roadway, in both cases between the Circle and the Mill.
- The AGM discussed the possible sale of the Avenue in view of its potential liability if building developments grew up on both sides of it.

1963

- The first year of Mr C W (Bill) Wilson as chairman.
- The AGM was attended by more than 20 people
- The AGM was told that correspondence from solicitors Potts & Ball relating to ownership legality of the 'Circle to Mill' road was available for inspection through the Hon Secretary.
- MANWEB provided £75 to assist in resurfacing the road and pathway from the Mill to Westview. The committee agreed to add £250 to this to undertake the work.
- A workman was sought to maintain the grass verges.

ABSTRACTS FROM THE MINUTE BOOK

- The committee agreed to submit to the Parish Council the following under the Public Health Act of 1936:
  - *under sec 58 (1b) That by reason of its delapidated condition the house occupied by Mr Scalley is seriously detrimental to the amenities of the neighbourhood.*
  - *under the approp section of the Act – that the Council enforce the liability of Letts Bros to ensure that the existing drainage from the Park is not impaired by their building project.*
- The AGM considered the desirability of renaming Upton Park to avoid confusion with adjacent building developments. It was agreed not to change the name but to seek Parish council help to press developers to change the name of their new estates.
- The AGM agreed to fit a lock to the gate, with residents holding keys at 2s 9d each and encouraged to occassionally lock the gate.
- On Miss Trant's suggestion it was agreed to ask the parish council to paint the lamp-posts dark green.
- 'Cul-de-Sac' signs were agreed upon as a further deterrent to traffic.

1964

- The officials and committee were retained
- The AGM was held in a private home (the Wilsons') but returned to the Village Hall the following year. The move to a summer AGM proved popular and was retained.
- The AGM lent its support to the residents of Mill Lane, including a donation of two guineas, in their legal action against Houlbrooks who were using the Mill as a factory with machinery.
- It was noted that the lamp-posts were still not painted and agreed that a reminder should be sent to the responsible authority.
- The AGM agreed to resurface the rest of the roadway (the Circle not Avenue) at a cost of £265. A later committee meeting requested quotes for pothole filling
- The proposed road work demanded a near doubling of the Park rate, which was agreed at the AGM despite several objections. The committee was later asked to write to these residents expressing the views of the committee. This expenditure led to a request to the bank for overdraft facilities up to £25.

1965

- The officials and committee were retained.
- The Circle resurfacing was carried out in April
- There was no reply yet from Austins regarding rate payment from the flats.
- The committee approved Starkie's plans for building Fosse Way.
- Park rate arrears continued despite the chasing-up of offenders. The subject was discussed at the AGM and the committee was asked to pursue and not write off the money owed. The new rate was reduced down to just above the rate of two years previously. The Avenue resurfacing was on hold due to

fund limits.
- Mr Morgan, Clerk of the Rural District Council, briefed the committee on Boundary Commission plans which would take Upton Park into the City. The UPPA committee agreed to write to the Commission voicing its objection.

1966

- Wilson wished to stand down as Chairman having done a reasonable term but he was persuaded to remain pending a willing candidate being found.
- Miss Martin joined the committee to provide a member from the Mill end.
- There was still concern about damage to the Circle road surface resulting from Austin's building work at the Mill end.
- Austin stated that his new house Park rates would be based on their council rateable values.
- There was the first AGM discussion of revising the Park rate from the long standing Council Rateable Value to a fairer system (NOTE – at this time the Council RV was based on the potential rentable income from a property. In view of the fact that tenants far preferred new property this meant that new property could often have an RV double that of a larger but old property). Owners of the new Park properties (Nos. 50 and 52) sought a fairer system but this was heavily defeated by the AGM. Mrs Sumption's proposal of equal shares was narrowly defeated – but was adopted years later.
- The rate increased by 20% due to road maintenance needs.
- The AGM discussed flats being charged half rates but no decision was made. It was left to the committee to approach flat occupiers to seek amicable arrangements. The next committee meeting agreed to charge flats at half rate in all cases where flats were seperately rated by the Council.
- Mr Pringle was now planning to build more new houses on the Mill site – these are assumed to be Nos. 98-104. Attempts were made by UPPA to gain some compensation payment from the developer but again these were stalled by the inability to prove title. By 1967 Mr Pringle did pay £100 into the Park fund for access to the privately funded road.
- Some difficulties were being experienced with the lock on the gate – it was agreed that the lock needed oiling.
- Damwood Properties obtained planning permission for three properties on the Orchard Plot (plot 15) and sold two plots to Woods & Whitehouse to build two properties. UPPA agreed to do all in its power to stop the breaking of the covenant to build a third property.
- Potholes were still causing concern and Mr Croghan was asked to fill these with bagged tarmac as well as clearing the leaves.
- The Mill wall privet hedge growth was giving problems so Mr Croghan was asked to trim these for UPPA. Other hedges belonging to proprietors were also of concern, being overdue for trmming back.
- Several deaths occurred in the Park and it was agreed that although

ABSTRACTS FROM THE MINUTE BOOK

funds were for the road it was right and proper to fund wreaths on behalf of UPPA.
- The Avenue was resurfaced by a contractor at a cost of £260 including some drain repair.
- Mr Wilson not wanting to restand as Chairman, the role was taken by Miss Mary Vincent Trant with Ron Lloyd as Vice-Chairman.
- The AGM agreed to tarspray the road after the reinstatement following completion of all the building work in the Park.

1967

- The Chairman plus two other members agreed to visit a ratepayer defaulter.
- One Avenue tree was blown down and another declared dangerous. The council had accepted responsibility for the proposed school side of the Avenue and decided to fell all the poplars – now concidered dangerous – and initiate a tree-planting scheme.
- It was agreed that when the new school was built it would be advisable to lock the gate more often.
- The first request was made to the council for mechanical road sweeping.
- The gate padlock again needed attention.
- The Avenue entrance signs were in need of repainting and consideration was given to changing the wording to 'no trespassing'. The matter was left on hold in view of proposed widening of Wealstone Lane.
- The Grants were thanked for their public spiritedness in planting trees on the grass triangle opposite their house. The AGM agreed to put up some fencing to stop car parking on it.
- Residents were again encouraged to attend to their frontages or use of contractors would increase the Park rate.
- There was more AGM discussion on the locked gate with suggestions of leaving it open during the start and end of day rush periods and the issue of discouraging people from giving extra keys to friends.
- Agreement was reached to paint the gate with luminous paint but this appears never to have been done. It was also agreed to latch the gate frequently without actually locking it.
- An estimate was requested from the local council for a road sign stating 'gated road' to be put up at the Mill entrance.
- Mrs Mitchell of Fern Bank was concerned about the safety of the beech trees outside The Beeches (No. 23). Expert advice responded with recommendation of lopping but this would be expensive. It was an issue to be resolved between the owner and Mrs Mitchell.
- The council proposed to relocate the Avenue gate further back as part of their Wealstone Lane widening programme.
- The Mill was now seen as a safety hazard to children playing.
- There was discussion around the case brought to the Council's rate appeal court by Messrs Rogers and Measures of Nos. 50 and 52. The appeal

centered on comparisons with similar properties in Church Lane.
- A printed circular was produced for newcomers to the Park informing them of UPPA, its implications and the names of officials.
- Land in front of the electrical substation was owned by Austins the builders but the committee agreed to tidy it and make a rockery.
- It was reported that the Mill gate post was getting into state of disrepair.

1968

- Mr Basil R Williams applied to Land Tribunal to have the covenant removed from the vacant building plot on plot 15. UPPA informed him that they would oppose this. The AGM agreed that if UPPA needed additional funds to fight this then an EGM would be called to raise the rate supplement.
- Willowdene (No. 12) was now in a bad state due to its absent owner and there was a suggestion of letter to the Public Health Dept. In 1969 owner returned and the issue was rectified.
- Two padlocks on the gate had now disappeared so consideration was given to an automatic locking device. This not being feasible a new lock was bought with new keys available at 2s 6d each. The Chairman encouraged car owners to lock them as often as possible.
- There was an AGM proposal to buy a Flymo for cutting the Avenue grass. It was defeated partly on grounds of lack of volunteers to drive it. However, a Flymo does then appear on the accounts for 1972
- There was a complaint of hotted-up Minis speeding through the Park. Mr Scalley accepted that this was probably one of his sons and he had already dealt with the matter.
- A proprietor complained of loose dogs causing a nuisance in the Park and requested owners keep them under control.

1969

- Mr Pye of No. 18 felt UPPA should oppose the proposed development of Wealstone Lane playing field. The committee saw no grounds for this.
- Planning permission was sought to plant Avenue trees to replace those felled.
- The gate lock was now out of action. The need to paint the signs was raised again.
- The road was in a bad state with potholes. Complaints were received about the footpath but the roadway was seen as a priority.
- Miss Trant stated that everyone should take their turn in helping run the affairs of UPPA and the committee should rotate. After two years she therefore resigned and Ron Lloyd took the chair. Two committee members were also replaced.
- The AGM agreed to a rate increase to allow some expensive work and to start building a reserve.
- Speeding through the Park was still a concern and residents were again encouraged to lock the gate.

ABSTRACTS FROM THE MINUTE BOOK

1970

- The council planted row of Cornish Elm trees along Avenue boundary with the school.
- Mrs Comyn only paid part of her rate on the basis of unauthorised traffic, dogs and the poor state of the road. It was agreed that everyone must be treated equally and so the balance was requested along with statement of the committee's plans to rectify the issues raised.
- Several residents complained about dogs, including fouling by accompanied dogs.
- It was said that the police were reluctant to impose a speed limit in the Park since no excessive speed could readily be achieved.
- The AGM attendance was 14 ladies and 12 gentlemen.
- Most Park arrears had now been paid.
- Ken Starkie was appointed Vice Chairman with a view to taking the chair after Ron Lloyd. The Hon Secretary changed after two years from Mrs Rigby to Mrs B J Jones. Accountant Morris took over as treasurer.
- Chester Water Company proposed a new water main through the Park.
- There was discussion at the AGM over what standard the road should be maintained at, with many members thinking that the higher standard encouraged more unauthorised through traffic.
- It was reported that road maintenance from the Mill to the orchard plot really needed £800 spent on it but financially this was not feasible yet. The rate was maintained.
- A suggestion to keep the Avenue entrance gate locked for periods of the day to deter through traffic was not widely supported and it was felt that any decision needed a larger Park vote.
- More road subsidence had occurred following building work – this time outside Nos. 50 and 52. It was the responsibility of the builder.
- The abolition of receipts for Park rate paid by cheque (presumably Schedule A tax now abolished) was agreed.
- It was noted that the gate lock was missing again
- Mr Twine sent a letter regarding general deterioration in appearance of the Park. Issues such as the Park entrance board, grass cutting, hedges etc, were all described as being in hand.

1971

- The Army was asked to complete reinstatement before finally leaving.
- The road maintenance reserve was now up to £700. There was a debate on the wisdom of building up a reserve when the rate was levied for maintenance and the maintenance needed now.
- Thanks were expressed to Mr Trelfa for tidying the Avenue verge, to Mr Twine for painting the Avenue lampost, and to Messrs Kermode and Giffin for trimming the Orchard plot hedge. The committee felt this self help was saving UPPA money and generally improving the Park appearance.

- New houses butting onto the Avenue requested some of the Avenue verge to increase their back gardens. The committee felt this could not be agreed to.
- The AGM was held with just over 20 ratepayers present. Wakefield took over as Chairman, continuing trend of a two-year period of office.
- Various concerns were expressed over the state of the path and road following the work carried out by the Waterworks.
- Decimalisation had recently taken place and so the rate was now 5p in the £, equivalent to the 1 shilling in the £ of recent years.
- The Treasurer proposed limiting the RV rate to £150 since the current system was hard on some highly-rated properties. The idea was defeated by 15 votes to 1 but it was agreed to inform residents of the issue for debate at the next AGM.
- The first AGM mention of the 'speed bumps saga'. There were also proposals for 'give way' road markings but it was agreed that a special meeting of proprietors was needed for any conclusions.
- There were proposals and discussion for signs for speed limits and 'dogs on a lead' but they were defeated by 14 votes to 2.
- Suggestions favouring more locking of the gate were also defeated.
- It was reported that some frontages were in a poor state.
- The start of lengthy committee consideration of traffic calming measures including road narrowing outside Mona Villa (No. 58).
- Committee debate continued over what state a private road should be in, since some wanted improvements while others thought the current situation was preferable.
- With the gate lock missing yet again there was a suggestion of trying to weld it to the chain
- Vandalism was perceived as increasing so approaches were made to the Parish Council.

1972

- Notice boards were in place at each end of the Park but a complaint was received from No. 2 that the Mill end sign embarrassed his view and should be resited.
- Fairly new resident and new chairman Jim Irvin drew attention to a map of the Park and its low housing density, stating that it was reasonable to expect the covenant to be tested over the next 10 years. (It was not until the late 1970s that Jim Irvin took a drive through his grounds to build a bungalow in landlocked ground behind).
- Mr Kermode of Westview (No. 80) informed the committee that he was "contemplating going to the Lands Tribunal for the discharge of the covenant" on his land. After lengthy discussion the committee agreed to recommend at the next AGM that this should be resisted.
- The AGM was held with 30 people in attendance.
- A method of levying the Park rate was modified to an RV ceiling of £150.

ABSTRACTS FROM THE MINUTE BOOK

This was seen as a small step towards a more equitable Park rate.

- The AGM had a lengthy debate on the merits of retaining the covenant. Mr Kermode saw it as ludicrous that he should be constrained on a low housing density when so close nearby there was high density with flats. The general feeling of the meeting was one of not setting a precedent but no action was needed as Mr Kermode was only at the contemplation stage.
- Some members were withholding their Park rate to make a point. This was seen as deplorable and unacceptable behaviour.
- There was the usual AGM discussion on another missing lock for the gate.
- AGM concerns were expressed over the building up of reserves while attention was needed to the road.
- Authority was given to the committee to spend up to the yearly Park income in any one year.
- The AGM agreed to buy the Flymo.
- The Park rate was increased by 40%.
- Thanks were expressed to Miss Cairns for clearing the weeds by the sub-station.
- The first concrete lamp-posts appeared unannounced, adding additional lighting along the Avenue. These were sodium rather than white tungsten. Concern was voiced over both issues and the precedent this set for the rest of the Park.
- Further concrete lamp-posts appeared around the Park without warning from the council. A special Park meeting was held to consider action after a Park questionnaire had resulted in 11 favouring the new lamp-posts with 16 against. Mr Starkie was asked to approach MANWEB.

1973

- There was a proposal for house to be built by Mr Bullock on plot 12 with no breaking of the covenant. The committee agreed that there was no need for approval of the full plans.
- The Chairman's report at the AGM noted that there was a trend towards younger families moving into the Park and this would lead to more noise – but it was not the function of UPPA to intervene in any differences of opinion between individuals.
- The gate lock was still off as attempts were made to secure it by welding it to a chain. However an AGM decision was taken to give a free key to all residents.
- The AGM decided that any resident seen speeding should be reported to the committee who would then write to them.
- The total RV of the Park was now £17,095 in 1973 from £6,707 in 1972. The Park rate was increased by 25%.
- Another planning application was received to build in the grounds of No. 58. As in the 1950s, this was opposed by UPPA and turned down by the Council.

1974

- Plans for the Mill development were discussed at length, with a sub-committee in negotiation with Beresford Adams. For many years now the UPPA committee had been involved in such issues and so it was right to do so for this proposed development.

And so the end of the Minute book and over to filed typed sheets – not to be published in line with the usual '30 year ruling'.

A typical indenture for initial plot(s) ownership with embedded covenant

The following is a transcript of the indenture when William Pitt acquired the full rights on plots 2 ,3, 4 and 30 from the initial tenants-in-common arrangement of Pitt, Shone and Wood. The **covenant** was defined at this point and was embedded **(highlighted in this transcript for ease of identification)** in the indenture. **NB** This precedes the 1870 release document which relaxed the building density clause.

The transcript follows:
This Indenture made in the second day of February in the year of our Lord one thousand eight hundred and fifty seven Between William Shone, Collector and Agent and Thomas Wood, Saw Stationer both of the City of Chester of the first part William Pitt of the same City Cashier of the second part and Evan Reece Evans of the said City Railway Clerk of the third part whereas by Indenture dated the fourth day of June One thousand eight hundred and fifty six and made between Richard Barker and Ann Brittain of the first part William Walker Brittain of the second part William Brittain and Thomas Brittain of the third part and the said William Pitt William Shone and Thomas Wood of the fourth part. All those three several Fields Closes or parcels of Land theretofore commonly called or known by the name of the Sower Fields situate lying and being in the Township of Upton in the County of Chester containing together by admeasurement Thirteen acres and a half or thereabouts statute measure numbered '1,2 and 3' and more particularly delineated or described in a plan in the margin of the now recited Indenture and thereon coloured Green Together with a right of road or way for the said William Pitt William Shone and Thomas Wood and their several and respective heirs and assigns with Horses Carts and Carriages to and from the said Fields Closes or parcels of Land through or over the Yard belonging to the Corn Mill and premises of William Carter called Upton Mill and which road or way was also delineated in the said plan and thereon coloured Brown with all other ways rights and appurtenances to the said Fields Closes or parcels of Land and hereditaments belonging were for the consideration therein mentioned conveyed and assured

unto and to the use of the said William Pitt William Shone and Thomas Wood as tenants in common and of their several and respective heirs and assigns for ever And Whereas the said William Shone and Thomas Wood have contracted with the said William Pitt for the sale to him of the inheritance in fee simple of their two individual third parts or shares of and in the plots of land and hereditaments herinafter described being parts of the said Land conveyed by the hereinbefore recited Indenture free from incumbrances at or for the price or sum of Three hundred and ninety pounds four shillings and it hath been agreed by and between the said parties to these presents that the same undivided parts or shares shall be conveyed to the said William Pitt his heirs and assigns in manner herinafter expressed Now this Indenture witnesseth that in pursuance of the said contract and for conveying the same into effect and in consideration of the sum of Three hundred and ninety pounds and four shilling to the said William Shone and Thomas Wood this day paid by the said William Pitt the receipt whereof they do hereby respectively acknowledge and from the same and every part thereof release and discharge the said William Pitt his heirs executors administrators and assigns for ever by these presents They the said William Pitt William Shone and Thomas Wood Do and each of them Doth by these presents grant convey and confirm unto the said Evan Reece Evans and his heirs All those several plots pieces or parcels of land situate in the Township of Upton in the County of Chester containing by admeasurement Seven thousand eight hundred and four square yards or thereabouts being part of the said Land and hereditaments conveyed by the described in the herein before recited Indenture of the fourth day of June One thousand eight hundred and fifty six and heretofore called or known by the name of the Sower Fields but which have been recently laid out in Building lots and form an Estate called 'Upton Park' and which several plots of Land intended to be hereby conveyed are as to the boundaries and situation thereof more particularly delineated and described in the Map or plan drawn on the back of these presents and numbered lots '2 3 4 and 30' and on the said Map coloured Green Together with all rights of road ways waters watercourses privileges advantages emoluments and appurtenances to the said several plots of land and hereditaments or any part thereof belonging or appertaining or with the same or any part thereof now or heretofore held used or enjoyed or reputed as part or member thereof or appurtenant thereto And all

TYPICAL INDENTURE

the Estate and Interest of the said William Pitt William Shone and Thomas Wood in the said premises and every part thereof To have and to hold the said several plots of land and all and singular other the premises hereby granted or expressed and intended so to be unto the said Evan Reece Evans his heirs and assigns To such uses for such Estates and in such manner as the said William Pitt shall by any Deed or Deeds with or without power of revocation and new appointment from time to time or at any time appoint and until and subject to any such appointment To the use of the said William Pitt his heirs and assigns for ever And the said William Pitt doth hereby for himself his heirs executors and administrators covenant promise and agree to and with the said William Shone and Thomas Wood and each of them there and each of their heirs and assigns in manner following (that is to say) that he the said William Pitt his heirs and assigns shall and will in conjunction with the said William Shone and Thomas Wood as owners of the said Estate called 'Upton Park' and which is delineated on the said Map or plan on the back of these presents **pay or proportionate part of the expense of constructing the several entrance roads shown on the said Map or plan and thereon coloured brown or such and so many of the said roads as shall be required and also all necessary fences gates drains sewers and cesspools and also shall and will pay and bear the expense of constructing one half of all the roads or streets opposite to the said Plots pieces or parcels of land hereby conveyed or intended so to be and marked on the said plan and thereon Coloured Yellow together with all fences drains and Cesspools necessary to the proper construction of the said Roads or Streets And also that he the said William Pitt his heirs and assigns shall and will from time to time and at all times hereafter in conjunction with the other owners of the said Estate pay a proportionate part of the expense of maintaining repairing and keeping in good order and repair the said roads drains sewers and Culverts and all necessary Public Gates and fences of and belonging to the said Estate The proportionate part of the expense to be borne by each owner as lastly before mentioned to be reckoned and computed according to the quantity of land in square yards purchased or held by him And also that he the said William Pitt his heirs and assigns shall not nor will at any time hereafter erect or build more than one Villa but which may be either single or double upon each of the said several plots of Land hereby conveyed and that such Villa if single shall not be of less annual**

value than Fifteen pounds and if double than Twenty four pounds And also that he the said William Pitt his heirs and assigns shall not nor will at any time hereafter erect build or set up any Cowhouse Stable pigsty or other offensive or unsightly Building or structure to the front of any of the said several plots of Land hereby conveyed nor use exercise or carry on any manufacture Trade or business which may in anywise be a nuisance or offensive to the neighbourhood Also each of them the said William Shone and Thomas Wood doth hereby for himself his heirs executors and administrators covenant with the said William Pitt his heirs and assigns that not withstanding any act or thing by them the said William Shone and Thomas Wood made done or executed or knowingly suffered they the said William Pitt William Shone and Thomas Wood now have good right and full power to grant the said hereditament and premises hereinbefore expressed to be granted To the uses and in manner aforesaid And that the same hereditaments and premises shall at all times hereafter remain and to be the uses hereinbefore declared and be quietly entered upon and held occupied and enjoyed and the rents and profits thereof received and taken by the said William Pitt his heirs appointees or assigns accordingly without any lawful interruption or disturbance by them the said William Shone and Thomas Wood or their heirs or any person lawfully or equitably claiming by from or in trust for them or any of them And that free and discharged or otherwise by them the said William Shone and Thomas Wood their heirs executors or administrators sufficiently indemnified from and against all Estates encumbrances claims and demands whatsoever either already or hereafter made occasioned or suffered by the said William Shone and Thomas Wood or either of them or heirs or any person lawfully or equitably claiming by from under or in trust for them or either of them And further that they the said William Shone and Thomas Wood and their heirs and every other person having or lawfully or equitably claiming any Estate right title interest properly claim and demand in to or out of the said hereditaments and premises hereinbefore expressed to be granted or any of them or any part thereof by from or under or in trust for them the said William Shone and Thomas Wood or their heirs shall and will from time to time and at all times hereafter upon the request and at the cost of the said William Pitt his heirs appointees or assigns do and execute every such lawful act thing and assurance for the further or more perfectly assuring the said hereditaments and premises and

TYPICAL INDENTURE

every part thereof to the uses hereinbefore declared and in manner aforesaid as by the said William Pitt his heirs appointees or assigns or his or their counsel shall be reasonably required In Witness whereof the said parties to these presents have hereunto set their hands and seals the day and year first above written

The Release of Covenant

The release of covenant (transcript below) states that William Shone held the document but signatories were entitled to request copies. The only certified copy known to the history compiler is dated 18 December 1874.

Besides Pitt, Shone and Wood, the third parties named on the release of covenant and new covenant are listed below. Whether this was all the stakeholders at the time is not known, although interestingly one significant name is missing – a name that is believed to have owned many plots at that time – namely Dickson, the surrounding nursery owner.

- William Jones of Upton (provision dealer)
- George Edward Roberts of Upton (clothier),
- John Bauchlin? Shone of Hoole (banker's clerk)
- Thomas Williams Pritchard of Chester (brewer)
- David Horsfield of Upton (railway guard)
- George Thomas Holland of Upton (railway clerk)

Of these:

- Roberts and Holland are known to have bought half plots, presumably sharing a double villa with Wood and Pitt
- Horsfield is known to have bought Pitt's first house (No. 84)
- Jones only has plot 29 which he then sells on to Roberts to build Spring Villa (No. 29)
- John Shone is related to William Shone, and possibly shares in some of his plot ownership
- Pritchard is often mentioned in various deeds but what he owned in 1870 is not clear

The 'Release of Covenant' document is fully titled as *'Release of Covenant as to the Houses to be erected on the Upton Park Estate and new covenant in lieu thereof'.*

The transcript follows:

This Indenture made the twelfth day of January One thousand eight hundred and seventy Between William Pitt of Upton in the county of Chester Cashier of the first part William Shone of the City of Chester Collector and Agent of the second part Thomas Wood of the same City Law Stationer of the third part William Jones of

RELEASE OF COVENANT

Upton aforesaid Provision Dealer of the fourth part George Edward Roberts of Upton aforesaid Clothier of the fifth part John Beaichlin Shone of the township of Hoole in the County of Chester Bankers Clerk of the sixth part Thomas Williams Pritchard of the said City of Chester Brewer of the seventh part David Horsfield of Upton aforesaid Railway Guard in the eight part and George Thomas Holland of Upton aforesaid Railway Clerk of the ninth part Whereas each of the several persons parties hereto is seized and possessed of a certain portion of the land and premises situate in the Township of Upton in the County of Chester laid out in Building lots and forming the Estate called the "Upton Park Estate" and which said Lots are numbered from 1 to 30 both inclusive and more particularly delineated in the Map or Plan drawn in the margin of these presents And whereas each of the said parties on his becoming so seized and possessed of his portion of the said Estate entered into a certain Covenant and Agreement that he his heirs and assigns should not nor would at any time thereafter erect or build more than one Villa but which might be either single or double upon any one Lot of land held by him or them and that such Villa if erected should be built in accordance with a Plan to be approved of by the said William Pitt William Shone and Thomas Wood or their Surveyor or Agent and should be in the position indicated on the said Map or Plan or as near thereto as might be unless the said William Pitt William Shone and Thomas Wood should by Writing under their hands or the hands of their Agent consent to any deviation from such position And that such Villa if single should be not be of less annual Value than Fifteen pounds and if double than Twenty four pounds And whereas the said several parties hereto deem it advisable and for the benefit of the said Estate that the Covenant should be released and a new Covenant entered into by them in lieu thereof enabling them to erect or build on any one of the said Lots of land of which they may be the owners either a Double Villa of not less annual value than Twenty four pounds or two single or separate Villas of not less annual Value than Fifteen pounds each and they have mutually agreed to release the said Covenant and enter into such new Covenant in 'lieu' thereof as hereinafter contained And whereas it has also been mutually agreed between the said parties that these presents shall be placed and remain in the Custody of the said William Shone on his entering into such Covenant for the production thereof as hereinafter contained Now this Indenture Witnesses that in pursuance of the

UPTON PARK, CHESTER

said Agreements each of them the said parties hereto Doth for himself his Appointees heirs executors and administrators remise release and for ever quit claim unto the other, and others of them his, and their Appointees heirs executors administrators and assigns and doth fully and absolutely exonerate and discharge him them and every of them of from and against All that the said Covenant and Agreement so entered into by him and them not to erect or build more than one Villa single or double upon any one Lot of the said land as aforesaid and all benefit and advantage to be had or taken of from or by means of the same And also of from and against all and all manner of Action and Actions Suit and Suits cause and causes of action and Suit and claims and demands whatsoever which the said Releasers or any or either of them their or any or either of their appointees heirs executors administrators or assigns can or may have claim or demand or if these present had not been made could or might have had claimed demanded or been entitled unto upon from or against the said Releases or any or either of them their or any or either of their Appointees heirs executors administrators or assigns or their or any or either of their lands tenements goods chattels or effects by reason or on account of the same or the breach or non-performance thereof or otherwise however in relation thereto so and in such manner as that they the said Releasers and each and every of them their and each and every of their appointees heirs executors administrators and assigns and all and every other person or persons claiming or to claim any estate right title or interest from through under or in trust for them or any or either of them shall not nor can nor may take have or derive any advantage or otherwise avail themselves or himself of the same in any manner howsoever And each and every of them the said Releasers doth hereby for himself his appointees heirs executors and administrators Covenant promise and agree with and to the said Releasees and each and every of them their and each and every of their Appointees heirs executors administrators and assigns that they the said several Releasers their and each and every of their Appointees heirs executors administrators and assigns and will from time to time and at all times upon every reasonable request and at the proper cost and expense of the said several Releasees their and each and every of their Appointees heirs executors administrators or assigns make do execute and perfect or cause and procure to be made done executed and perfected all and every such further and other lawful and reasonable acts deeds matters and

RELEASE OF COVENANT

things whatsoever for the further better more perfectly and absolutely remising releasing exonerating and discharging the said several Releases their and each and every of their appointees heirs and assigns of from and against the said Covenant and Agreement and also of from and against all claims and demands of them the said several releasors their and each and every of their Appointees heirs executors administrators or assigns for or in respect or otherwise howsoever in relation thereto as by them the said Releasees their and each and every of their Appointees heirs executors administrators or assigns or their or his Council in the Law shall be reasonably advised and required And each of them the said several parties hereto doth hereby for himself his Appointees heirs executors and administrators Covenant and agree with and to each and every of the others of them and his and their several and respective appointees heirs and assigns that he the said Covenanting party his Appointees heirs and assigns shall not nor will at any time hereafter erect or build more than one double Villa or two single or separate Villas upon any one of the said Lots of land belonging to him or them and that such Villa or Villas if erected shall be built in accordance with a plan to be approved of by the said William Pitt William Shone and Thomas Wood or their Surveyor or Agent and shall be in the position indicated in the said Map or Plan or as near thereto as may be unless the said William Pitt William Shone and Thomas Wood shall by writing under their hands or under the hand of their Agent consent to any deviation from such position And that such Villas if single shall not be of less annual Value than Fifteen pounds or if double than Twenty four pounds And the said William Shone for himself his Appointees heirs executors administrators and assigns – hereby Covenants with each of the said several other parties hereto his Appointees heirs and assigns that he the said William Shone his appointees heirs or assigns (unless prevented by inevitable accident) will at all times hereafter at the request in writing and at the costs of any or either of the said parties their or his Appointees heirs or assigns produce or cause to be produced in England or Wales and not elsewhere unto them or any or either of them their or his Appointees heirs or assigns or to their or his Attorney Solicitor Counsel or Agent or in the course of any Judicial proceeding or otherwise as occasions shall require this present Deed of Release and Covenant And at the like request and costs furnish the said several parties or any or either of them their or his Appointees heirs or assigns with

Copies or extracts (attested if required) of the same Deed and permit any person or persons appointed by them or him to examine the same Copies or extracts with the Original In witness whereof the said parties to these presents have hereunto set their hands and seals the day and year first above written Signed by all those named above in the presence of Clerk with Mr G Tibbits? Solicitor Chester

The writing contained in this and the two preceding sides of Paper is a true copy of the Original Indenture of Release of Covenant of which it purports to be a copy the same having been carefully compared and examined therewith this eighteenth day of December One thousand eight hundred and seventy four by us: And we hereby certify that the said Deed was duly stamped with a One pound fifteen shillings Stamp. J Bridgeman(?) Solicitor Chester.

Census Records

When all the 19th century censuses were taken, Upton Park residences had not been assigned house numbers although several of them had house names. It appears that most of the pairs of semis went under single house names, such as "Grafton Villas". This is supported by the 1872 OS survey. Many of the house names used in the 1870s and '80s are no longer used but research has largely enabled the buildings to be traced back through their changing names.

Census information is recorded as consecutive houses (i.e. neighbours) and the Upton Park list flows around the park anti-clockwise from the north.

Unfortunately, no census data can be guaranteed as correct. People's ages where they are shown refer to their age in the census year.

1861 census

The 1861 census records only four households – all unnamed houses. Two of these are founding fathers of the Park and are still in the 1871 census with no house names. The other two households do not feature in the 1871 census.

Unnamed but deduced to be No. 84:
Founding father **William Pitt** (35yrs) formerly a farmer from Salop now recorded as a cashier and clerk & wife Margaret (32yrs); daughters Alice Jane (6yrs), Edith Margaret (1yr), and Clara (4yrs), who is not re-recorded in 1871; mother-in-law Margaret Evans (74yrs); servant Sarah Lloyd (22yrs) who may be related to farmer Lloyd.

Unnamed but deduced to be No. 13:
Founding father **Thomas Wood** (37yrs) Registrar of births & deaths, also law stationer & wife Sarah; son Thomas (18yrs) railway clerk; stepmother Elizabeth Wood (55yrs); niece (7yrs).

Unnamed dwelling:
Richard Wyatt (34yrs) managing clerk of telegraph office & wife (28yrs); son Richard (2yrs); lodger Augustus Bonyard? millener; servant (27yrs).

Unnamed dwelling:
Thomas Meredith (47yrs) nurseryman & wife Mary (46yrs); children Hannah (21yrs), Elizabeth (18yrs), John (16yrs) confectioner; Thomas (13yrs).

1871 / 1872 – the census and the OS survey

The spring 1871 census aligns well with the 1872 survey of the first edition OS map. The latter shows two single properties outside the circle

(**Westview** and unnamed **Millside**); five double villas on the inner circle (**Chatham; Hawthorne; Laburnum; Portland/Lily** and unnamed **Hollies/Derrymore**) and two double villas (**Grafton** and unnamed **Fernbank/Lowther**) on the outer circle.

The 1871 census records eight households against the 16 dwellings on the 1872 survey. It is reasonable to assume some of these other eight were uninhabited since the 1871 census for Newton/Upton/ Moston/Bache records 11 uninhabited dwellings and one still being built, while Upton Park was believed to be the only major development in the area. The following record is derived from the 1871 census but with some assumptions in aligning to current Park houses.

Unnamed (No. 84) known to be Millside from old indentures:

David Horsfield (33yrs) railway goods guard & wife Mary (32yrs); nephew David Horsfield Dodd; lodger the curate Miles Hodgson Towers.

Unnamed (No. 5?):

Spinster Miss Hilton living on an annuity; sister widow Margaret Dean (70yrs) possibly Edward Dean's mother; nephew Robert Hilton (18yrs) banker's apprentice.

Unnamed (No. 7) known to be Lilley House from the 1881 census record:

Spinster Anne Evans (34?yrs) artist in watercolours; her widowed mother Laura Evans (72yrs), both of moneyed means; general servant Elizabeth Willow (22yrs).

Westview (No. 80):

William Beswick (48yrs) schoolmaster & wife Mary (46yrs); children all born in Chester, Ann (17yrs pupil teacher), Harry (15yrs), Frank (13yrs), Jessie Maude (11yrs), Hugh (9yrs), Ernest (7yrs), Kate Edith (5yrs), Leonard (3yrs). No servants are recorded.

Unnamed (No. 13) in 1881 census Sarah recorded in Ivy Cottage:

Founding father Thomas Wood (46yrs) Registrar of births & deaths, also accountant and law stationer & wife Sarah (56yrs); niece Martha A Pover (16yrs, whose age doesn't tally with the 1881 census); niece Helen L Pover (4yrs).

Unnamed but other records suggest No. 9:

This household later moved into Spring Villa (29) which was built after the 1872 OS survey.

George E Roberts (32yrs) clothier (tailor & draper) & wife Mary (30yrs); children, Eliza (6yrs), Charles E (4yrs), George (2yrs); brother-in-law Henry Farnworthy (18yrs) bookseller's apprentice; and domestic servant Sarah Hughes (35yrs).

CENSUS RECORDS

Unnamed dwelling (deduced to be No. 19 but possibly Nos. 23/25):
Founding father William Pitt (45yrs) and recorded as a railway agent now a widower; daughters Alice Jane (16yrs), Edith Margaret (11yrs), Jessie Hannah (9yrs), Caroline (7yrs); sister Mary Ann Pitt (27yrs) housekeeper.

Unnamed but other records show Hawthorne Villa (No. 21):
George Thomas Holland (44yrs) railway clerk & accountant – later became a coal merchant (1881) & wife Mary Anne (47yrs); children Maria (17yrs), Elizabeth (16yrs), Margaret (13yrs), Frederick (6yrs).

Upton Mill:
William Carter (60yrs) miller baker and farmer & wife Elizabeth (58yrs); son-in-law Edward Dean (31yrs) miller; daughter Elizabeth (31yrs); grandson Edward (5yrs); Elizabeth Carter (68yrs) living on an annuity. Workers/servants not noted.

Neighbouring Upton Park
Upton Villa (now demolished):
Widow Selina Dickson (76yrs); son Thomas (34yrs); also the Freeman family.

From the 1881 census

There were 17 occupied houses and four unoccupied. The census also recorded place of birth. Of the 17 people recorded as 'heads of households' half these were local (within 30-mile radius) while the others were from all around the UK including Hampshire, Ireland and Northampton.

Unnamed house known to be Rose Cottage, later Millside (No. 84):
James Prince (42yrs) rate collector (municipal) & wife Elizabeth H (36yrs); daughter Dora Louise (1yr).

Westview (No. 80):
William Smith (59yrs) & wife Margaret (45yrs) with daughter Cecelia (8yrs). Also Miles H Towers (42yrs) bachelor, resident parson of Upton; his niece Mary Towers (17yrs); Elizabeth Bithell (25yrs) spinster general servant.

Vron Deg (No. 3 – but possibly 1 & 3):
Sarah Richardson (35yrs) wife of a missionary; her children, Emily (7yrs), John (6yrs), Henry (3yrs) all born in Madagascar, William (1yr) born in Chester. Her two servant girls, nursemaid Louisa Venables (14yrs); general servant Mary Langton (15yrs).

Portland Villa (No. 5):
Thomas Bate (58yrs) retired from cheese factory & wife Alice P (62yrs); his daughter Margaret R Bate (21yrs); general servant girl Tibitha A Markland (15yrs).

UPTON PARK, CHESTER

Grafton Villa (No. 40):
Widower Joseph Denson (67yrs) retired chemist & druggist; two servants, housekeeper Eliza Reese (51yrs) and Mary Fleet (41yrs).

Grafton Villa (No. 42 or back of 40):
Evan R Evans (49yrs) unemployed commercial clerk & wife Elizabeth (43yrs) occupied letting apartments; boarder Thomas Morgan (22yrs) packer in the nursery; lodger Allen Jasper (19yrs) apprentice to nurseryman.

Grafton Villa (nos: 42 or back of 40):
John Hamilton (27yrs) market gardener & wife Alice (26yrs).

Lilley House (No. 7):
Spinster Ann Evans (50yrs) artist/painter; general servant Annora Flynn (16yrs).

Laburnum Villa (No. 9):
William Wannop (42yrs) railway cashier & wife Emily (38yrs); daughter Ann E (7yrs); general servant Ann Blake (14yrs).

Also – Laburnum Villa (No. 9):
Samuel J Carr (32yrs) railway manager's assistant & wife Sarah Ann (32yrs); children, Joseph E (9yrs), Percy J (7yrs), Annie Louisa (5yrs); brother-in-law Joseph C Ellesby (30yrs) nurseryman's clerk; **Founding father William Pitt's** daughter Jessie H Pitt (19yrs) companion (domestic servant).

Ivy Cottage (No. 13):
Founding father Thomas Wood's widow Sarah Wood (67yrs) living on rents & dividends; niece Martha A Pover (38yrs) domestic servant; niece Helen L Pover (4yrs); guest (visitor) Alexander Stirton (44yrs) market gardener.

Hawthorne Villa (No. 19) name later became **Parkstone**:
Widow Fanny Wannop (64yrs) living on an annuity and possibly mother of William in No. 9; guest (visitor) Fanny Wilson (16yrs) a farmer's daughter; general servant Fanny Bennett (15yrs).

Hawthorne Villa (No. 21):
George T Holland (55yrs) coal merchant & agent & wife Mary A Holland; son Frederick T Holland (16yrs) commercial clerk

No house name (possibly the railway cottage No. 56 or 58):
Edward T Pugh (34yrs) widower chief railway booking clerk; children Edward W (7yrs); Edith A (4yrs); housekeeper domestic Emma Morris (33yrs).

No house name (possibly the other railway cottage No. 56 or 58):
Charles Wess (27yrs) commercial clerk & wife Margaret C (27yrs); children born in the Park – Charles H (2yrs) and Frederick W (4mnths);

boarder Austin McKean (60yrs), forester.

Chatham Villa (No. 25):
The census recorded as unoccupied – believed to be owned by founding father William Pitt.

Sunneyside (No. 23):
Widow Jane Harris (72yrs) living on an annuity; her two nieces Rose McK Aspinall (26yrs) and Louise T. Aspinall (24yrs) both British citizens but born in Shanghai; general servant Jane Price (19yrs).

No house name (Park records indicate Oaklea No. 68):
William Shone (33yrs) estate agent and accountant & wife Grace (30yrs); son William (1yr); two domestic servants, cook Mary Dodd (30yrs); housemaid Mary Dodd (16yrs).

Spring Villa (29):
George E Roberts (42yrs) tailor & draper & wife Mary (40yrs); eight children, Eliza (16yrs) housekeeper, Charles E (14yrs) shop assistant & errand boy, George (11yrs), Sarah A (9yrs), Mary (7yrs), Marsha (5yrs), Theodora (3yrs), Joseph T (10m).

No house name (likely to be No. 33) – a new house since 1871:
Widow Diana Burnett (75yrs); three spinster daughters, Diana (41yrs), Margaret E (39yrs), Elizabeth (37yrs) all unemployed; houseguest Adelaide Retemeyor (37yrs) a daily governess; general servant domestic Caroline Pitt (17yrs).

Mayfield Villa (No. 31) a new house since 1871:
Spinster Mary Clark (60yrs) living on investments; brother James Clark (58yrs) living on an annuity; general servant Esther Ballis (60yrs).

Also a further three unoccupied premises.

Upton Mill:
Edward Dean (42yrs) farmer baker and miller & wife Elizabeth (41yrs); five children, Edward (15yrs), Joseph (11yrs), Bessie (9yrs), Helen (3yrs), Charles (1yr); widowed mother-in-law Elizabeth Carter (68yrs) living on an annuity; nephew William Carter (13yrs); five servants, general servant Lucy Roberts (31yrs), John Dain (23) and Edward Dodd (21) both indoor farm servants, Henry Cain (44yrs) and Frederick Quin (20yrs) both bakers.

Neighbouring Upton Park:
Widow Selina Dickson lived in **Upton Villa** (now demolished) with her daughter, granddaughters and three servants.

From the 1891 census

This census falls between the two OS surveys of 1872 and 1898. In the large turnover of residents since 1881 only the following remain: Smiths of No. 80; Roberts of No. 29; Clarks of No. 31; Bates of No. 5; Shone of No. 68; and the Deans in the Mill.

Twenty-four households are named (plus the further Fern Bank). The number suggests that Nos. 28 and 32 may have been built between 1891 and the 1898 survey.

Unnamed house (may have been No. 19?):
Edward Dean Jnr (26yrs) son of miller Edward Dean of the Mill; his brother Joseph (21yrs).

Westview (No. 80) – number of inhabitants reduced since 1881:
William Smith (69yrs) retired railway contractor & wife (his second, see 1881 census) Jane (52yrs); daughter Cecelia(18yrs).

Vron Deg (No. 3) – new residents since 1881:
Widow Jane Ruthren (75yrs) from Co. Down Ireland, living on investments; widowed daughter Louisa Bell (43yrs); widowed daughter Harriett Fritsch? (38yrs); granddaughter Maud Bell (17yrs); grandson Henri Fritsch (4yrs); visitor Jane Ryan (45yrs)

Fammau View (No. 76) – .assumed as new property since 1881:
John Griffiths (46yrs) retired corn dealer & wife Jane; their children, Hannah (14yrs), Thomas (14yrs), John (9yrs), Jane (7yrs); general domestic servant Ellen Roberts (20yrs).

Roade Villa (No. 74) – assumed as new property since 1881:
John Davies (34yrs) bank clerk & wife Esther (29yrs); their sons John (3yrs), Robert (1yr); servants Lena Brown (17yrs); Jane Gillam (15yrs).

The Hollies (No. 1) – assumed unoccupied in 1881 census:
Two households named: Thomas Cox (??) retired Clerk in Holy Orders, servant Mary Rowlands (49yrs) spinster;

also: ????? *name of head difficult to read*, living on investments; sister Kate (44yrs), widowed sister Louisa (40yrs), niece Constance (15yrs), servant Elizabeth Davies (20yrs).

Portland Villa (No. 5) – same family but changes since 1881:
Thomas Bate (68yrs) retired from cheese factory, his married daughter Mrs Pritchard (39yrs), her children Constance (6yrs), Jessie (4yrs), 1mnth baby; general servant Ann Pritchard (17yrs).

Grafton Villa (Nos. 40 or 42) – new inhabitants since 1881:
William Holland (38yrs) road surveyor & wife Mary (36yrs); their children George (14yrs), William (13yrs), Albert (11yrs), Eva Mary (8yrs), Frederick (6yrs), Henry (4yrs); general domestic servant Mary Humphreys (19yrs).

Grafton Villa (nos: 40 or 42) – new inhabitants since 1881:
John Whelan? (45yrs) Civil Air Ordnance Survey depot & wife Esther (44yrs); their children Thomas (15yrs), Francis (13yrs), Ellen (9yrs),

Esther (6yrs), Edward (3yrs).

Lilley House (No. 7) – new inhabitants since 1881:

William Ballance (36yrs) Inspector of Schools & wife Ada (36yrs); their children George (12yrs), Harold (9yrs), James George (6yrs), Olive Doreen (2yrs), Reginald (5mnths); servant general domestic Elizabeth Hughes (17yrs).

Laburnum Villa (No. 9) – new inhabitants since 1881:

Alfred Williams (36yrs) railway clerk (recorded as married but no wife recorded); son William (8yrs), brother Frederick Darius (19yrs) railway clerk; housekeeper widow Elizabeth Roberts (56yrs).

Unnamed – but probably No. 13:

Founding father Thomas Wood's widow Sarah (76yrs); now no others recorded with her.

Holly Bank (No. 17) – new property since 1881:

Widow Mary Beaumont (60yrs) living on investments; her daughters Mary (34yrs), Florence (27yrs). son James (19yrs) theology student.

Norton Villa (No. 15) – new property since 1881:

William John Morris (43yrs) manager of leadworks & wife Marion (43yrs); their children William Palmer Morris (11yrs), Hugh Augustus Morris (9yrs), Marion Dorothea (6yrs); sister-in-law Adelaide Palmer, spinster living on investments; domestic servant Elizabeth Atkinson (25yrs).

Hawthorne Villa (No. 21) – new occupants since 1881:

William Fitch (62yrs) retired hairdresser & wife Susannah (57yrs); niece Susannah Sheen (43yrs) lady's help; servant Albert Over? (20yrs).

(The other **Hawthorne Villa** is not recorded but may be under a new name).

Fern Bank (No. 56 or 58 – new inhabitants since 1881:

Owen Robinson (37yrs) railway clerk & wife Ann (39yrs); their daughters Edith (8yrs), Ellen (6yrs), Amy (4yrs), Cecelia (1yr); boarder Jane Ellen Vaughan (13yrs).

Fern Bank (No. 56 or 58) – new inhabitants since 1881:

Margaret Lewis (48yrs) retired mantle maker, daughter Elizabeth (23yrs) mother's help, daughter Gertrude (20yrs) mantle maker; boarder James Coombs, compressed air engineer/draughtsman.

Unnamed (believed to be No. 23 or 25):

John Jones (72yrs) retired grocer & wife Eliza (71yrs); indications are that the above were tenants.

Woodbine (believed to be No. 23 or 25):

Edmund Baillie (39yrs) merchant nurseryman & wife Harriett (39yrs); their children Edmund (17yrs), John (16yrs), Harriett Eliza (14yrs),

UPTON PARK, CHESTER

Charles (12yrs), Rose (10yrs), Leonard (7yrs), Daisy (5yrs), Ivy (2yrs); servant Mary Jane Hitchen (20yrs); indications are that the above were tenants.

No house name (Nos. 68 & 66 from Park records) – .daughter since 1881 census:

William Shone (43yrs) estate agent & accountant & wife Grace (41yrs); son William (11yrs), daughter Grace (7yrs); domestic servants cook Mary Dodd (38yrs), kitchen maid Catherine Bebbington (19yrs).

Spring Villa (29) c.f.1881 – same family less 3 children:

George E Roberts (52yrs) tailor and draper & wife Mary (50yrs); five of their children, George (21yrs), Sarah A (19yrs), Mary (17yrs), Theodora (14yrs), Joseph T (11yrs); servant Mary Eliza Roberts (14yrs).

Mayfield Villa (no 31) – minor change since 1881 census:

Spinster Mary Clark (70yrs) living on investments, her married brother James Clark (68yrs) living on an annuity; great nephew Ernest Clarke (6yrs); general servant Elizabeth Blake.

Rose Cottage (No. 84) – same family since 1881 census:

James Prince (52yrs widower) collector of rates & taxes; children Dora (11yrs), Violet (9yrs), Philip (7yrs), Maggie (4yrs); aunt Elizabeth (72yrs) living on investments; servant Margaret Jones (33yrs).

Upton Mill – the two oldest sons have moved out, grandmother died and all workers/servants changed since 1881:

Edward Dean (52yrs) farmer baker and miller & wife Elizabeth (50yrs); their three youngest children, Bessie (19yrs), Helen (13yrs), Charles (11yrs); sister-in-law Hannah Stockton (54yrs) living on investments; four servants, baker John Middleton (44yrs), and general servants Elizabeth Roberts (22yrs), Edward Oldfield (16yrs), William Dough (15yrs).

Another Fern Bank is recorded which may have been just outside the park:

James Woodward (65yrs) retired poulterer & wife Elizabeth; their sons George (30yrs?) farm labourer, Thomas (25yrs) barber; grandson James (21yrs) barber.

Electoral Registers - 1901 and 1911

NB: Only men had the vote and voting rights went with ownership and with occupancy. Many other names are given only as residing in Upton and are not included below. The 1901 census becomes public domain from 2 January 2002 and will be referenced to update the **uppa.org** website.

(Bracketed text) has been added by the history author drawing on other sources.

1901	1911
Richardson, James Vron Deg (No. 3)	Richardson, James Manchester landlord (of No. 3)
Robinson, Owen Mona Cottage (No. 58)	Robinson, Owen Mona Cottage (No. 58)
Wannop, William Stockport landlord (of No. 9)	Wannop, William Laburnum Cottage (No. 9)
Cole, Peter Halifax landlord of Fernbank (No. 56)	Cole, Peter Halifax landlord of Fernbank (No. 56)
Dean, Edward Jnr Upton Mill	Dean, Edward Jnr Upton Mill
Bullock, James Maxwell also owned Upton schools	
Balance, William	
Cox, Thomas (of No. 1 / 3)	
Fitch, William (of No. 21)	
Forester, Walker Claud	
Hughes, Robert William (of Nos. 23 / 25)	Hughes, Robert William (of Nos. 23 / 25)
Hughes, Reginald Gilbert Lodger in the Limes (No. 25) to Mr Hughes. Sole use of bedroom and use of f sitting room.	Hughes, Reginald Gilbert Lodger in the Limes (No. 25) to Mr Hughes for services rendered. Sole use of bedroom and use of ground floor.
Mason, John	
Prince, James (of No. 84)	Prince, James (of No. 84)
Shone, William (of Nos. 66/68)	Shone, William (of Nos. 66/68)

UPTON PARK, CHESTER

1901	1911
Pearson, William Lodger in Westview (No. 80) to Mrs Smith. Sole use of u/f bedroom and use of other f rooms	Pearson, William Lodger in Westview (No. 80) to Mrs Smith. Sole use of u/f bedroom and 2nd floor, use of grd floor
	Haselden, James Henry (of No. 12)
	Woodward, Henry London landlord of Ranmere (No. 18)
	Thorn, Henry William Mold landlord of Rock Cottage (No. 32)
	Buck, Archibald
	Burgess, John of Grange House (No. 76)
	Cochran, Walter (believed to be Cockram of No. 13)
	Cowie, George
	Dyson, Edward
	Foster, Harry
	Gilroy, Andrew Bolton
	Griffiths, John
	Johnson, Robert Sedgewick (of The Briars No. 28)
	Jones, Thomas Henry
	Kendall, Edward Chambers
	Warner, Lionel Ashton Piers
	Wase Thomas Edglow
	Wood, Charles
	Crane, George Frederick Lodger in Grafton Villa (No. 40) to Mrs Mary Crane for 15/-p.w. board & lodging. Sole use of bedroom and use of rest.
	Crane, Percy Lodger in Grafton Villa (No. 40) to Mrs Mary Crane for 15/-p.w. board & lodging. Sole use of bedroom and use of rest.

Electoral Registers – Autumn 1921 and May 1929

Where the UPPA accounts ledger shows a different name responsible for the Park Rate, this name is shown under the house name. The implication is that electoral roll name is the tenant.

HOUSE		Autumn 1921		May 1929	
84	**Millside**	Gowings	Leonard James	Smith	John Sidney
		Gowings	Winifred Violet	Smith	Kathleen Lily
80	**Westview**	Pearson	Cecilia	Pearson	Cecilia
		Pearson	William	Pearson	William (J)
		Wall	James	Smith	Mary Louisa
				Smith	Hermione Mary
76	**Grange Hse**	Gardner	Ralph Wilson	Gardner	Ralph Wilson (SJ)
		Gardner	Elizabeth Emma	Gardner	Elizabeth Emma
74	**Roade Villa**	Crane	Mary	Crane	Mary
	(W Pearson)	Crane	George Frederick	Crane	George F
68	**Oaklea**	Matthias	Elsie	Mathias	Esther Sophia
	(Brook Hurst & Co in 1921)	Matthias	George Daniel James	Mathias	Thomas
	(A W S Firley in 1929)				Gwynne
				Mathias	Gwen
66	**Firdene**			Furley	Arthur Walter Snead (J)
	(Brook Hurst & Co in 1921, A W S Firley in 1929)			Furley	Daisy Rebecca
58	**Mona Villa**	Whaley	Horace	Whaley	Horace
		Whaley	Lizzie	Whaley	Lizzie
56	**Fernbank**	Fletcher	Albert Kirton	Fletcher	Albert K
	(H E Crane then H Dean)	Fletcher	Sarah Ann	Fletcher	Sarah A

UPTON PARK, CHESTER

HOUSE	Autumn 1921		May 1929	
	Fawcett	Edward George	Swarbrick	Ernest
42 The Nook	Wynne	Elizabeth	Wynne	Elizabeth
(W Haswell then J Crosby)	Wynne	Alun		
	Wynne	Ernest		
40 Grafton Villa	Crosby	John	Crosby	John
	Crosby	Ada Charlotte	Crosby	Ada Charlotte
	Dudgeon	Charles	Crosby	Barbara Betsy
	Jones	Cyril		
32 Rock Cottage	Martyn	Dorothy	Martyn	Dorothy
	Martyn	Gerald Stephen	Martyn	Gerald S
			Martyn	Dorothy Loveday
			Devoy	Katie
28 The Briars /	Johnson	Robert Sedgewick	Longworth-Dames	Kathleen
Garden Hse	Johnson	Alice	Roberts	Eva
18 Ranmere	Jones	Edward Twist	Jones	Edward Twist (J)
(Edith Clarke then Woodward)	Jones	Henrietta	Jones	Henrietta
16 Fairfield	Singleton	William		
(Woodward then Edith Clarke)	Singleton	Mary Jane		
	Singleton	Arthur Stanley		
	Singleton	William Horace		
14 Laverstock	Jones	Alfred Litherland	Kellett	Florence Mary
(Shearer from Nicholson then Austin Jones) Jones		Effie Muriel		
12 Willowdene	Haselden	James Henry	Haselden	James Henry (J)
	Haselden	Sophy	Haselden	Sophy

ELECTORAL REGISTERS

HOUSE		Autumn 1921		May 1929	
8	**Heatherlea** (B J Willis)			Lindesay	Walter B
				Margery	May Maud
6	**Woodcroft**			Pinnington	Emma
				Pinnington	George
				Pinnington	Richard
				Pinnington	Edith
4	**Rhossilli**			Compston	Charles Hartwell
				Compston	Margaret Penny
				Compston	Kathleen
2	**The Westings**			Randles	Frank
				Randles	Phylis May
1	**The Hollies** (SOllerhead)	Cowie	George	Cowie	George (J)
			Margaret May		Margaret May
					Harold E
					Wilhelmina
33	**Belmont**	Whitley	Norah Evelyn (O) (J)	Whitley	Norah E
		Whitley	William Thomas	Whitley	William Thomas
		Richmond	Joseph William		
31	**Mayfield** (reps of FMaddocks)	Davies	Thomas Harold	Williams	George
				Williams	Kathleen
		Maddocks	Stanley	Maddocks	Stanley
				Maddocks	Dorothy
				Dutton	Joseph
				Dutton	Annie Elizabeth

UPTON PARK, CHESTER

HOUSE	Autumn 1921	May 1929
29 Spring Villa (For 1921 SDavies)	Griffiths / Griffiths / Griffiths — John / Clara (sen) / William Jones	Griffiths / Griffiths — John (J) / Clara
25 The Limes (CBlandford took over in 1921)	Carbutt / Carbutt — Benjamin / Anne May	Blandford Charles — Annie Jane
23 The Beeches	Sabine / Sabine — HWTC / Rose	Sabine / Sabine — Harold (J) / Rose / Higley Mary
21 Hawthorns (Mrs Margaret Davies)	Crane / Crane — Henry Ebrey / Mabel Boswell	Crane / Crane / Cruise — Henry Ebrey / Mabel Boswell / Mary
19 Hawthorne Villa / Parkstone	Dean / Dean — Charles / Helen	Dean / Malpas — Helen / Ethel
17 Hollybank	Speed / Speed — Henry / Sarah	Griffiths / Griffiths / Griffiths / Griffiths — William (J) / Emily (J) / Arthur (J) / Edwin (J)
15 Norton Villa / Carden Bank	Weaver — Arthur	Anderson / Anderson — Edward Sansbury / Edith
13 Laburnum Bank / Lyndale	Furley / Furley — Arthur Walter Snead / Daisy Rebecca	Hylton-Stewart / Hylton-Stewart / Rowan — Eric William / Miriam / May
9 Laburnum Cottage	Trant — Alfred William Vincent	Trant / Trant — Alfred William Vincent / Ann Eliza

HOUSE		Autumn 1921		May 1929	
9	**Lab Cott (cont)**			Trant	Mary Vincent
7	**White Cottage**	Dickson	Guy Tritton	Brown	Margaret
	(Albert Dean then WJeff)	Dickson	Ella	Brown	John
5	**Ravensworth**	Catchpole	Lewis	Moore	Sydney J
	(in 1921 Thos Edwards)	Catchpole	Maude Helen	Moore	Margaret
3	**Anchorage**			Catchpole	Louis Frederick J
	(SOllerhead)			Catchpole	Maude Helen
				Catchpole	Donald W
	Mill House	Dean	Edward	Dean	Edward
		Dean	Martha	Dean	Martha
	Upton Villa	Gardner	Ernest Hilton	Gardner	
	(o/s the Park)	Gardner	Nora		

Footnote

(J) indicates Juror (but not always shown)
(S.J) indicates Special Juror

NB 1929 roll records Coleman, Selina and Arnold Bertram of Ferndale

Electoral Registers – 1939 and 1945

The UPPA accounts ledger responsible rate payer is shown under the house name if different from the roll name. This implies that the roll name is a tenant.

HOUSE		1939		October 1945	
84	**Millside** (Flavell)	Flavell Barton	Henry Erasmus May Margaret	Harris Harris Reeks Williamson	Joan M George J Edna L Edna L
80	**Westview**	Pearson Blundstone Lawson Hoole Florence	Constance Hilda Margaret Christine Florence Kate	Harris Harris Harris	Magdeline Robert Olwen M (M)
76	**Grange House** (I T Williams in 1945)	McEldowney Mountney Mountney	William Joseph Donald Rosalind	Williams Williams Cowe Pugh	Ivor T Elizabeth K C Margaret E Dorothy A
74	**Roade Villa** (M S Pearson)	Crane Crane	George Frederick (J) Florence May	Pearson Pearson Bishop	Leonora Marshall S Rita E
70	**The Cedars** (in 1945 with Shell)	Foden Foden	William (J) Florine May	Foden	William Aubrey
68	**Oaklea** (Furley)	Coleman Coleman	George Francis Winifred	Cook Cook	Evelyn Maynard C

ELECTORAL REGISTERS

HOUSE		1939		October 1945	
	Oaklea (cont)	Williams	Annie E	Cook	John M (M)
				Sinclair	William J
				Sinclair	Louise A
66	Firdene	Taylor	Jack Hepworth (J)	Tregoning	Celia M A
	(Furley)	Taylor	Hermione	Tregoning	George E
		Speed	Caroline	Peake	Agnes B
64	Wyeby	Furley	Arthur Walter Snead (J)	Wardle	Isla M
	(in 1945 L Marcuss)	Furley	Daisy Rebecca	Wardle	Mark K
58	Mona Villa	Thelwell	Francis A	Thelwell	Francis A
		Thelwell	Maria E	Thelwell	Maria E
56	Fernbank	Fletcher	Albert Kirton	Fletcher	Albert K
	(Helen Dean)	Fletcher	Sarah Ann	Fletcher	Sarah A
48	Lindum	Herbert (O) (J)	Hardy Earnest	Hardy	Earnest H
		Herbert	Gwendoline Sarah	Hardy	Sarah G
		Jones	Nellie	Wynn	Lily
42	The Nook			Blagden	Dorothy L
	(N Crosby)			Coleman	Roy E
40	Grafton Villa	Crosby	Eugene Nettie (J)	Crosby	Eugene N B B
		Crosby	Betsy Barbara	Barker	Violet
				Hill	Patricia M
32	Rock Cottage	Martyn	Dorothy (J)	Martyn	Dorothy
		Martyn	Gerald Stephen	Martyn	Gerald S
				Prince	Thomas
28	Garden House	Longworth-Dames	Kathleen		
		Roberts	Eva	Roberts	Eva

UPTON PARK, CHESTER

HOUSE	1939		October 1945	
18 Ranmere	Jones	Edward Twist (J)	Carbutt	Annie M
(Miss H G Clark)	Jones	Henrietta	Oldham	Betty M
	Jones	Gwyneth Twist	Oldham	Frederick R
16 Fairfield	Singleton	William	Singleton	Mary Jane
(H G Clark then Mrs Schofield)	Singleton	Mary Jane	Singleton	William
14 Laverstock	Jones	William Austin	Matthews	Dorothy
(still Jones in 1945)	Jones	Mildred	Matthews	Frederick (M)
	Harrison	Anne		
12 Willowdene	Haselden	Sophia	Davies	Alfred O
	Matterlead	Edith	Davies	Elsie
			Davies	Ethel J
			Rose	Eric L
10 The Garth	Evans	Edward (J)	Best	Albert F (M)
(Loadman)	Evans	Marion	Best	Gladys A
8 Heatherlea	Warner	Albert Joseph (J)	Warner	Albert J
		Maude		Maude
		Philippa Marjorie		Philippa (M)
6 Woodcroft	Loadman	Caroline	Loadman	Mary C
	Loadman	Winifred Crompton	Loadman	Wilfred C
			Loadman	Robert E (M)
			Loadman	Mary A (M)
			Loadman	James C (M)
4 Rhossilli			Sumption	J Constance
(Compston)				

252

ELECTORAL REGISTERS

HOUSE		1939		October 1945	
2	The Westings (Lightfoot)	Cox	Garfield Lionel (J)	Cox	Dorothy M
		Cox	Dorothy May	Cox Garfield (M)	
				Terry	David G
1	The Hollies (Ollerhead)	Griffiths	Ellen Alexander	Griffiths	Ellen A
		Griffiths	Mary Daphne Auburn		Esme J G
		Clay	Thomas William Lloyd		Mary D A
		Clay	Violet Patricia	Harris	George J
		English Lucy			
33	Belmont	Whitley	Norah Evelyn (J)	Whitley	Norah E
		Lovett	Vera May	Lorett	Vera M
				Jones	Blanche R
				Williamson	Margaret
				Icke	Joan O (M)
31	Mayfield (1945 still Brocklebank)	Brocklebank	Robert Gardner	Dubbock	Ruth C
		Brocklebank	Marjorie Barnes	Gilbert	Gwendoline
29	Spring Villa	Griffiths	John		
		Griffiths	Clara (sen)	Griffiths Clara	
		Griffiths	Dalzie	Comyn	Dalzie
		Griffiths	Gwyneth		
		Griffiths	Marjorie	Griffiths	Marjorie
		Griffiths	John Seldon	Griffiths	John
25	The Limes	Blandford	Annie Jane	Blandford	Annie J
23	The Beeches	Sabine	Barbara	Sabine	Barbara
		Sabine	HWTC (J)	Sabine	Harold

253

UPTON PARK, CHESTER

HOUSE	1939		October 1945	
The Beeches (cont)				
	Sabine		Sabine	Pamela H
		Rose	Sabine	Rose
			Sabine	Brenda L
	Higley	May	Higley	Mary
21 Hawthorns	Craig	Doris Evelyn	Craig	Doris E
	Craig	Willaim Archibold	Craig	William A
	Craig	William Arthur Desmond		
19 Parkstone	Dean	Helen	Fergusson	May W
(1945 still H Dean)	Malpas	Ethel Mary		
17 Hollybank	Griffiths	Arthur	Astle	Celia A
	Griffiths	Edwin	Astle	Arthur
15 Carden Bank	Anderson	Edward Sonsbury	Anderson	Edward S
	Anderson	Edith	Anderson	Edith
13 Lyndale	Musgrave	Raymond (J)	Musgrave	Raymond
(Hylton Stewart now of Queens Park)	Musgrave	Elsie Mabel Woolesey	Musgrave	Elsie M W
			Musgrave	John R (M)
			Clague	John C
			Clague	Margaret
9 Laburnum Cottage	Trant	Anne Eliza	Trant	Ann E
	Trant	Mary Vincent	Trant	Mary V (M)
	Trant	Margaret Patricia	Trant	Margaret P
			Roberts	Irene M
7 White Cottage	Parker	James Cecil (J)	Parker	James C
	Parker	Elsie May	Parker	Elsie M

ELECTORAL REGISTERS

HOUSE	1939			October 1945	
5 Ravensworth	Moore	Sydney (J)		Evans	Marjorie
	Moore	Ada		Evans	Frederick (M)
				Williams	Mary
				Mallalieu	Lavinia (M)
3 Derrymore				Moore	Sydney
(Mrs F Ollerhead)				Moore	Ada
Land	Cheers	Harold		Shaw	George D
				Shaw	Ruth

Footnote
(J) is juror but not always shown
(M) on military roll

2000 YEARS OF BUILDING
A Festival for the Millennium

CELEBRATING CHESTER'S DEVELOPMENT THROUGH TIME

Chester Civic Trust is a voluntary organisation with an equal concern for the past, present and future of this unique city. Our Millennium Festival '2000 YEARS OF BUILDING' has been a successful celebration of Chester's development through time, and in that context we are delighted to support local history publications which contribute to the greater enjoyment and appreciation of our heritage. Upton Park is an important part of the story, spanning 150 years from the middle of the 19th century when Chester grew rapidly both in prosperity and size. We congratulate all those involved in the production of this book and hope that many who read it will be inspired to take an active interest in their local environment and in the future of Chester.

STEPHEN LANGTREE
Chairman
Chester Civic Trust
Bishop Lloyd's Palace
51/53 Watergate Row
Chester CH1 2LE
www.chestercivictrust.org.uk